ENGLAND'S MISSION

ENGLAND'S MISSION

THE IMPERIAL IDEA IN THE AGE OF GLADSTONE AND DISRAELI 1868–1880

C. C. Eldridge

Lecturer in History, Saint David's University College, Lampeter

Macmillan

First published 1973 by

THE MACMILLAN PRESS LTD

London and Basingstoke
Associated companies in New York
Dublin Melbourne Johannesburg and Madras

SBN 333 14797 9

Printed in Great Britain by

A. WHEATON & CO.
Exeter

TO RUTH

Contents

List of Illustrations

All the above appeared in *Punch* between 1872 and 1880.

List of Maps

Preface

VICTORIAN imperialism has been the subject of intensive research in the last two decades and the traditional framework of British colonial policy in the Victorian age has come under heavy fire. In fact no part of the old orthodoxy has been safe from attack. Landmarks have been swept away, basic concepts have been challenged and the inadequacy of labels attached to movements and men by previous historians demonstrated. However, no new structure has been established, few new ideas have achieved general acceptance and the framework of British imperial history in the nineteenth century remains a topic of intense controversy. The purpose of this book is a modest one. It is an attempt to reinterpret in the light of current research the events of the years 1868–80 (which are said to have witnessed the alleged 'climax of anti-imperialism', the 'turn of the tide' in favour of the empire and the exotic imperialism of Disraeli) and, if possible, to place them in a different context and, it is hoped, a clearer perspective. The University of Edinburgh kindly awarded me a Post-Doctoral Fellowship during the years 1966–8 to begin research on this project.

Needless to say, like all students of imperial history at Edinburgh I have benefited greatly from the vast knowledge and friendly counsel of Professor G. Shepperson, under whose guidance this study first took shape. I also wish to record a special debt of gratitude to Professor W. David McIntyre of the University of Canterbury, Christchurch, New Zealand, who has been as a teacher, critic and friend a constant source of inspiration and encouragement. He has read many drafts of the present work, suggested numerous revisions and saved me from many errors. The errors that remain are entirely my own responsibility.

It is also my pleasure to thank Professor C. D. Chandaman

of St David's University College who read the entire manuscript and made a number of helpful suggestions; also Mrs Inez Crowdy who, despite many more important demands on the time of a departmental secretary, produced two handsome typescripts typed to perfection. Mr C. I. Lewis drew the maps, the Revd D. T. W. Price and Mrs Susan Willmington helped with references, and Miss Mair James cheerfully assisted in the final stages of typing the manuscript. To all these people I wish to record my thanks.

The Pantyfedwen Fund of St David's University College has been generous in providing financial assistance to meet the cost of preparing part of the manuscript for publication, and I also wish to acknowledge most gratefully the valuable assistance given to me over a number of years by the officers and staffs of Edinburgh University Library, the National Library of Scotland, the British Museum, the Public Record Office, the Institute of Historical Research, the National Registry of Archives, the Royal Commonwealth Society, Nottingham University Library and Manuscripts Department, the Methodist Missionary Society, Rhodes House, the National Library of Wales and St David's University College Library.

My greatest debts of gratitude, however, are to my mother, who did not live to see the publication of the present work, and above all to my wife. She has lived with this manuscript, read the proofs, checked references, compiled the index and put up with much else besides. It is in love and gratitude that I dedicate this book to her.

February 1973 G.C.E.

List of Abbreviations

GENERAL

A.P.S.	Aborigines Protection Society
A.S.S.	Anti-Slavery Society
B.M.	British Museum
C.H.B.E.	*Cambridge History of the British Empire*
C.O.	Colonial Office
encl.	enclosed
F.O.	Foreign Office
G.A.A.C.	General Association for the Australian Colonies
M.M.S.	Methodist Missionary Society
N.C.M.H.	*New Cambridge Modern History*
Parl. P.	*Parliamentary Papers*
P.R.O.	Public Record Office
R.C.S.	Royal Commonwealth Society
Treas.	Treasury
W.O.	War Office

PERIODICALS

A.H.R.	*American Historical Review*
C.H.R.	*Canadian Historical Review*
C.M.	*Camden Miscellany*
C.S.S.H.	*Comparative Studies in Society and History*
E.H.R.	*English Historical Review*
Econ.H.R.	*Economic History Review*
H.J.	*Historical Journal*
H.S.(A.N.Z.)	*Historical Studies (Australia and New Zealand)*
J.A.H.	*Journal of African History*

J.B.S.	*Journal of British Studies*
J.C.P.S.	*Journal of Commonwealth Political Studies*
J.E.H.	*Journal of Economic History*
J.P.R.A.H.S.	*Journal and Proceedings of the Royal Australian Historical Society*
N.Z.J.H.	*New Zealand Journal of History*
P.&P.	*Past & Present*
P.R.C.I.	*Proceedings of the Royal Colonial Institute*
P.S.Q.	*Political Science Quarterly*
R.M.S.	*Renaissance and Modern Studies*
T.N.A.P.S.S.	*Transactions of the National Association for the Promotion of Social Science*
T.R.H.S.	*Transactions of the Royal Historical Society*
V.S.	*Victorian Studies*

Introduction:
A Definition of Terms

IMPERIALISM, we were told long ago, is no word for scholars. It does not convey a precise meaning and confuses rather than communicates. Unfortunately it is a word scholars seem unable to dismiss. It is essential, therefore, to begin by defining the sense in which a word with so many associations according to time and place is used throughout this study.

In the mid-Victorian period imperialism was a recent addition to the English language. Professor Richard Koebner and Helmut Schmidt have traced its origins to the 1840s when it was used to blacken both the adventurous schemes of Prince Louis Napoleon of France and his aggressive policies as Emperor Napoleon III. From the very beginning the word had rather unpleasant connotations. Its English usage grew up in the period under discussion and in the late 1870s, in particular, it became a smear-word to stigmatise the policies of Disraeli. By 1880 'imperialism' was well established as a slogan in British political life.

But imperialism was not used at this time in a derogatory sense alone. There was an alternative interpretation. In 1868 the *Spectator* referred to 'Imperialism in its best sense' which signified 'the consciousness that is sometimes a binding duty to perform highly irksome and offensive tasks'. Disraeli's Colonial Secretary, the Earl of Carnarvon, frequently spoke along similar lines and after his resignation in 1878 he lectured on 'a true and a false brand of Imperialism'. For Carnarvon the 'true strength and meaning of Imperialism' lay, on the one hand, in creating 'a great English-speaking community, united together in a peaceful confederation, too powerful to be molested by any nation, and too powerful and too generous, I hope, to molest any weaker State' and, on the other, in restoring law, order and liberty to backward and warring societies, thus creating a system 'where the light of morality and religion can penetrate into the darkest dwelling places'. This was a brand of imperialism to be proud of.

Throughout the major part of this study, therefore, imperialism denotes what Lord Rosebery dubbed 'a greater pride in Empire'. Comparatively few 'imperialists' in the mid-Victorian years were interested in imperial expansion : their main objective was to preserve and consolidate the existing British empire. Not until the 1880s did the real struggle develop between the consolidationist and expansionist schools.

In recent years, however, imperialism has also been used by several historians in relation to the 'informal' empire of trade and influence. It has been freely used to describe the expansion of British commercial and financial power beyond the formal boundaries of political jurisdiction. While this usage probably stretches the term too far, it does serve to remind us that the Victorians were more interested in trade than in territory and that the mid-Victorians were no exception.

The term 'mid-Victorian' also requires definition. Professors J. A. Gallagher and R. E. Robinson, in their discussion of the 'imperialism of free trade', loosely refer to the years 1840–70 as the mid-Victorian age – a usage accepted by their critics and adopted by many subsequent writers. The acceptance of such terminology can only lead to confusion, especially as it implies the existence of an early Victorian era yet effectively limits its duration to three years. Mathematically, of course, the years 1869–70 saw the mid-point of Victoria's reign. A clear distinction can therefore be drawn between the middle decades of the century (1840–60) and the mid-Victorian decades (1860–80), which can logically be dubbed the early and mid-Victorian periods – especially as 'late-Victorian' normally refers to the years after 1880.

Unfortunately historians seem unable to agree on the use of such terminology. Professor W. P. Morrell, for example, bases his discussion of *British Colonial Policy in the Mid-Victorian Age* (London, 1969) on the years 1852–72, and similarly, writers in other fields of nineteenth-century history adopt the divisions which suit their subject best. It needs to be explained, consequently, that the present writer uses the term 'mid-Victorian' with reference to the years from the beginning of Palmerston's last ministry to the end of Disraeli's second administration (1859–80).

Happily a definition of the 'imperial idea' has been firmly established. A. P. Thornton blazed the trail in *The Imperial Idea and its Enemies: A Study in British Power* (London, 1959). Unhappily the ensuing description of the empire spirit in an earlier age is no more than a pale reflection of Professor Thornton's masterly study of the imperial idea in the late-Victorian period.

1

Imperialism in the Free Trade Era

IN THE last two decades the mid-Victorian years have achieved a certain notoriety in the history of the British empire. Long regarded as the 'Little England' era, they have now been dubbed, amid much controversy, the golden age of British expansion overseas. This new-found glory, however, has not been without its detractors, and the debate concerning both the 'imperialism of free trade' and Victorian arguments about empire has by no means ended.

The Victorian age saw the heyday of British trade, finance and naval power. Already by the early years of the nineteenth century the gigantic and unparalleled British industrial revolution had given Great Britain, for the time being at least, a monopoly of the new modes of production and for the foreseeable future a monopoly of large sections of world trade. During the first half of Queen Victoria's long reign British commerce and industry led the world. Indeed, the other trading nations, unable to rival British power, were eager to share in British wealth. The markets of the United Kingdom and her empire lay open to them. This stimulated economic activity, reduced international tensions and encouraged acquiescence in the British hegemony. The beginnings of a global economy, centred on Great Britain, seemed to offer to all nations the optimal chance of exploiting both their own domestic resources and the possibilities of foreign trade in a world policed by the Royal Navy and serviced by British capital exports. Thus Great Britain became not only the leading industrial and commercial nation but the self-appointed policeman as well.[1]

It is not surprising, therefore, that the Victorians closely identified the era of the 'workshop of the world' and of the *Pax Britannica* with the principles and practice of free trade. Since in a free market the British were able to undersell their competitors with comparative ease, the doctrines of free trade understandably became a faith from which any deviation was characterised as a fall from grace. 'The commercial vice of Protection . . . is the natural resort of ignorant cupidity, and ignorant cupidity is the besetting sin of communities intensely commercial and wanting in education', wrote Goldwin Smith, Regius Professor of Modern History at Oxford, in 1863.[2] The whole world should be opened up to free trade. Professor Smith was not alone in concluding that the fragments of empire inherited by the Victorians were now superfluous. In Parliament, Cobden and Bright argued that colonies, especially those with responsible government which were apparently destined for independence, had become a burden. Not only had they refused to take any more British convicts and, even more dubiously, refused to follow Great Britain's lead in the management of their commerce, but their very existence weakened Great Britain's defensive power and acted as a constant drain on the British Treasury.

With such views being so forcefully expounded in the leading academic and political centres, it was easy to believe that the majority of British economists, politicians and writers in the middle decades of the nineteenth century subscribed to similar beliefs and held colonies in low esteem. According to later commentators this was the great 'Age of Separatism', and the 1860s, specifically, were said to have seen the 'climax of anti-imperialism' when the extreme theories of Goldwin Smith and the separatist ideas of the so-called Manchester School held the

---

[1] For a survey of British industrial growth in the early nineteenth century and the expansion of the Victorian economy in general, see E. J. Hobsbawm, *Industry and Empire* (London, 1968); A. H. Imlah, *Economic Elements in the Pax Britannica* (Cambridge, Mass., 1958); W. W. Rostow, *The British Economy of the Nineteenth Century* (London, 1948); and L. H. Jenks, *The Migration of British Capital to 1875* (New York, 1927).

[2] G. Smith, *The Empire: A Series of Letters Published in the Daily News, 1862–3* (London, 1863) p. 42.

day. In fact it became a commonplace to write of the middle decades of the last century as though they were dominated by an aversion to empire. Not until the last quarter of the nineteenth century, when Great Britain's future economic strength, political primacy and military security seemed in danger, did the empire become a necessity. Indeed, it seemed to many later observers that for half a century the political morality of free trade, closely linked with *laissez-faire*, internationalism and pacifism, provided a peaceful and prosperous interlude between the mercantilist imperialism of the eighteenth century and the violent, neo-mercantilist 'New Imperialism' of the late-Victorian age.

For nearly fifty years historians of British colonial policy accepted such a framework of ideas, based upon a purely legalistic concept of empire, which permitted the nineteenth century to be divided into periods of 'anti-imperialism' and 'imperialism' according to the amount of territory annexed and the degree of belief expressed in British rule overseas. The century was neatly separated into two contrasting phases. After 1815 there was an age of anti-imperialism when the old colonial system was gradually dismantled and the doctrines of mercantilism slowly gave way to the free trade, *laissez-faire* and pacific principles of the Manchester School, whose adherents so decried the existence of colonies and called for the dismemberment of the empire. This was an age of stagnation if not of disintegration. The years after 1870, however, witnessed an age of belligerent expansionism when Great Britain, confronted by changing world conditions which challenged her industrial supremacy, commercial prosperity and military security, once again found solace in empire. This hypothesis, endorsed by such authorities as A. P. Newton, H. E. Egerton and Sir Charles Lucas, and popularised in the 1920s by such distinguished scholars as C. A. Bodelsen, R. L. Schuyler and P. T. Moon, soon established itself as the orthodox view of nineteenth-century British imperial history. Age sanctified these generalisations and the thesis subsequently found a place in most standard works on the British empire.[3]

[3] This framework of ideas was used extensively in A. P. Newton and J. Ewing, *The British Empire since 1783: Its Political and Economic Development* (London, 1929); H. E. Egerton, *A Short History of British Colonial Policy* (London, 1897), subsequently revised by Newton in 1932; and A. P. Newton, *A Hundred Years of the British Empire* (London, 1942).

The neat divisions established by one generation of historians generally tend to be viewed with distrust by their successors. But the first full-scale attack on this narrow political interpretation did not come until 1953 when two Cambridge historians, John Gallagher and Ronald Robinson, adopted a fundamentally different approach in their now famous article 'The Imperialism of Free Trade'.[4] This new approach heralded the complete collapse of the traditional framework of British colonial policy in the Victorian age. Two decades later it still has not been satisfactorily replaced.

In particular, the age of Gladstone and Disraeli remains at the heart of the controversy concerning the development of the imperial idea in nineteenth-century England. According to the older view, the years 1868–80 (beginning with the 'empire scare' of 1869–70) witnessed a revulsion against the 'Little England' ideas of the Liberals and an upsurge of imperial sentiment expressed in the 'tawdry imperialism' of the Conservatives in the late 1870s. According to the new view, these years witnessed the vital era of transition from the 'informal' concept of empire of Palmerston's age to the new urge towards imperial expansion evident from the 1880s. In either view they are key years of change.

The place of the empire in British foreign policy certainly loomed large in the exchanges between the two leading political protagonists of the day. By the 1870s both party leaders had developed their own notions of empire. Gladstone looked to the continuing free association of largely independent colonies of

---

It was enlarged upon in three important works: C. A. Bodelsen, *Studies in Mid-Victorian Imperialism* (Copenhagen, 1924); R. L. Schuyler, 'The Climax of Anti-Imperialism', *P.S.Q.*, xxxv (1921) 537–60, reproduced with additional material in the same author's *The Fall of the Old Colonial System: A Study in British Free Trade, 1770–1870* (New York, 1945) pp. 234–84; P. T. Moon, *Imperialism and World Politics* (New York, 1926). Subsequently, the idea of an age of 'anti-imperialism' before 1870 dominated by separatist thought has been reproduced in a large number of standard histories of the British empire. See, for example, J. A. Williamson, *The British Empire and Commonwealth* (London, 1935); C. E. Carrington, *The British Overseas: Exploits of a Nation of Shopkeepers* (Cambridge, 1950); A. L. Burt, *The Evolution of the British Empire and Commonwealth from the American Revolution* (Boston, 1956); E. A. Walker, *The British Empire* (Cambridge, Mass., 1956).

[4] J. A. Gallagher and R. E. Robinson, 'The Imperialism of Free Trade', *Econ.H.R.*, 2nd ser., vi (1953) 1–15.

A BAD EXAMPLE.

DR. PUNCH. "WHAT'S ALL THIS? YOU, THE TWO HEAD BOYS OF THE SCHOOL, THROWING MUD!
YOU OUGHT TO BE ASHAMED OF YOURSELVES!"

British settlement held together by ties of kinship and affection; Disraeli concentrated on the 'eastern' empire of trade and defence, a centralised military unit backing up Great Britain in her role on the world's stage. And just as Disraeli attacked Gladstone's ideas in his Crystal Palace speech of 1872, so Gladstone, with rather more success, criticised Disraeli's actions in his Midlothian campaigns of 1879–80. Nevertheless, Disraeli made a significant contribution to the character of British imperialism and his concept of empire greatly influenced later generations.

There are still a large number of unsolved problems, however, which it is the purpose of the present study to explore. Its purpose is twofold : to trace the re-emergence of the empire during the years 1868–80 as an important factor in British politics, and also to trace the gradual transformation of mid-Victorian ideas about empire into that nexus of attitudes and motives normally dubbed late-Victorian imperialism. According to Professor C. A. Bodelsen, the late-Victorian movement for empire unity began 'as a protest against the separatist tendencies which were so powerful about the middle of the nineteenth century'.[5] But were the critics of Lord Granville's alleged policy associated with the pioneers of the 'New Imperialism'? Recent research suggests that many of Bodelsen's assumptions about policy, and to some extent about opinion, were misconceived and that there was no dramatic change in British policy or attitudes towards the empire during the early 1870s. The opponents of Lord Granville certainly had comparatively little to do with the birth of the 'New Imperialism' and there was no sudden change in British colonial policy after Disraeli became Prime Minister.

On the contrary, most recent writers have stressed the *continuity* of British imperial expansion overseas, denied the existence of any period of anti-imperialism in nineteenth-century England, and associated the formal expansion of the years after 1880 with developments in the field of foreign politics and economics. But as yet there has been no detailed examination, in the light of the current debate concerning mid-Victorian policy and thought, of the activities of the Gladstone government in the years 1869–71 or of the events of Disraeli's later years. No

[5] Bodelsen, *Studies in Mid-Victorian Imperialism*, p. 7 (henceforth abbreviated to Bodelsen).

attempt has been made so far to fit the so-called 'climax of anti-imperialism' into the new framework, and no convincing explanation of Disraeli's imperial policy has been established.

Certain obvious questions immediately arise. What was the basis of the colonial policy of Gladstone's first administration? Who formed the opposition to Granville's policy and what did their subsequent activities in campaigning for the empire amount to? Where did the impulses for imperial expansion come from in the 1870s? And above all, what was Disraeli up to during the years 1877–80 and what difference did his term of office make to the character of British imperialism? In fact, how did the imperial idea come to assume the character attributed to it in the late-Victorian age? Before answers to such questions can be attempted, it is necessary to put the years 1868–80 into their proper context and to establish what the imperial idea amounted to in an earlier age. It is necessary, therefore, to begin by analysing the recent debate concerning mid-nineteenth-century policy and attitudes towards the empire begun by Gallagher and Robinson in 1953.

I

In their article 'The Imperialism of Free Trade' Gallagher and Robinson rejected the long-held assumption that the period 1840–70 was one of anti-imperialism, when statesmen and officials alike distrusted expansion and were indifferent to the maintenance of the existing empire. Defining imperialism as the 'process of integrating new regions into the expanding economy', they asserted :

> Far from being an era of 'indifference', the mid-Victorian years were the decisive stage in the history of British expansion overseas, in that the combination of commercial penetration and political influence allowed the United Kingdom to command those economies which could be made to fit best into her own.[6]

Thus, viewing the empire in the context of an expanding British economy, and taking British political and economic expansion in the 'informal' empire into account, Gallagher and Robinson

[6] Gallagher and Robinson, *Econ.H.R.*, VI 11.

postulated a fundamental continuity in British expansion during the Victorian years. As one of their most formidable critics admits, it was an argument attractive not only for its novelty of interpretation but for the skill with which it was presented.[7]

Gallagher and Robinson began by showing the inadequacies and inconsistencies of the orthodox hypothesis. They drew up a list of additions to empire in the age of 'indifference' and raised several awkward questions. Why had the colonies all been retained, new ones obtained and new spheres of influence established in this 'Age of Separatism'? They pointed out that while it was true that Great Britain had abandoned formal control of the South African interior by withdrawing from the Orange River Sovereignty and the Transvaal, effective supremacy over the whole region had still been maintained, ending in the annexation of Basutoland in 1868 and Griqualand West in 1871. This extension of empire for the declared purpose of ensuring 'the safety of our South African possessions' had been made, significantly enough, by the Gladstone government at the height of the so-called 'climax of anti-imperialism'. Were these the actions of men intent on liquidating the empire? Moreover, in the age of *laissez-faire* the rapidly expanding economy of India had been developed by the state along the best mercantilist lines. Surely this was conclusive proof that free trade had not made the empire superfluous. And above all, why in the so-called 'Age of Imperialism' after 1870 was there such continued reluctance on the part of the British government to annex territory? All these contradictions, the proponents of the new thesis argued, could be resolved by accepting a basic continuity in nineteenth-century British imperial expansion.

Gallagher and Robinson drew a clear distinction between the 'mercantilist use of power to obtain commercial supremacy and monopoly through political possession' and the imperialism of free trade which was content to limit 'the use of paramount power to establishing security for trade'. Consequently, they wrote, 'whether imperialist phenomena show themselves or not is determined not only by the factors of economic expansion, but equally by the political and social organisation of the regions brought into the orbit of the expansive society, and also by the

---

[7] D. C. M. Platt, 'The Imperialism of Free Trade: Some Reservations', *Econ.H.R.*, XXI (1968) 296.

world situation in general'.[8] On this basis British imperial expansion was not likely to be chronological or even linked to phases of economic growth, since the level of economic integration and the type of political control required varied with each region. Accordingly, mercantilist techniques of formal empire could be employed to develop India at the same time as the informal techniques of free trade were being used to the same end in Latin America and China. Thus, Gallagher and Robinson argued, the difference between formal and informal empire was one not of fundamental nature but of degree – both being variable political functions of an expanding British industrial society. To this extent they were linked and even interchangeable. Informal means were always preferred to direct rule, but 'mid-Victorian as well as late-Victorian policy-makers did not refuse to extend the protection of formal rule over British interests when informal methods had failed to give security'. It just so happened, in the circumstances of the middle decades of the century, when British trade and industry led the world and rivals were few, that informal techniques were usually sufficient.[9]

By citing examples of British intervention in South America and China, Gallagher and Robinson sought to show that throughout the whole century 'British governments worked to establish and maintain British paramountcy by whatever means best suited the circumstances of their diverse regions of interest'. They concluded that the usual summary of the policy of the free trade era, 'trade not rule', should be amended to read 'trade with informal control if possible; trade with rule when necessary'.[10] Although the imperialists of the late-Victorian period were driven to annex more often than their mid-century counterparts, their aims were basically the same. To label one period 'imperialist' and the other 'anti-imperialist', therefore, was not only entirely irrelevant but mistaken, since British interests were always protected and extended.

This new thesis had great appeal. It caused many leading scholars to have second thoughts on the nature of British imperialism in the nineteenth century. It rapidly gained acceptance. Not only did all the contradictions inherent in the

---

[8] Gallagher and Robinson, *Econ.H.R.*, vi 6.
[9] Ibid. p. 12.
[10] Ibid. p. 13.

traditional conception appear to be removed, but it seemed to provide a comprehensive framework for British overseas expansion throughout the nineteenth century, embracing both 'formal' and 'informal' concepts of empire as well as bringing the Indian empire, hitherto regarded as a separate case, under the same roof as the Crown colonies and the colonies of British settlement. Indeed, it was clearly a scholarly way of stating the obvious. Mr Gallagher and Dr Robinson went on, in fact, to contribute several new aspects to the general theory of imperialism in subsequent writings in the *Cambridge History of the British Empire*, in the *New Cambridge Modern History* and, in conjunction with Alice Denny, in their book *Africa and the Victorians.*[11]

But murmurs of dissent were heard as the 'Gallagher–Robinson thesis' was still in the process of elaboration. No substantial counter-attack on the 'imperialism of free trade' was mounted, however, until Professor Oliver Macdonagh entered the lists with his article 'The Anti-Imperialism of Free Trade'.[12]

II

Professor Macdonagh objected both to the rigidity of the Gallagher–Robinson thesis and also the looseness of its terms : the conception of formal and informal empire as variable political functions, he explained, 'merely replaces the old conceptual difficulties with new'. First, the definition of 'informal' empire was not exclusive enough. One of the main recipients of British overseas trade, emigration and culture was the United States. Would it not be extravagant to include that country as part of the 'informal' empire, he asked, and equally odd to drain Canada of colour on the map while painting the Balkans off-red? And what about Ireland – was she exploiter or exploited?

[11] R. E. Robinson, 'Imperial Problems in British Politics, 1880–95', *C.H.B.E.* (Cambridge, 1959) III 127–80; R. E. Robinson and J. A. Gallagher, 'The Partition of Africa', *N.C.M.H.* (Cambridge, 1962) XI 593–640; R. E. Robinson and J. A. Gallagher, with Alice Denny, *Africa and the Victorians* (London, 1961). It is noteworthy that the authors shift their ground in each of these contributions.

[12] O. Macdonagh, 'The Anti-Imperialism of Free Trade', *Econ.H.R.*, XIV (1962) 489–501. Prior to this, criticism of the thesis had been voiced in D. S. Landes, 'Some Thoughts on the Nature of Economic Imperialism', *J.E.H.*, XXI (1961) 496–512. An alternative to the economic explanation has been argued by D. K. Fieldhouse, ' "Imperialism": An Historiographical Revision', *Econ.H.R.*, XIV (1961) 187–209, and *The Theory of Capitalist Imperialism* (London, 1967).

Ireland was indeed the prime exporter of population from the United Kingdom; but she was also the major exporter of French Revolutionary ideology, Roman Catholic religion, and anti-British sentiment. In fact 'overseas trade, investment, migration and culture' were not four battalions in the same regiment: they did not even march in the same direction.[13]

Macdonagh also objected to the de-personalisation and universality of the thesis. It did matter which party and men were in power. The existence of an implacable opposition to imperialism had been ignored; the relationship of the economic and political arms of government was not simply one of master and servant; imperial problems were often inextricably interwoven with domestic issues; and finally, the Victorian attitude towards empire was compounded of more elements than self-interest.[14]

Macdonagh's main aim, however, was to question the connection which Gallagher and Robinson had sought to establish between British imperialism and free trade policy during the mid-nineteenth century. He pointed out that free trade was only part of a general political attitude – a political morality – which included economy, pacifism, anti-*rentier* and anti-aristocratic prejudices. Basing his argument primarily on quotations from the writings and speeches of Richard Cobden, he sought to prove that 'Cobden was both sensitive and opposed to imperial growths and exercises *because* of his adherence to Free Trade'. The natural attitude of doctrinaire free-traders, Macdonagh asserted, was anti-imperialist. The 'imperialism of free trade', therefore, was a misnomer which could only mislead; in fact, he concluded, it suggested the opposite of the truth.[15]

This broadside did not necessitate a fundamental revision of the Gallagher–Robinson thesis. The framework could be modified to remove the rigidity – to admit variations, within certain limitations, according to which party and men were in power and to allow for the existence of a strong, but, as Macdonagh admitted, largely ineffective counter-current of anti-imperialism. Definitions could also be adjusted to make them more exclusive, although Macdonagh had ignored the fact that Gallagher and Robinson used the term 'informal' empire only for areas (unlike

[13] Macdonagh, *Econ.H.R.*, xiv 489.
[14] Ibid. pp. 500–1.
[15] Ibid.

the United States) in which a 'power solution' was possible.
Moreover, it could be contended that Macdonagh had mainly
taken issue with the appellation 'imperialism of free trade'. He
was intent on denying that the free-traders promoted empire; the
phrase 'the imperialism of the free trade era', it seems, would
have been perfectly acceptable. Macdonagh can also be criticised
for concentrating almost solely on the writings of Cobden, who
freely acknowledged that he held 'opinions of a somewhat
abstract kind and not adapted for the practical work of the day'.
By following Cobden's thought too exclusively, one critic has
suggested, Macdonagh exaggerated the anti-imperialism of free
trade at the level of practical politics.[16]

Indeed, one is left wondering whether the extremely sophisti-
cated theories of Richard Cobden were really representative of
the Manchester School's attitude, and even whether Manchester's
ideas so completely dominated the mid-Victorian decades. As
Macdonagh himself wrote : 'The British people, it was evident,
were not ready to follow the doctrinaire disciples of the Manchester School.' All in all, Macdonagh's attack left too many
loose ends to be convincing, especially in view of his admission
that 'it was the achievement of Mr Gallagher and Dr Robinson
to establish the essentially imperialist character of British policy
and public sentiment in the years 1845 to 1860, and to dissipate
the contrary myth'.[17] Thus the Gallagher–Robinson thesis survived largely unscathed – with a few modifications written into
the framework – and the middle decades of the nineteenth
century still appeared as an important age of expansion.

III

More recent criticism has been much more damaging to the
thesis. In several recent works D. C. M. Platt has attacked the
Gallagher–Robinson view of British official policy in relation to
overseas trade and investment. While agreeing that the British
government in the century before 1914 regarded itself as bound,

---

[16] Cobden to H. Ashworth, 16 Oct. 1857, quoted in J. Morley, *The Life
of Richard Cobden* (London, 1903) p. 671. R. J. Moore cites this statement
(which refers solely to India) in criticism of Macdonagh's arguments in his
'Imperialism and "Free Trade" Policy in India, 1853–4', *Econ.H.R.*, xvii
(1964) 145.

[17] Macdonagh, *Econ.H.R.*, xiv 500.

so far as possible, to open the world to trade, Dr Platt denied that government action ever amounted to the energetic promotion and intervention described by Gallagher and Robinson.[18] Force was not a common or acceptable instrument in the British search for commercial paramountcy. In fact he was able to demonstrate his own thesis by a careful examination of British policy throughout the nineteenth century in South America and the Far East. He even cited the very examples Gallagher and Robinson had used to support their own case and showed them not to have been typical of British policy, but the reverse of what Gallagher and Robinson claimed. Everywhere, said Platt, there seemed to be a general reluctance on the part of the British government to intervene. British 'paramountcy', he claimed, was automatic. It was the creation of a British industrial and financial lead, through the agency of British traders and investors, without government intervention. Not surprisingly, therefore, his conclusions challenged the findings of the two Cambridge historians and appeared to shake the very foundations of their thesis. Nonintervention and *laissez-faire*, Platt asserted, were the characteristic attitudes of Victorian officialdom and these attitudes were faithfully reflected overseas. In direct contradiction of Gallagher and Robinson's conclusions, he stated :

> It is *not* true, for example, that British government policy in Latin America was to obtain 'indirect political hegemony over the new regions for the purposes of trade', or to create 'a new and informal empire' in the interests of future British commercial expansion. It is *not* the case that the mid-Victorian Foreign Office, in any positive or consistent sense, encouraged stable governments in Latin America, in China, and in the Balkans as good investment risks, and coerced weaker or unsatisfactory states into more co-operative attitudes. It can *not* be argued that Britain had a 'political hold' on China, nor can it be denied that the government was reluctant to intervene over a wide field of British trade and financial interest and was particularly anxious to avoid the use of force to promote trade. Above all, the policy of a *laissez-faire*, non-interventionist

[18] D. C. M. Platt, *Finance, Trade and Politics in British Foreign Policy, 1815–1914* (London, 1968); 'The Imperialism of Free Trade: Some Reservations', *Econ.H.R.*, xxi 296–306; and 'Economic Factors in British Policy during the "New Imperialism" ', *P.&P.*, xxxix (1968) 120–38.

government can *not* realistically be described as 'trade with informal control if possible; trade with rule when necessary'.[19]

Where had Gallagher and Robinson gone wrong? Platt concluded that they had overestimated the scope of government in the first half of Victoria's reign and the limits within which, in the age of *laissez-faire*, it was possible for the British government to work. No British government was prepared to extend its responsibilities beyond the minimum required to guarantee equal favour and open competition overseas. And this unwillingness to intervene in the realm of trade was paralleled by an equally strong tradition in British diplomacy : non-intervention in the internal affairs of foreign states. Force was 'rarely and only exceptionally employed for the promotion of British trade and investments'.[20]

What then was the British government prepared to do? Platt answered that it was always ready to negotiate 'open door' commercial treaties, compile and transmit commercial intelligence, and use its diplomatic and consular stations for the defence of British subjects against 'outrage and injury'. But there its functions ceased. Did this constitute 'imperialism' in the mid-Victorian era? Platt argued that it did not. After all, free trade was simply *laissez-faire* applied to overseas trade policy – and who has ever heard of the 'imperialism of *laissez-faire*'?[21]

The last quarter of the century, however, was a different matter. Here Platt agreed that the Gallagher and Robinson formula, 'trade with informal control if possible; trade with rule when necessary', did have some meaning, for he admitted that the late-Victorians were prepared to take much greater steps in defence of British trade. Platt argued that in the interests solely of commerce and finance, previously treated in such a cavalier fashion, British governments now found it necessary to enlarge the scope of government responsibility to the extent of outright annexation and the establishment of political spheres of influence:

The pressure of renewed protectionism, the partition of the world into colonial or semi-colonial enclosures surrounded by high tariff barriers, and the development of a new form of

---

[19] Platt, *Econ.H.R.*, xxi 305.
[20] Ibid. p. 297.
[21] Ibid. p. 305, n. 2.

American reactions than by the local oil interest – by politics rather than commercial needs.[23] Similarly in China, where concern for future markets and for equal treatment were at the forefront of British policy, it was in reality the old political battle being fought with new economic weapons that brought the British government into the race for concessions and spheres of influence. Equally in Africa, the Foreign Office often intervened only when considerations of strategy and foreign policy or strong domestic pressure existed alongside the economic factor. Moreover elsewhere, in Turkey and Persia for example, economic considerations were clearly subordinated to the maintenance of British security. Thus while Dr Platt has performed a valuable service in restoring to prominence the economic factors in British policy during the 'New Imperialism', we must remember that commercial interests were only one factor in a more general political context and that, as Zara Steiner has recently reminded us, the protection of markets never achieved the same weight in the calculations of officials in Whitehall as that maintenance of British security which Gallagher and Robinson so fully concentrated upon in *Africa and the Victorians*.[24]

Dr Platt's thesis may also be questioned in other ways. Little attention has been paid to the role of the Colonial Office. That department certainly knew much more about local transgressions of the policy of non-intervention than other departments in Whitehall, and the policy of 'qualified restraint'[25] on the imperial frontier was rather different from the attitude Platt describes. However much successive British Foreign Secretaries might

[23] Platt, *Finance, Trade and Politics*, pp. 325–9.

[24] See the stimulating review of Platt's book by Zara Steiner, 'Finance, Trade and Politics in British Foreign Policy, 1815–1914', *H.J.*, XIII (1970) 545–52. The central thesis of *Africa and the Victorians* has itself attracted much criticism. The principal reservations, apart from those of Platt, are outlined in J. Stengers, 'L'Impérialisme colonial de la fin du XIXᵉ siècle: Mythe ou Réalité', *J.A.H.*, III (1962) 469–91; C. W. Newbury, 'Victorians, Republicans and the Partitions of West Africa', *J.A.H.*, III (1962) 493–501; G. Shepperson, 'Africa, the Victorians and Imperialism', *Revue Belge de Philologie et d'Histoire*, XL (1962) 1228–38; E. Stokes, *Imperialism and the Scramble for Africa: A New View* (Historical Association of Rhodesia and Nyasaland, 1963); R. Hyam, 'The Partition of Africa', *H.J.*, VII (1964) 154–69.

[25] For an excellent survey of the problem, see W. D. McIntyre, *The Imperial Frontier in the Tropics, 1865–75: A Study of British Colonial Policy in West Africa, Malaya and the South Pacific in the Age of Gladstone and Disraeli* (London, 1967).

interventionist financial diplomacy made any less active poli
an abandonment of an obligation to which all British gover
ments subscribed – the official duty to maintain a 'fair fie
and no favour' for British interests at home and abroad.[22]

This amounted to a breach in the theory of continuity. In Plat
eyes, it was Gallagher and Robinson's error to have translate
this newly acquired scope of government action back in time
the mid-Victorian period, to have assumed that mid-nineteent
century statesmen and officials were as ready as their successo
to undertake 'informal control if possible, direct when necessar
in the interests of British trade. It was as simple as that. Mi
Victorian imperialism was a very weak affair.

What then remains of Gallagher and Robinson's thesis at th
stage in the argument? More than appears at first sight, as I
Platt's own interpretation has yet to be fully substantiated. Firs
as regards the theory of continuity, he has made a very stron
case for his view that officials in the Foreign Office throughou
the nineteenth century were averse to extending political respon
sibilities in the interests of trade and that British diplomats over
seas were more than reluctant to act for particular firms. Th
'formal' and 'informal' areas of British paramountcy were not s
interchangeable as Gallagher and Robinson thought. We ma
also agree that in the post-1880 era the Foreign Office was force
to readjust its policies to the new political and economic climat
but it is by no means clear how significant a departure th
represented in the traditional principles and practices of Briti
diplomacy. The Cobdenite Board of Trade, the Foreign Offi
and the Gladstonian garrison at the Treasury were extrem
hesitant in abandoning their *laissez-faire* stand. Older patterns
thought – purely negative attitudes – certainly persisted into
late nineteenth century.

The assertion that after 1885 the Foreign Office often in
vened solely in the interests of commerce and finance does
ring true. In his chapter on Latin America, Platt insists that,
the contrary, in this region British policy developed 'hardl
all from the time of Castlereagh to that of Sir Edward Gr
And when the British government did become involved, a
Mexico in 1913, their policy was dominated more by fea

[22] Ibid. p. 306.

preach open competition and talk piously of not wanting any exclusive rights, British policy as carried out on the spot added up to much more than this. Professor A. P. Thornton stated over a decade ago :

> The policy later known as that of the 'Open Door' in China was one that had long been pursued in the eastern seas by private persons who had every intention of ensuring that it was they themselves who would act as custodian of the door once they got it open. (Whose door it was in the first place, they did not consider a matter of importance; and their discovery that the United States saw some moral obligation in the policy to keep the door open for whomsoever might wish to pass peaceably through it, gave these eastern traders a shock from which they were slow to recover.) Similarly, when the British 'opened' the Karun River in Southern Persia in 1889, in the hope that it would become a highway of regional commerce, Salisbury the Foreign Secretary took pains to assure his opposite number at St Petersburg that England sought no special advantage, that the commerce of the area in question would be open to all the world. The answer he got was sharp enough. 'C'était là', said Giers, 'une manière de parler.'[26]

However fair and selfless the principles enunciated seemed, the continued dominance and prosperity of British trade were the end in view. Platt seems to have accepted the government's enunciation of principles at face value. But the policy they initiated worked differently in different areas. In India, a particular case for example, government policy supported by the majority of the Manchester School was the very reverse of *laissez-faire*. And elsewhere the minimal aims of the British government did not always mean that local intervention was prevented. When it came to the test, no British government could afford to ignore the future well-being of British overseas trade, and there was a large indefinable area between what local agents could do and what the Foreign and Colonial Offices would veto. The men of the 'turbulent frontier' proved a constant headache to those two departments in London and a kind of 'sub-

[26] A. P. Thornton, *The Imperial Idea and its Enemies: A Study in British Power* (London, 1959) p. 14.

imperialism' often developed which they found difficult to suppress.[27]

Platt's classifications, therefore, seem in some ways too precise, too neat. Such rigid divisions cannot be drawn between the authority of Whitehall and the man on the spot; between political independence and economic involvement; between 'official' and 'unofficial' action. Economic involvement on the periphery of empire too often led to political intervention as political instability in areas of trade led local officials to take sides in civil wars or intervene to re-establish conditions conducive to commercial prosperity. Too often officials in Whitehall could do no more than condone actions already undertaken.

Nor does such a rigid division between the mid-Victorian empire and the years after 1880 seem acceptable. To emphasise this, Platt would largely remove the economic factor from the formal expansion of the earlier period :

> Actual imperial annexations in Africa and the East during the mid-Victorian period were seldom directly connected with the interests of British trade; they were designed primarily to safe-guard existing frontiers and to establish government control and discipline over existing British communities.[28]

But surely the mid-Victorian obsession with security, defence of the routes to the east and the 'keys' of India was but the economic argument at one remove : Palmerston was frequently as much concerned with trade as with defence.[29] And it seems equally difficult to accept Platt's contention that political spheres of influence 'had no relevance to the needs of British trade and finance'[30] when we remember the situation of Singapore, Lagos, Zanzibar and Hong Kong. Great Britain was not always so successful in keeping her promotion of 'a fair field and no favour' trade policy apart from politics – as she apparently

[27] J. S. Galbraith, 'The "Turbulent Frontier" as a Factor in British Expansion', *C.S.S.H.*, II (1960) 150–68.

[28] Platt, *Econ.H.R.*, XXI 305.

[29] 'It is the business of Government to open and secure the roads for the merchant': Palmerston to Auckland, 22 Jan. 1841, quoted in C. K. Webster, *The Foreign Policy of Palmerston* (London, 1951) II 751. See also R. J. Gavin, 'Palmerston's Policy towards East and West Africa', unpublished D.Phil. thesis (Oxford, 1958), and the same author's 'Nigeria and Lord Palmerston', *Ibadan* (1961) 24–7.

[30] Platt, *Econ.H.R.*, XXI 305.

was in South America, the case study on which Platt builds so much. As Zara Steiner has commented, throughout the century good offices and protection were often exceedingly difficult to distinguish from 'unqualified diplomatic intervention'.[31]

What then is left? Have the middle decades of the last century been stripped of their new-found glory? Not entirely. While we must agree that Gallagher and Robinson's formula, 'trade with informal control if possible; trade with rule when necessary', over-emphasises the steps the British government was prepared to take in the mid-Victorian period, Platt's formula 'fair field and no favour', while representing the pious platitudes of Foreign Secretaries and the Cobdenite Board of Trade, takes too little notice of the amount of political involvement such a policy could entail. These historians, by concentrating so exclusively on British trade policy in what C. R. Fay termed the 'informal' empire,[32] have ignored developments in the formal empire, where the economic stake already established, coupled with unstable local conditions, often led to further political intervention beyond the area of government. Nor has any notice been taken of that new body of economic theory supporting the formal empire which Bernard Semmel has dubbed 'free trade imperialism'.[33] In fact it is obvious that there was a fundamental continuity in British overseas trade and territorial expansion throughout the nineteenth century. But the continuity was one of direction rather than time. As Professor W. D. McIntyre has written:

> British expansion proceeded by a series of uneven thrusts, which began for particular reasons at different times and in different areas . . . within a general continuity of direction, movements of greater or lesser activity must still be recognised.[34]

[31] Steiner, *H.J.*, xiii 547.

[32] C. R. Fay, 'The Movement Towards Free Trade', *C.H.B.E.*, ii 399. Fay first coined the phrase 'informal empire' to describe the expansion of Great Britain's commercial and financial power beyond the bounds of her political jurisdiction in his *Imperial Economy and its Place in the Foundation of Economic Doctrine, 1600–1932* (Oxford, 1934).

[33] B. Semmel, *The Rise of Free Trade Imperialism: Classical Political Economy, the Empire of Free Trade and Imperialism, 1750–1850* (London, 1970); see also Semmel, 'The Philosophic Radicals and Colonialism', *J.E.H.*, xxi (1961) 513–25.

[34] McIntyre, *Imperial Frontier*, p. 374.

Nevertheless all British governments in the Victorian era recognised their duty to establish security for British trade. This Platt accepted. That in the late-Victorian period more forceful intervention – an enlarged scope of government responsibility – was needed to achieve this end, does not, however, necessarily indicate a breach in the theory of continuity but rather a change of gear in government activity. To argue that there was 'no continuity as between the mid- and late-Victorians in the steps that they were prepared to take in defence of British trade' because the later period 'saw pre-emptive annexation and the outright delimitation of spheres of interest and influence *in the interests of commerce and finance*'[35] is surely to underestimate the role of the economic factor in the mid-Victorian period. The mid-Victorians had also annexed territory and established spheres of influence – had used the same means – in the general British interest and the economic factor was an important thread in the general political context.

Recently, Dr Platt has to some extent tacitly recognised this position. While he still asserts the importance of the new direction in British policy in the late-Victorian age after 1880, he has come to see several important developments occurring in the mid-Victorian years. The whole debate on the 'imperialism of free trade' has advanced once more and taken yet another path with the publication of his most recent article, 'Further Objections to an "Imperialism of Free Trade", 1830–60', in the *Economic History Review* for February 1973.

In this article, Dr Platt (now Professor of the History of Latin America at Oxford) attacks the Gallagher–Robinson model from a different angle. The concept of 'informal' empire has always rested on three basic assumptions: the readiness of the British government to establish or, at least, to maintain British paramountcy by whatever means suited the circumstances; the determination of British manufacturers and merchants to penetrate world markets; and the economic subordination of the countries producing primary products to Great Britain in her role as the workshop of the world. Having already questioned whether the political arm functioned in this way, Platt has now challenged the idea of economic aggression in the early Victorian age. Was there ever any 'blue-print' or grand design for estab-

[35] Platt, *Econ.H.R.*, XXI 305.

lishing British paramountcy in remote parts of the world? Platt
thinks not. By analysing the export figures for 1830–60, he
demonstrates that in this period northern Europe and the U.S.A.,
British India, Australasia and Canada were the main British
export markets. Latin America, the Levant and China were
relatively unimportant areas. There was little prospect for two-
way trade with these regions, the purchasing power of the local
populations was small, and to some extent the internal markets
were self-sufficient. The ability of British traders to break into
distant markets and to meet the challenge of local handicraft
production and cottage industry has been grossly exaggerated. In
fact, Platt believes the whole idea of complementary satellite
economies is wrong. There was no vigorous expansion into the
regions of alleged 'informal' empire in the early Victorian age :

> There are, indeed, absurdities in attributing a modern, neo-
> colonial relationship between subordinate primary producers
> and developed industrial powers, to a period and to trades
> where primary products were not, as yet, in demand, and
> where exports of British produce and manufactures to the
> entire continent of Spanish America and Brazil, 1841–50,
> averaged £5.7 million per annum, to Turkey (including
> Wallachia and Moldavia, Syria and Palestine) £2.6 million,
> and to the massive population of China only £1.6 million.[36]

Platt concludes that in a period of short booms, disastrous slumps
and long periods of exceedingly slow growth there was a marked
general indifference to marginal markets.

Was this, then, a period when Great Britain 'practised active
imperialism over the whole breadth of the world, "informal" in
pattern but no less aggressive or enthusiastic for that'? Did this
age, he asks, see the high point of Great Britain's 'Empire of Free
Trade'? On the contrary, the scale of government intervention,
the size of the trade involved, the extent of interest displayed by
British traders and investors, and the nature of the stakes do not
seem to warrant this interpretation. Indeed, once the degree of
dependence of those distant territories on imported manufactures
and the true place of exports in their mid-nineteenth-century
economies is assessed, the 'imperialism of free trade' is revealed as

[36] Platt, 'Further Objections to an "Imperialism of Free Trade", 1830–60',
Econ.H.R., xxvi (1973) 84.

a sham. Gallagher and Robinson, he concludes, antedated by several decades the importance of the 'informal' empire not only as a destination for British investment but as a supplier of foodstuffs and industrial raw materials. The concept of 'informal' empire, therefore, is inapplicable to the years before 1860.

Platt agrees, however, that the concept is applicable to the relationship between the primary producers and Great Britain in and after the later decades of the nineteenth century. Then, he argues, a new range of local demand developed from the outflow of British investment. This permitted the purchase of coal, iron, machinery and railway materials and thus changed the character of British exports to some of the more distant markets in the last decades of the century. An increased demand for British manufactures followed from a subsequent increase in the demand for industrial raw materials and foodstuffs in Great Britain. Platt indicates this change in direction of British exports by contrasting the evidence of witnesses before the Select Committee on Import Duties in 1840, who looked towards extending British sales in northern Europe and the U.S.A., with that of witnesses before the Royal Commission on the Depression of Trade and Industry in 1885–6, who by this time had begun to look towards markets in India, the white colonies and the Far East. Once again he returns to the argument that the British government was only forced into an active promotional policy towards trade and investment overseas by international pressure in the last decades of the century – new methods in new circumstances:

The timing of the new period and of the new attitudes is obvious. Any truly *aggressive* expansion of British trade and investment at a national level into distant, non-colonial territories had to await the development of genuine markets for British manufactured goods. It was necessarily dependent on the emergence, within the United Kingdom, of a greatly enlarged demand for imported foodstuffs and industrial raw materials, which finally spilled out into the furthest ends of the world. It was forced and promoted by strong foreign competition within the traditional outlets for British trade and investment in Europe and North America. It developed out of a reserve of British capital in search of higher yields in the newly emergent nations. It was indeed, in every respect, a product of the last four decades of the Victorian era.[37]

It is interesting to note that Professor Platt in placing such emphasis on the last four decades of the century has absorbed the mid-Victorian decades (1860–80) into his argument. The years he has recently written about embrace the early Victorian age alone.

Thus in the present debate Platt certainly seems to have come off best in one part of the argument at least. It would seem that 'informal' empire (as defined by Platt)[38] is not a term which can be applied generally with any historical accuracy before 1860. He has also established that there was a change in the attitudes of the British government and business towards economic expansion into distant markets in the late nineteenth century. But was there such a sharp break as he postulates in the character of British imperialism from 1880? After all, economics is but one thread in that argument. Platt's thesis that the British government's reluctance to intervene was largely removed and that economic motives dominated British policy in the last quarter of the century remains to be substantiated. Indeed, when one recalls that in the fifty years before 1865 the British empire had expanded by an average of about 100,000 square miles per annum, an average annual expansion not far below that of the subsequent half-century, it becomes clear that there are many other considerations and even new criteria to take into account in broader discussions which involve the 'formal' empire. As regards the mid-Victorian years, they still emerge as important years of trade expansion, but certainly not as 'the decisive stage in the history of British expansion overseas' outlined by Gallagher and Robinson.[39]

One thing is quite obvious, however, even though the debate will not end here:[40] never again will it be possible to characterise

[37] Ibid. p. 90.

[38] For conceptual difficulties involved in the use of this term, see Katharine West, 'Theorising about "Imperialism": A Methodological Note', *The Journal of Imperial and Commonwealth History*, I (1973) 148–9.

[39] See Hobsbawm, *Industry and Empire*, pp. 113–16. Statistics are to be found in B. R. Mitchell and P. Deane, *Abstract of British Historical Statistics* (London, 1962) pp. 274–337; and in *Parl. P.* 1868–9 LVIII and 1881 LXXVII.

[40] Further contributions to the debate, not mentioned in this chapter, are: P. Harnetty, 'The Imperialism of Free Trade: Lancashire and the Indian

the mid-Victorian years as an age of anti-imperialism. Clearly, many of the basic assumptions about policy made by earlier writers on this period were misconceived. Ideas as well as events have to be placed in an entirely different framework. To date, the scholarship of Professors Bodelsen and Schuyler has dominated research on mid-Victorian thought, but now the material once covered apparently so exhaustively, needs to be reassessed. Not only have their assumptions about the mid-Victorian era been challenged, but their conclusions about mid-Victorian attitudes towards empire also need to be reviewed in the light of the advances made in the research of the past decade.

Cotton Duties, 1859–62', *Econ.H.R.*, xviii (1965) 333–49; W. M. Mathew, 'The Imperialism of Free Trade: Peru 1820–70', *Econ.H.R.*, xxi (1968) 562–79; and A. G. Hopkins, 'Economic Imperialism in West Africa: Lagos, 1880–92', ibid., 580–606. The latter article has provoked a reply by J. F. A. Ajayi and R. A. Austen, 'Hopkins on Economic Imperialism in West Africa', *Econ.H.R.*, xxv (1972) 303–6 and A. G. Hopkins, 'Economic Imperialism in West Africa: A Rejoinder', ibid., 307–12. Another recent contribution to the debate is P. Harnetty, *Imperialism and Free Trade, India and Lancashire in the Mid-Nineteenth Century* (London, 1972).

2
Mid-Victorian Pragmatism

IF IT IS obviously no longer satisfactory to write of the middle
decades of the last century as though British policy was dominated by an aversion to empire, what did the imperial idea
amount to at this time? Unfortunately mid-Victorian thought
about empire, colonies, trade, and influence in general, is also
surrounded by much controversy. Even in the late 1950s, when
the general outline of the Gallagher–Robinson thesis of continuity began to be accepted in many quarters, several writers
continued to draw a clear distinction between general attitudes
towards empire and the actual policies Great Britain pursued in
administering her colonial possessions.[1] The myth of mid-Victorian
'indifference' took much longer to dissipate.

The view of nineteenth-century British imperial history
popularised in the 1920s – of a period of stagnation followed
after 1870 by a phase of belligerent expansionism – was buttressed
by a whole theory concerning mid-nineteenth-century thought.
Once the economic reason for empire was removed by free trade
and the constitutional link undermined by responsible government, the mid-Victorians, it was argued, saw no need for maintaining the imperial tie and became intent on shedding the
financial burdens and trappings of empire. The teachings of those
groups of economists, like the Manchester School, who preached
the uselessness of empire were assumed to have dominated the
age, and the writings and speeches of politicians and publicists
were searched to prove the rule. The works of those who insisted
that the empire was an expensive anachronism were cited;

[1] See, for example, J. R. M. Butler, 'Imperial Questions in British Politics,
1868–80', *C.H.B.E.*, III 18–26.

partisan judgements – such as labels of derision used against opponents and Disraeli's harangue against the Liberals in his Crystal Palace speech – were accepted at face value; and the odd word spoken in an outburst of irritation, the sentence taken out of context and any casual remark which could be interpreted as a criticism of empire were all used to buttress the thesis. Thus isolated comments concerning the burden of imperial defence, the expense of certain colonies and the embarrassing position of Canada were formulated into a general philosophy relating to the outlook on the whole empire during the 1860s. The mid-nineteenth century was an age of pessimism and lack of interest in the empire. In short, it was an 'Age of Separatism'. Such an interpretation was difficult to shift, especially when it was apparently documented so fully in the detailed works of such historians as C. A. Bodelsen and R. L. Schuyler.

I

There was some truth in the statement. Critics of empire had always existed and in the mid-Victorian era the assumption that independence was the natural destiny of the colonies of British settlement was tacitly accepted by all. Nobody suggested that troops should be employed to retain a colony against its will. What the argument was about was the pace and conclusion of this process of historical change : evolution or dissolution? Professor Koebner pushed his argument too far when he asserted that 'most thinking men in those days had little doubt about the impending dissolution of the British Empire'.[2] Not everybody agreed that the framework of empire need disintegrate, or that the moment of separation need arise in the foreseeable future. Such views were ignored by the older school of historians; but as the concept of continuity in British overseas expansion was gradually accepted, a revision of the traditional view became necessary. Eventually the 'myths of the Little England era' were laid bare.

Mercantilism – 'the use of power to obtain commercial supremacy and monopoly through political possession' – had always been associated with imperialism. Therefore those who attacked the commercial and political restrictions of the old

[2] R. Koebner and H. D. Schmidt, *Imperialism: The Story and Significance of a Political Word, 1840–1960* (Cambridge, 1964) p. 83.

colonial system and declared colonies to be economically worthless, were, it was assumed, anti-imperialist in outlook. After all, in 1776 Adam Smith had declared that Great Britain derived nothing but loss from the dominion which she assumed over her colonies, and Josiah Tucker, another pioneer of the free trade movement, and Jeremy Bentham, the Utilitarian philosopher, entertained similar views. In 1793 Bentham cried *Emancipate Your Colonies* and Ricardo, James Mill and J. R. McCulloch agreed. A superficial identification between the movement for free trade and colonial self-government was soon established. Subsequently, many historians, following the lead of Professors Schuyler and Bodelsen, argued that mid-nineteenth-century British politicians, with the American War of Independence in mind, agreed that colonies were worthless and that the British public should be prepared for the dissolution of the empire. All other ideas about empire to the contrary were ignored. Thus it remained a matter of puzzlement to those who adopted this line of reasoning, why 'in view of this current of separatism and indifference and the much stronger one of not wanting to augment the encumbrance of empire by extending its boundaries even the period from 1815 to 1850 produced imperial . . . expansion'.[3] No wonder recent writers have devoted more attention to those other justifications for empire previously ignored.

The classical economists and Philosophic Radicals were not so 'anti-colonial' in sentiment as was previously thought, nor were the ideas of the Colonial Reformers led by Edward Gibbon Wakefield as unique as this rather self-important group would have us believe. As Bernard Semmel has shown, the Benthamite Radicals 'were advocates of positive programmes of empire and, grounding their arguments upon the new economic science, constructed and maintained a set of doctrines of which the keystone was the necessity of empire to an industrial England'.[4] In short, the old conception of empire based on colonial trade was replaced

[3] K. E. Knorr, *British Colonial Theories, 1750–1850* (Toronto, 1944) p. 411.

[4] Semmel, *J.E.H.*, xxi 513. Notable contributions to this line of argument have been made by L. Robbins, *Robert Torrens and the Evolution of Classical Economics* (London, 1958); R. N. Ghosh, *Classical Macroeconomics and the Case for Colonies* (Calcutta, 1967); D. Winch, *Classical Political Economy and Colonies* (London, 1965); and E. R. Kittrell, 'The Development of the Theory of Colonisation in English Classical Political Economy', *Southern Economic Journal*, xxxi (1965) 189–206.

by a new emphasis on the importance to Great Britain of
migration and colonial investment, so that the maintenance of
empire remained a basic feature of British policy. Indeed,
Professor Semmel has even gone so far as to assert that 'the
period of the fall of the Old Colonial System may be viewed as
one of the rise of free trade imperialism'.[5]

During the years of periodic unemployment and trade depression after the Napoleonic wars, when much talk was heard of
the danger of social revolution, colonisation was advocated as a
means of alleviating the widespread pauperism, the abject
poverty and distress in the English agricultural counties, as well
as over-population in Ireland. The colonies would be of great
benefit to the mother country in taking some of her 'redundant'
population, especially if the cost of emigration could be financed
by selling their Crown lands. This line of argument, urged by
Robert Torrens, Wakefield, Charles Buller and Robert Godley,
and enthusiastically supported by Nassau Senior, Archbishop
Whately, J. R. McCulloch, John Stuart Mill and Wilmot
Horton, became one of the new props in defence of colonies.

An equally important line of argument developed by Wakefield
and Torrens was the importance of overseas investment, especially
in the colonies. Many economists at the time feared that the
normal rate of profit in post-war England was tending to decline,
according to the law of diminishing returns, as too much capital
was seeking investment. The export of surplus capital for colonisation was proposed, therefore, to keep up the rate of profit on
domestic investment. John Stuart Mill suggested that by opening
up new territories the cost of producing food would be reduced
and Great Britain's terms of trade improved. This would raise
the rate of profit at home, broaden the British economy and thus
increase domestic investment beyond its former level. 'The ex-
portation of capital is an agent of great efficacy in extending the
field of employment for that which remains : and it may be said
that up to a certain point the more capital we send away, the
more we shall possess.'[6] Thus emigration and colonial investment
became twin pillars of a new economic theory supporting empire,

[5] Semmel, *Rise of Free Trade Imperialism*, p. 4.
[6] J. S. Mill, *Principles of Political Economy* (London, 1909) pp. 382,
739–41, quoted in A. G. L. Shaw (ed.), *Great Britain and the Colonies,
1815–65* (London, 1970) pp. 13–14.

and in fact after 1830 no prominent classical economist, J. R. McCulloch apart, ventured an over-all attack on the new doctrines of colonisation. Professor A. G. L. Shaw has concluded:

> After Mill's enthusiastic backing, it would appear that accusations that the early Victorian economists opposed imperial development could be made only by those who had never read the *Principles.* This would be more surprising if such a neglect of sources was not so common among those who confidently pronounce on what is (or is not) contained in them.[7]

In the early and mid-Victorian periods, then, economists were not by any means unanimously opposed to the continued existence of empire: in certain circumstances this was actually favoured.

Even the characteristics of the Manchester School have been largely misrepresented. Very few of its members were informed about the British colonies and it possessed no coherent philosophy concerning empire. In fact the 'Manchester School' (so dubbed contemptuously by Disraeli) was not a coherent body at all, but rather a disparate group of economists expressing divergent views. This group was admittedly concerned above all with the principles of free trade, but they did not expound any general theory of *laissez-faire.* This was attributed to them by their critics.[8] And it was the pacifist wing led by Richard Cobden, opposing the use of power in foreign policy, that gave the group its anti-colonial reputation. This was not at all representative of other elements of the school.[9] As Professor Shaw has written: 'Far more Mancunians supported the "imperialism of free trade" in China by ceaselessly memorialising the Foreign Office to take strong action there than backed Cobden and Bright in opposing it.'[10] Even Cobden and Bright disagreed over British policy towards India. Here, it has been asserted, the Manchester Radicals actually contributed to the strength and endurance of Great Britain's imperial connection. Dr Robin Moore has shown that, despite Cobden's convictions of the 'worthlessness and futility of

[7] Ibid. p. 17.
[8] W. D. Grampp, *The Manchester School of Economics* (Berkeley, 1960) p. 131.
[9] Ibid. pp. 7–8.
[10] Shaw, *Great Britain and the Colonies*, pp. 19–20.

British rule in India', many leading members of the Manchester group, including Bright, propounded

> a policy of internal development through the promotion of communications and public works. There is good reason to suggest that this policy was inspired by the motive of obtaining Indian cotton, and that the espousal of it involved condoning improvements being effected by private capital upon which the returns were secured against the public revenue of India. That is to say, in anti-imperialist terms, the Manchester School were associated with the 'exploitation' of India as a source of raw material, and as a field for the guaranteed investment of 'finance capital'.[11]

Thus even the alleged centre of 'Little Englandism' did not always hold Little England views! Perhaps it is nearer the truth to say that those economists whose ideas were based on a class-conscious and pacifist anti-imperialism had greater influence over a later generation than they did in their own day. Goldwin Smith admitted in 1863 that the doctrines of free trade had yet to be generally accepted: 'the same arguments are current at this very day respecting the superior profit of Colonial commerce, and the wealth arising from Colonial dominion, which were in everyone's mouth before that great event [the American War of Independence] occurred'. Cobden certainly bemoaned the fact that 'there is as much clinging to colonies at the present moment amongst the middle class as among the aristocracy; and the working people are not wiser than the rest'.[12] Even Professor Macdonagh was forced to admit that the years 1845–60 were essentially imperialist in character:

> There was perhaps no clearer case of mid-Victorian imperialism than the *Arrow* episode and the Canton bombardment; and no mid-Victorian electorate spoke its will more clearly than that which endorsed Palmerston at the general election of the same year, and drove Bright, Cobden, Miall,

[11] Moore, *Econ.H.R.*, xvii 135–6. See also A. Redford, *Manchester Merchants and Foreign Trade* (Manchester, 1956) ii 21–31; and P. Harnetty, 'The Indian Cotton Duties Controversy, 1894–96', *E.H.R.*, lxxvii (1962) 684–702.

[12] Smith, *The Empire*, pp. 166–7; Cobden to Bright, 23 Dec. 1848, quoted in Morley, *Life of Cobden*, pp. 502–3.

Milner Gibson, and Fox, the Manchester Radicals, bag and
baggage, from the House of Commons.[13]

Clearly, Little England ideas were not universally accepted or
even popular at this time. As J. S. Galbraith has pointed out,
'Little Englander' is of doubtful value as a description of a
significant British attitude at mid-century. Palmerston, not
Cobden or Bright, was the true representative of the age.[14]

II

In fact the labels 'Little Englander', 'Colonial Reformer' and
'Liberal Imperialist' are all part of that terminology used by the
older school of historians to depict a clash of ideas about empire
in the mid-nineteenth century. To this extent, it has been said,
'they frustrate rather than facilitate comprehension of British
colonial policy'.[15] For there never was such a clash of opposites.
The Colonial Reformers, by no means the coherent body they
made themselves out to be, unfairly caricatured the views of
others and created their own image of their opponents in order
to destroy them. 'Little Englandism' was always a term of
derision applied to political opponents, never a rallying cry
warmly embraced by any but the most extreme of theorists. The
divergence of opinion was not so great as the language of partisan
politics would suggest. Even William Molesworth, a leading
Colonial Reformer, could be attacked for holding Little England
ideas, and after one spirited exchange with the Russell government in 1851, the London *Evening Mail* noted :

> if actions rather than words were to be trusted, Molesworth
> had no more ardent supporters than the very Ministers who
> denounced him for his 'Little England' views, for all agreed on
> the principle of colonial self-government and reduction of
> British expenditures for colonial purposes.[16]

And so they did. By 1852 the grant of responsible government
to colonies of British settlement, thereby reducing the burden on
the imperial exchequer, had been accepted by both political

[13] Macdonagh, *Econ.H.R.*, XIV 500.
[14] J. S. Galbraith, 'Myths of the "Little England" Era', *A.H.R.*, LXVII
(1961) 39–42.
[15] Ibid p. 42.
[16] Ibid.

parties. Throughout the 1860s ways were being sought for disposing of the remaining burdens, principally the cost of Great Britain's overseas garrisons. The crux of the mid-Victorian debate was where and how this process should end. Was the concession of internal self-government to end in complete independence? Could the empire be retained by loose ties of kinship and affection? Was there to be an abrupt separation or some sort of continuing association after political independence? Few denied that eventual independence was the goal of colonies of British settlement, but equally few urged their immediate abandonment. Most British statesmen, including Gladstone, preferred to leave that decisive step to the initiative of the colonial governments. At any given moment their attitude seems to have been that the time for such an event had yet to come.

It is wrong, therefore, to characterise the period 1840–70 as 'years of indifference'. That would be to accept the biased assertions of certain contemporaries upon whose statements the older school of historians placed so much reliance. The Colonial Reformers were not impartial observers. They were only too ready to attribute indifference to those who ignored or did not accept all their own (often ill-advised) proposals. Debates on matters concerning the colonies were much less rare, unpopular and ill-attended than was once thought. Professor Shaw's recent survey has shown that during the years 1830–50 a fairly sizeable proportion of parliamentary time was devoted to colonies, amounting to about 8 per cent of the columns in *Hansard*. And if a fairly 'thin' house be accepted as normal, the numbers attending were not so bad. In fact the division lists reveal, on average, more members voting in colonial debates than in those on non-colonial matters. Professor Shaw concludes:

the overwhelming impression remains that the colonial reformers' complaints about parliamentary indifference to the Empire were thoroughly ill-founded, however often they may have been repeated ever since . . . both houses during this period showed in their debates far more concern about colonial than foreign affairs, although there were no complaints about Parliament's ignorance or lack of concern for the latter.[17]

[17] A. G. L. Shaw, 'British Attitudes to the Colonies, *ca* 1820–50', *J.B.S.*, IX (1969) 81.

Colonial affairs also received considerable attention in the 1860s. It has recently been calculated that some 18 per cent of the questions raised in the Commons in 1864 concerned imperial matters.[18] Repeated crises covering almost the whole area of the empire occurred at this time. The American Civil War raised the problem of relations with the North and the perennial difficulties concerning the defence of Canada. Maori uprisings throughout the 1860s attracted the attention of those who objected to British troops being used for the maintenance of internal security in self-governing colonies. The Ashanti war of 1863–4 nearly resulted in the overthrow of the Palmerston administration and indirectly led to the 1865 Select Committee on the West African Settlements. In the West Indies, criticism of Governor Eyre's heavy-handed quelling of a race riot in Jamaica ended in a much-publicised trial at the Old Bailey. Governor Sir Charles Darling was recalled from Victoria and, in Australia generally, the tariff controversy raged once again. The late 1860s also saw Fenian raids on the new Dominion of Canada and Riel's rebellion on the Red River. Finally, the decade closed amid heated arguments concerning the withdrawal of the last British regiments from Canada and New Zealand.

Clearly, colonial problems were constantly coming to the fore and were frequently discussed in Parliament. And so while it is commonplace to cite the comments of the Canadian delegates on the British Parliament's lack of interest in the British North America Act of 1867, it is also quite obvious that at this time the substantial and extremely articulate minority of members interested in colonial affairs, and the few enthusiasts who constituted 'public opinion', were becoming increasingly active, though lacking the effective organisation of other pressure groups and lobbies. Too much has been heard of mid-Victorian separatism, pessimism and indifference. A. G. L. Shaw has concluded : 'It seems doubtful if there was any period of anti-imperialism in nineteenth-century England. There were always anti-imperialist writers, but at no period did they represent the mood of very powerful political groups.'[19] There is nothing wrong with

[18] See P. M. Amey, 'The Nature of the Concern with the Empire of Parliament and Some Leading Journals during Palmerston's Second Ministry', unpublished M.Phil. thesis (London, 1971) Appendix 1.

[19] Shaw, *Great Britain and the Colonies*, p. 25.

Bodelsen's categories – optimists, pessimists and separatists – but separatism was a far less prevalent attitude than some commentators, after a hasty review of Bodelsen's book, have mistakenly suggested.

Most 'separatists', apart from the few extremists like Goldwin Smith and Richard Cobden, did not advocate the immediate abandonment of the British empire. Often the critics of empire decried the system by which the colonies were governed rather than the actual existence of colonies. What activated Cobden and Lowe was the belief that the system according to which colonial affairs were conducted was one of 'unmixed evil, injustice and loss' to the people of this country. But many critics of the existing imperial relationship who agreed with this argument were too often dubbed as 'separatists' by their opponents without just cause. Very few Victorian politicians and writers had a consistent philosophy concerning imperial relations. On occasion Robert Lowe could insist (in 1846) that he was not 'one of those who looked forward to separation from Great Britain as the only means of freedom. . . . He could never see that, under proper government, in any time the necessity could arise for separation from the great country of their birth.' And even in 1865, after his ideas had undergone further modification, he could still advocate that in the event of an American attack on Canada, Great Britain should attack the United States by sea.[20] Similarly, Cobden could fall from grace. He once emphasised in the House of Commons that he was

not opposed to the retention of Colonies any more than the hon. Gentlemen opposite. He was as anxious as anyone that the English race should spread themselves over the earth; and he believed colonisation, under a proper system of management might be made conducive to the interests of the mother country as to the emigrants themselves.[21]

Even Goldwin Smith would probably have been indignant at being termed a 'Little Englander'. He had a large vision of a new

---

[20] Lowe, 26 Jan. 1846, quoted in J. F. Hogan, *Robert Lowe, Viscount Sherbrooke* (London, 1893) pp. 230–1; also 3rd ser., *Hansard*, 13 Mar. 1865, CLXXVII 1578–9.
[21] 3 *Hansard*, 22 June 1843, LXX 205.

empire – a moral association of English-speaking nations. In his
view :

> That connexion with the Colonies, which is really part of our
> greatness – the connexion of blood, sympathy and ideas – will
> not be affected by political separation. And when our Colonies
> are nations, something in the nature of a great Anglo-Saxon
> federation may, in substance if not in form, spontaneously
> arise out of affinity and mutual affection.[22]

In this sense, Smith's vision was not so dissimilar from that of
the 'optimists' who hoped that, as the colonies grew, developed
and matured, the imperial framework would somehow hold
together. The question at issue between the two groups was
whether any formal bonds of empire would last. And bearing in
mind the American War of Independence, the collapse of the
old colonial system and the ever-increasing sphere of colonial self-
government, the practical possibility of continuing imperial unity
did indeed seem remote. On the other hand, Gladstone, and
many like him, did not regard the future unity of the British
empire 'as bound up essentially in the maintenance of any
administrative function whatever'.[23] To this extent the mid-
Victorians were realists.

Yet the policy of peaceful disengagement they adopted did not
amount to anything like 'separatism'. Hitherto the withdrawal of
British garrisons from self-governing colonies following the 1861
Select Committee on Colonial Military Expenditure, the decision
not to accept the proffered cession of the Fiji Islands in the same
year, the cession of the Ionian Islands in 1864, and the report
of the 1865 Select Committee on the West African Settlements
which recommended ultimate withdrawal from all British West
African possessions except, perhaps, Sierra Leone, have often
been regarded as aspects of that alleged 'anti-imperialism' attributed to British governments in the 'Little England era'. But in
fact the withdrawal of the British military presence was advocated
in the 1860s not only in the interests of economy and efficiency,
but for what were believed to be sound strategic reasons. The
question of annexing additional territory was always considered
on the purely practical basis of expedience, as the deliberations

---

[22] Smith, *The Empire*, p. 6.
[23] 3 *Hansard*, 26 Apr. 1870, cc 1905.

concerning Fiji clearly showed. The Ionian Islands were ceded to Greece for entirely diplomatic considerations.[24] And despite the recommendations of the 1865 committee, Britain did not evacuate the West African settlements which continued to expand under the discretion permitted to the Colonial Secretary in that very same Select Committee's report. What the 1860s did see, however, was the full realisation by British statesmen of the implications of responsible government.

Responsible government had been rapidly extended to the colonies of British settlement, save those in South Africa. The concern of the Colonial Office soon became not whether a colony was ready for constitutional advancement, but whether local demands could be resisted. The initial reserved areas for imperial control – control of Crown lands, amendment of colonial constitutions, control of tariff policy – had also been rapidly undermined, a process which continued in the 1860s with the passing of the 1865 Colonial Laws Validity Act and the handing over of the interests of both Maoris and Canadian Indians to the local settler governments. It was a hurried and disorganised act of disengagement, the implications of which the politicians of the 1860s had to face and to rationalise. Consequently much talk was heard during this decade of the corollaries of self-government: self-defence, self-reliance and the privileges of 'freemen'. The loose ends of responsible government had to be tidied up and the most important of these remained the cost of Great Britain's overseas garrisons. As these garrisons were gradually withdrawn, the realisation dawned on British politicians that it was now necessary to look ahead to the formation of cohesive national units in Canada, Australia and South Africa to make these colonies truly capable of an independent existence. Gladstone, for example, asserted:

we must not conceal it from ourselves, that if up to this time the sentiments of British North Americans with regard to self-

[24] On these aspects of what used to be called the 'Little England' era, see my articles: 'Forgotten Centenary: The Defence Review of the 1860s', *Trivium*, v (1970) 85–103; 'The Myth of Mid-Victorian "Separatism"': The Cession of the Bay Islands and the Ionian Islands in the Early 1860s', *V.S.*, xii (1969) 331–46; and 'The Imperialism of the "Little England" Era: The Question of the Annexation of the Fiji Islands, 1858–61', *N.Z.J.H.*, i (1967) 171–84.

defence have to some extent separated the burdens of freedom from the spirit of freedom the fault has been mainly ours. . . . We have to bring about a different state of things. The best way to do it is to raise their political position to the very highest point we can possibly bring it, in order that with the elevated position their sense of responsibility may likewise grow. It cannot be too distinctly stated that it is in this light that we look upon the plan for uniting the Provinces of British North America.[25]

Edward Cardwell also affirmed that it was British policy to form 'great and powerful communities' overseas, capable of defending themselves and standing on their own feet.[26] Thus by the 1860s a policy of separation by consent, radically different from what the older school of historians regarded as 'separatism', had come to be accepted by the British government. John Bright was quick to detect this in a debate on the army estimates in March 1865 :

I suspect from what has been stated by official Gentlemen in Government and in previous Governments, that there is no objection to the independence of Canada when ever Canada may wish for it. I have been glad to hear those statements, because I think they mark an extraordinary progress in sound opinions in this country.[27]

Palmerston confirmed this opinion later in the debate.

Indeed, the gap between public opinion and policy was much narrower than we have been led to believe. For most so-called separatists looked for the gradual relaxation of ties – usually by mutual consent over an unspecified period of time – as a prelude to the grant of independence which, although regarded as inevitable, did not preclude some form of continuing association. Even Cobden confessed : 'People tell me I want to abandon our colonies; but I say, do you intend to hold your colonies by the sword, by armies, and ships of war? That is not a permanent hold upon them. I want to retain them by their affections.'[28] Few statesmen, however, were prepared to take the positive line of

---

25 3 *Hansard*, 28 Mar. 1867, CLXXXVI 753–4.
26 3 *Hansard*, 28 Feb. 1867, CLXXXV 1178.
27 3 *Hansard*, 23 Mar. 1865, CLXXVIII 168–74.
28 R. Cobden, *Speeches on Questions of Public Policy*, ed. J. Bright and J. E. Thorold Rogers (London, 1870) I 485.

action Cobden advocated. As John Bright admitted : 'I have no dread of separation but I would avoid anything likely to provoke it.'[29] In this sense, Bright was more representative of the views of the majority of the Manchester group of economists than Cobden and Goldwin Smith. Although opposed to the extension of imperial commitments and additional expense, he was not in favour of the dismemberment of the empire – except by mutual consent. 'Give up all the colonies & dependencies of the Empire? Can any Statesman do this, or can any country do this? I doubt it.'[30] Clearly, retrocession was too damaging a political position for him to adopt.

Indeed, if the views of the few extreme theorists are put on one side, there is much common ground among the mid-Victorians in their attitudes towards the future development of the self-governing colonies. The suggestions for the gradual relaxation of imperial ties advocated by the majority of the separatists, the idea of separation by consent preached by the exponents of the 'voluntary tie' school of thought, and the policy the British government followed throughout the 1860s were not so very far apart. Indeed, if the term 'separatism' is to remain of any value as the description of a significant British attitude in the mid-Victorian scene, it can only be used to indicate a permissive attitude towards separation *should the colonies wish for it*. It cannot infer any deliberate intention, except among a few outspoken theorists, to inaugurate the immediate dismemberment of the empire. Similarly, the 'anti-imperialism' of the so-called 'Little England era', about which so much has been written, never amounted to anything more than a correspondingly negative assumption that if the colonies were destined for eventual independence, colonial expenditure should be cut to a minimum and further expansion avoided – an attitude adopted by several British statesmen but one never accepted as the basis for British policy. It is refreshing, therefore, to be reminded of some of the positive aspects of the mid-Victorian age. Professor Cell records in his survey of the policy-making process in the middle years of the nineteenth century :

[29] Bright to E. Ellice, 16 Dec. 1859, *Ellice Papers*, National Library of Scotland, MSS. Acc. 1993.

[30] Bright to E. Sturge, 24 Sept. 1857, quoted in J. L. Sturgis, *John Bright and the Empire* (London, 1969) p. 92. For a summary of Bright's position, see ibid. pp. 90, 101–2, 183–4.

The achievement of the mid-Victorians ought not to be overlooked. In the twentieth century decolonisation has been shown to be a process at least as dangerous and as complex as colonisation. Between 1840 and 1870 Great Britain peacefully disengaged herself from a substantial portion of her empire. There was no precedent for this : no imperial power in modern times had ever done such a thing before. The graceful way in which she did it, leaving behind her a residue of goodwill instead of bitterness ought rather to be the cause of admiration than contempt.[31]

This was an achievement of which the mid-Victorian policy-makers could be proud.

III

What then did the imperial idea amount to at this stage in the evolution of Great Britain's empire? While most mid-Victorian thinkers recognised the gradual growth of the settlement colonies towards eventual independence and may even, on occasion, have objected aloud to the existence of 'these colonial deadweights which we do not govern', it would be a mistake to infer that the majority of mid-Victorian statesmen had no faith in empire. Lord Robert Cecil, later third Marquis of Salisbury, believed in 1860 that 'any proposition to abandon our Colonies would be hooted out of the House'.[32] Obviously the imperial idea was still in existence. This is not to deny that some aspects of empire were extremely unpopular in the 1860s, or to suggest that only cranks thought the empire added nothing to British strength. But even the leading Manchester Radicals, Goldwin Smith included, accepted the existence of the Indian empire. Bright's prognosis of its abandonment was that 'the whole country, in all probability, [would] lapse into chaos and anarchy and into sanguinary and interminable warfare'.[33] Thus even those who regarded the colonies as a burden could subscribe to the belief that the empire was a trust, however costly and undesirable, handed down

[31] J. W. Cell, *British Colonial Administration in the Mid-Nineteenth Century: The Policy-Making Process* (London, 1970) pp. 211–12.

[32] 3 *Hansard*, 31 May 1860, CLVIII 1835.

[33] G. M. Trevelyan, *Life of John Bright* (London, 1913) pp. 265–6.

to them by their forefathers. The pragmatic acceptance of obligations once they had been incurred seems to have been almost universal. Imperialism could mean civilisation as well as exploitation. To the mid-Victorian generation the empire entailed a duty, and for many the imperial idea was beginning to assume a sense of mission.

No Victorian statesman was more aware of this than Gladstone. Despite his well-known aversion to imperial expansion and his firm belief that 'the lust and love of territory have been among the greatest curses of mankind'[34] – views which earned for him the title of 'Little Englander' – he was by no means opposed to the existence of colonies. On the contrary, he informed the members of the Mechanics' Institute at Chester in November 1855 :

> In my opinion, and I submit it to you with great respect, they are desirable both for the material and for the moral and social results which a wise system of colonisation is calculated to produce. As to the first, the effect of colonisation undoubtedly is to increase the trade and employment of the mother country.

The second, the moral aspect, involved the duty to provide for the extension of good laws. Gladstone was an enthusiastic admirer of the British constitution :

> We think that our country is a country blessed with laws and a constitution that are eminently beneficial to mankind, and if so, what can be more to be desired than that we should have the means of reproducing in different portions of the globe something as like as may be to that country which we honour and revere? I think it is in a work by Mr Roebuck that the expression is used 'that the object of colonisation is the creation of so many happy Englands'.[35]

It was not over the existence of colonies that Gladstone argued with his opponents, but about the method of their management. Steeped in classical tradition, he believed the only 'moral' way to govern colonies was to adopt the Greek model – 'perfect free-

---

[34] 'An Address delivered to the Members of the Mechanics' Institute at Chester, 12 Nov. 1855', quoted in P. Knaplund, *Gladstone and Britain's Imperial Policy* (London, 1927) p. 193.
[35] Ibid. p. 202.

dom and perfect self-government'.[36] He believed in the moral virtues of self-government and self-defence, wished to apply these things as widely as possible, and devoted the later part of his political career to trying to secure them for Ireland. It was a philosophy which made Gladstone many political opponents, who were only too willing to distort his views and accuse him of being a separatist. This was far from correct. He was concerned with the principles of 'freedom and voluntaryism':

> Govern them upon the principle of freedom – let them not feel any yokes upon their necks – let them understand that the relations between you and them are relations of affection; even in the matter of continuing the connection, let the colonists be the judges, for they are the best judges as to whether they ought to continue to be with you or not, and rely upon it you will reap a rich reward in the possession of that affection unbroken and unbounded in all the influence which the possession of such colonies will give you, and in all the grandeur which it will add to your renown. Defend them against aggression from without – regulate their foreign relations (those things belong to the colonial connection, but of the duration of that connection let them be the judges) – and I predict that if you leave them that freedom of judgment it is hard to say when the day will come when they will wish to separate from the great name of England.[37]

Such was the basic supposition of those who formed the 'voluntary tie' school of thought. Great Britain should reduce 'not political influence, but power over colonies to a minimum'. The tie would then be one of sentiment, kinship and affection.

As to the empire of trade and strategy, those parts which Sir Charles Adderley dubbed the 'Roman' as opposed to the 'Grecian' elements of empire, Gladstone was opposed to their extension. Great Britain already had burdens enough. He had no liking for British rule over alien races. Nevertheless, Gladstone did accept the 'moral trusteeship' of backward peoples where it had already been incurred. Great Britain, for example, had 'no interest in India except the well-being of India itself'. India was, indeed, 'a capital demand upon the national honour', a burden

[36] Ibid. p. 204.
[37] Ibid. p. 225.

that Great Britain should aim one day to shed. It was only with
the greatest reluctance that Gladstone could entertain any concept of empire not based on the classical model of Greece. Yet
while constantly reiterating his ideas on the independent future
of the settlement colonies, he never forgot, and remained proud
of, 'that great and glorious fabric of truly civilised society which
it is our duty and task and high privilege to administer throughout the vast regions of the world'. 'While we are opposed to
imperialism', he declared, 'we are devoted to empire.'[38]

Gladstone possessed little political imagination. He tended, in
his thoroughness, to push every principle to its logical conclusion. Many mid-Victorian statesmen, however, who accepted
Gladstone's basic position were much more pragmatic in outlook.
Gladstone's theoretical views on the empire were not always in
agreement with the more practical approach of most of his
generation.

More in tune with the outlook of his age were the ideas of the
much-maligned fifth Duke of Newcastle, a Peelite who held the
seals of the Colonial Office from 1852 to 1854 and again from
1859 to 1864, a slightly longer period than any of his mid-
Victorian colleagues. Like Gladstone, Newcastle's main political
beliefs embraced free trade, *laissez-faire* and responsible government for the settlement colonies. The duke knew from experience
that 'the normal current of colonial history is the perpetual
assertion of the right to self-government'.[39] Unlike the third Earl
Grey, he was even prepared to subject his other beliefs, such as
free trade, to this one great principle. Like Gladstone, Newcastle
envisaged the gradual development of colonial nationhood
through the spread of local self-government, yet he found it
difficult to accept that political independence was possible in the
immediate future. Newcastle looked for the continuance of the
empire on the basis of responsible government and local independence, control of foreign policy and empire defence providing
the main links with the mother country. In an after-dinner
speech to the Australian Association in 1862, he declared can-

[38] 3 *Hansard*, 21 Aug. 1883, CCLXXXIII 1539; and speech at Leeds, 7 Oct.
1881, quoted in Sir P. Magnus, *Gladstone, a Biography* (London, 1954)
p. 287.
[39] C. B. Adderley, *Review of 'The Colonial Policy of Lord John Russell's
Administration' by Earl Grey, 1853; and of Subsequent Colonial History*
(London, 1869) p. 3.

didly that he hoped Great Britain would never attempt to retain the colonies by force and that the days when 'a single redcoat should fire a shot or point a bayonet in hostility at any British colonist' were long past :

> If any colony wished to separate from us – if they thought their strength was sufficient to allow them to stand alone – we should not seek to restrain them by force. . . . But he believed that the present attachment between Great Britain and her colonies was such that it would be a long day ere the union between them was severed, or sought to be severed by either of them.[40]

Newcastle was convinced that the bonds of 'mutual affection and interest' were so strong that in time of crisis the colonies would be 'ready to fight with us and for us to a man'.[41] A prophetic assertion for the 1860s, fully justified by the events of the first half of the twentieth century!

Yet in private Newcastle was prepared to admit the logical *possibility* of an early separation. Canada, for example, could 'not for ever – perhaps not for long – remain a British colony'. Therefore he regarded it as Great Britain's duty to ensure the creation of a powerful state out of the disjointed British North American provinces. Then Canada

> would become to us a strong and self-reliant Colony so long as her present relationship with the Mother Country continues and when she separates she would be a powerful and independent Ally and a most valuable, and I believe essential, makeweight in the Balance of Power on the American continent.[42]

Newcastle advocated a policy of conciliation. He bluntly informed Palmerston :

> You speak of some supposed theoretical gentlemen in the Colonial Office who wish to get rid of all Colonies as soon as possible. I can only say if there are such, they have never

[40] *The Times*, 13 Feb. 1862.
[41] Newcastle to Gladstone, 5 Dec. 1861 (copy), *Newcastle Papers*, Nottingham University Library, Manuscripts Department, NeC C.2/105.
[42] 'Remarks on a Memorandum on the Intercolonial Railway' by Newcastle, undated (early 1862), private and confidential, *Newcastle Papers*, NeC 11,260.

ventured to open the opinion to me – if they did so on grounds of peaceful separation I should differ from them so long as Colonies can be retained by bonds of mutual sympathy and mutual obligation.[43]

Newcastle had no dread of future political separation, but in the meantime he was proud of the moral values embodied in the British concept of empire and wished to see it continue for as long as mutual agreement and friendly association could endure. He had equally strong views on the 'dependent' empire : additional obligations should not be lightly undertaken nor existing burdens hastily shed. Such an attitude led Goldwin Smith to regard the duke as a 'decided Imperialist'.[44]

Nevertheless, Newcastle's liberal attitude towards empire was the prevalent one among mid-century statesmen not over-inclined to place too much emphasis on the pecuniary aspect of empire. It was in fact the position the government had adopted ever since Lord John Russell's speech on colonial affairs in 1850. At that time an authoritative declaration of government policy seemed necessary as Great Britain's new free trade policy had caused discontent in some colonies and the new constitutional venture of self-government had raised doubts at home about the value of continuing the connection. Russell affirmed : 'I consider it to be our bounden duty to maintain the colonies which have been placed under our charge.' In the body of the speech he came out strongly against separation. But at the end came the famous peroration designed to meet the views of his critics :

I anticipate indeed with others that some of the colonies may so grow in population and wealth that they may say – 'Our strength is sufficient to enable us to be independent of England. The link is now become onerous to us – the time is come when we can, in amity and alliance with England, maintain our independence.' I do not think that that time is yet approaching. But let us make them as far as possible, fit to govern themselves – let us give them, as far as we can, the capacity of ruling their own affairs – let them increase in wealth and population, and whatever may happen, we of this great empire

[43] Newcastle to Palmerston, 11 Nov. 1861 (copy), *Newcastle Papers*, NeC C.2/94–8.
[44] G. Smith, *Reminiscences* (New York, 1911) pp. 185–6.

shall have the consolation of saying that we have contributed to the happiness of the world.[45]

This 'time-honoured formula of stoic self-satisfaction',[46] looking forward, like Gladstone, to the creation of 'so many happy Englands', provided successive British governments with a policy of minimum controversy to which even those hostile to the existing commitments could freely subscribe. Politicians with such diverse views as Cobden, Gladstone, Adderley, Earl Grey and Disraeli, and leading exponents of such different points of view as Goldwin Smith and Wakefield, were united in support of a policy of self-government, self-defence and reduced colonial expenditure. For the extreme critics of empire the gradual liquidation of the old colonial system and the extension of self-government were the first step towards the empire's dissolution; for the majority it provided an opportunity for building a new set of relationships with the colonies of British settlement. Those who warmly embraced the idea of responsible government looked forward to a free association of virtually independent states. This was the imperial idea most consistently expressed throughout the 1860s: 'To ripen those communities to the earliest possible maturity – social, political and commercial – to qualify them, by all the appliances within reach of a parent state, for present self-government and eventual independence', asserted Arthur Mills, the Colonial Reformer, 'is now the almost universally admitted aim of our colonial policy.'[47] Few would have disagreed with this.

But the British government's policy of conciliation was to some extent ambivalent. It amounted to the paradoxical policy of separation by consent, with the aim of maintaining the existing bonds for as long as possible. In the mid-Victorian years the logical inevitability of separation was acknowledged, but it was also popularly believed, as Lord Kimberley wrote in 1870, that 'the question of independence ought not to be regarded as a practical one in our time. It is reduced to a mere speculation as to the future.'[48]

[45] 3 *Hansard*, 8 Feb. 1850, cviii 535–67.
[46] Koebner, *Imperialism*, p. 71.
[47] A. Mills, 'Our Colonial Policy', *Contemporary Review*, xi (June 1869) 217.
[48] Kimberley, 22 July 1870, in 'Journal of Events during the Gladstone Ministry, 1868–74', ed. E. Drus, *C.M.*, xxi (1958) 17–18.

IV

Clearly, the 1860s were not dominated by an aversion to empire. The mid-Victorians, as W. D. McIntyre has recently written, 'for all their love of doctrinal controversy about empire, retained a pragmatic approach' to colonial developments.[49] The mid-Victorians were realists. Professor Cell concludes : 'It is not the realism of the 1860s that needs to be explained. It is the rise in the late nineteenth century of the belief that some other outcome, such as imperial unity, was really a practical possibility in the long run.'[50]

Little was heard about imperial consolidation in the 1860s. Even the critics, like Disraeli, who regarded the unplanned extension of self-government to the majority of the settlement colonies as hasty and premature and regretted that the policy of colonial devolution had not been accompanied by some attempt to delineate more fully local and imperial responsibilities, rarely reverted to ideas of imperial consolidation. Most empire-conscious observers were aware of the fragility of the traditional colonial links, yet seemed content with the British government's policy since it did not aim at severing those ties. Most empire enthusiasts refused to believe that local independence would lead to the inevitable dissolution of the empire. As Herman Merivale, when Professor of Political Economy at Oxford, had written in his classic *Lectures on Colonisation and Colonies* :

> It does not follow as a necessary consequence that the attainment of domestic freedom is inconsistent with continued dependence on the Imperial sovereignty. The epoch of separation is not marked and definite, a necessary point in the cycle of human affairs, as some theorists have regarded it. . . . The mere political link of sovereignty may remain, by amicable consent, long after the colony has acquired sufficient strength to stand alone. Existing relations may be preserved, by very slight sacrifices, on terms of mutual goodwill. But this can only be by the gradual relaxation of ties of dependence. The union must more and more lose the protective, and approximate to the federal character. And the Crown may remain, at last, in solitary supremacy the only common authority recognised by

49 McIntyre, *Imperial Frontier*, p. 385.
50 Cell, *British Colonial Administration*, p. 211.

many different legislatures, by many nations, politically and socially distinct.[51]

Thus in the 1860s, while the British government continued its existing policy towards the colonies of settlement and continued to shoulder its obligations towards the Crown colonies, and while men like Palmerston, Newcastle, Disraeli and Carnarvon continued to uphold imperial interests, there seemed little need for the supporters of empire to enter into a detailed argument in its defence. And in the House of Commons there always existed a sufficient number of back-benchers, committed to the cause of empire, to check the influence of Cobden and his few associates who favoured the writings and extreme theories of Goldwin Smith.

The 1860s did, however, see a large increase in separatist literature. The events of that decade, the American Civil War, the Anglo-Maori wars and the Ashanti expedition, and the problems associated with them – the defence of Canada, colonial military expenditure and territorial expansion in West (as well as South) Africa – all helped to emphasise the cost of empire, and consequently its disadvantage for the British taxpayer. It was also maintained that the state of dependence was a humiliating condition and the political tie retarded colonial economic growth. Anthony Trollope, one of the few authors of fiction to write on the colonies at this time, adopted this stance in his *North America* (1862);[52] and Goldwin Smith, with compelling logic, spelt out his own position for all to see in several letters to the *Daily News* published, in book form, under the title of *The Empire* in 1863. Two years later Henry Thring, Home Office counsel, in a pamphlet *Suggestions for Colonial Reform* (London, 1865), drew up a uniform scheme for the constitutional development of colonial government in four stages, whereby a colony might withdraw from the empire whenever it desired to do so. And at the same time Viscount Bury produced a two-volume work entitled *The Exodus of the Western Nations* (London, 1865), in which he concluded that separation was only a matter of time and ought to be prepared for in advance to ensure a peaceful

[51] H. Merivale, *Lectures on Colonisation and Colonies* (London, 1841) II 293.
[52] A. Trollope, *North America* (London, 1862) I 129–31. See also J. H. Davidson, 'Anthony Trollope and the Colonies', *V.S.*, XII (1969) 305–30.

parting amid mutual goodwill. Believing Thring's idea of the future relations between Great Britain and her independent ex-colonies to be inadequate, he prepared a draft treaty in the form of 'Articles of Separation', regulating Great Britain's relations with a colony after independence had been recognised.[53] So complex were the problems raised by the events of the 1860s, and such were the uncertainties relating to Great Britain's future connection with her colonies, that colonial commentators, some of whom at least were proud of the empire, could freely contemplate a rupture of the relationship.

A curious admixture of the ideas of the Manchester Radicals and of latter-day imperialists is to be found in the work of Sir Charles Dilke, who published in 1868 his two-volume account of a journey through the English-speaking world, entitled *Greater Britain*. Dilke was frankly separatist as regards Canada. In his opinion the political connection benefited no one. He could see no reason why Great Britain should be more friendly towards Canada than the United States. Dilke did not believe in the idea of empire as an organised system of political relations between mother country and colonies; his allegiance was to a wider nationalism, to 'Anglo-Saxondom'. Dilke included the United States in 'Greater Britain' and thought the American Republic offered the English 'race' the 'moral dictatorship of the globe, by ruling mankind through Saxon institutions and the English tongue'. Although he was less hostile to the connection with the Australasian colonies, provided they paid for their own defence, he believed there was no advantage to be gained in the military, commercial and emigration spheres from the links with self-governing colonies. They certainly did not add to Great Britain's prestige. He concluded :

Any relation would be preferable to the existing one of mutual indifference and distrust. Recognising the fact that Australia has come of age and calling on her, too, to recognise it, we should say to the Australian colonists : 'Our present system cannot continue; will you amend it, or separate?' The worst thing that can happen to us is that we should 'drift' blindly into separation. After all, the strongest of the arguments in

[53] See Bodelsen, pp. 50–7; Schuyler, *Fall of the Old Colonial System*, pp. 247–50.

favour of separation is the somewhat paradoxical one that it would bring us a step nearer to the virtual confederation of the English race.[54]

Dilke did not follow Goldwin Smith, however, in suggesting that Great Britain should force separation on the colonies. On the contrary, the retention of Australia and New Zealand was an onerous duty: the Australians would prosper to a greater degree in connection with the mother country and this was in the interests 'both of our race and of the world'. Instead he wished the mother country to insist on the colonies undertaking a fair share of the burden of imperial defence. Then separation, 'though infinitely better than a continuation of the existing one-sided tie, would, in a healthier state of our relations, not be to the interest of Britain, although it would perhaps be morally beneficial to Australia'.[55] Thus it seems that Dilke was not opposed to colonisation after all, but to the retention of colonies of British settlement in a state of dependence after they were capable of standing alone.

As regards the Crown colonies and the Indian empire, Dilke was fervently in favour of their retention:

The possession of India offers to ourselves that element of vastness of dominion which, in this age, is needed to secure width of vision and nobility of purpose; but to the English our possession of India, of the coast of Africa, and the ports of China offers the possibility of planting free institutions among the dark-skinned races of the world.

Dilke possessed a much stronger conception of the civilising mission of the 'Anglo-Saxon race' than most of his contemporaries who were not so concerned with trusteeship of the backward peoples of the world. Although Dilke felt that the British administration of India was not without its faults, he maintained: 'The only justification of our presence in India is the education for freedom of the Indian races.'[56] He insisted it was England's mission to plant free institutions among the dark-skinned races. If Great Britain should withdraw from the sub-

---

[54] C. W. Dilke, *Greater Britain* (London, 1868) II 157. See Bodelsen, pp. 60–75.

[55] Dilke, *Greater Britain*, II 156–7.

[56] Ibid. pp. 381, 407.

continent, trade would collapse and anarchy prevail. Thus he became preoccupied with 'the conception, however imperfect, of the grandeur of our race, already girding the earth, which it is destined, perhaps, eventually to overspread'.[57] This was the sort of boisterous pride in empire which Goldwin Smith and the extreme theorists of separation so much disparaged.

It may seem strange that Dilke could boast about Great Britain's imperial expansion and the spread of English civilisation, yet contemplate with indifference the breakaway of the self-governing portions of that empire. But unlike Henry Thring and Viscount Bury, he did not merely accept the inevitability of separation in a purely negative manner. As Professor Koebner has noted, Dilke's book 'combined a forceful, suggestive language with a strong appeal to the pride and values of the mid-Victorian Englishman. It opened up new vistas to an English world and new directions of progress.' By its appeal to the Anglo-Saxon race and English civilisation, 'it purged the idea of separation from the spirit of resignation and instilled it with expansive vitality'.[58] In reviewing the book, only the *Edinburgh* and *Quarterly Reviews* found it necessary to rebuke Dilke for advocating colonial emancipation.

In the 1860s, then, the question of the future development of the British empire was well aired. Most daily newspapers as well as the weekly and monthly reviews at some stage dealt at length with the 'colonial question', as it had come to be called. The Defence Review of the 1860s was a prominent aspect of government policy. The mid-Victorians were well aware that the traditional colonial links were no longer satisfactory and that new paths lay ahead. Joseph Howe, the ex-Nova Scotian politician, for example, prefaced the pamphlet he wrote on *The Organisation of Empire* in 1866 with the words:

Under the Providence of God, after centuries of laborious cultivation, the sacrifice of much heroic blood, the expenditure of a vast amount of treasure, the British Empire, as it stands, has been got together, and the question, which is presented to us, in some form of Parliamentary or newspaper disputation almost every week is, what is now to be done with it.

[57] Ibid. p. 406.
[58] Koebner, *Imperialism*, p. 89.

For his part, Howe advocated consolidation of the empire, a uniform defence and finance policy, with the colonies possessing responsible government represented in a 'Parliament of the Empire'. This was a rather unusual position to adopt in the 1860s. Becoming more common was C. B. Adderley's idea that 'between the alternatives of dependence and separation lies the real secret of a lasting connexion – that of common partnership'.[59] Most serious writers, accepting the logical development of colonial independence, regarded the alternatives as being between planned separation and a policy of 'drift'. The British government's colonial policy, since it made no specific arrangements for separation, was usually stigmatised as the latter. Hence the abundance of 'separatist' literature in the late 1860s suggesting future paths for the government to take.

It was only the few outspoken theorists who advocated the immediate dismemberment of the empire. As has been seen, mid-Victorian separatism in general involved a permissive attitude towards separation should it occur, rather than a direct attempt to begin the dismemberment of the empire. And so, throughout the 1860s, the British government continued to follow a policy of separation by consent, refusing to make concrete plans for hypothetical developments in the future or to force the pace of colonial independence.

At least it did so until 1868. In December 1868 Gladstone formed a ministry consisting of a number of politicians who were suspected of being strongly against the continuance of the colonial connection. A sudden fear blew up that the new Liberal government was preparing to apply some of the more extreme separatist notions to colonial policy. The dissolution of the empire, far from being in the vague future, appeared to be at hand. It was Granville's insistence in carrying through to its logical conclusion the withdrawal of the British garrisons from self-governing colonies, despite the special circumstances of New Zealand and Canada; the language of his despatches; and the government's initial refusal to guarantee a loan to New Zealand for the purpose of internal security, that led to the cry of 'the empire in danger' being taken up by certain sections of the press and to much of the controversy of 1869–70. It was the 'empire scare' of these years that the older school of historians designated

[59] Adderley, *Review*, p. 420.

the 'climax of anti-imperialism', the watershed between the 'Age of Separatism' and the dawn of the 'Age of Imperialism'.

But how far was the contemporary assessment of the situation correct? As has been seen, there was enough conflict of views about the future of the British empire in the late 1860s. Nobody was sure about the path that lay ahead. What then did this 'crisis of opinion' in 1869–70 really amount to? Did the Gladstone administration depart from established policy and really intend to dismember the empire? If not, how should the alleged 'climax of anti-imperialism' be interpreted in the light of the current debate concerning mid-Victorian policy and thought? Why did an 'empire scare' occur at all at this time? Clearly, the policies followed and the thoughts expressed during these two momentous years warrant close examination : they are fundamental to the debate concerning the nature and continuity of Victorian imperialism.

3

The Climax of Anti-Imperialism:
A Crisis of Opinion

THE years 1869–70 witnessed a controversial upheaval in imperial relations. The government's policy was suddenly attacked in Parliament, the press, at public meetings and in the colonies themselves. The new Colonial Secretary, Earl Granville, was thought by many contemporary observers, and indeed by some subsequent writers, to have contemplated dismembering the empire. And it was this reaction to the apparent trend of Granville's policy that led, it has been suggested, to an imperialist revival in the 1870s.[1]

What was the cause of this unprecedented agitation? Did the Gladstone administration try to implement a separatist policy? Or was the government merely unfortunate in having to deal with several crises which arose at one and the same time? There is plenty of evidence to suggest, for example, that a showdown with New Zealand was inevitable unless the British taxpayers were prepared to tolerate imperial troops being used at their expense, in combating the results of a policy which the imperial government had consistently deprecated. Granville's decision to withdraw the British military presence while Maori resistance

[1] Bodelsen, pp. 7–9. Granville's term of office has received little detailed attention from historians. Knaplund, *Gladstone and Britain's Imperial Policy*, pp. 95–139, devotes a chapter to Gladstone's first administration. But while dealing exhaustively with the Australian tariffs question, he ignores the crisis in relations with New Zealand and mentions only briefly the difficulties with Canada. By far the most balanced account of colonial policy during these years is contained in Butler, 'Imperial Questions in British Politics, 1868–80', *C.H.B.E.*, III 18–40.

continued, naturally aroused the opposition of a vocal group in London interested in New Zealand. And the government's determination to apply the same policy to Canada – at a time when the United States apparently harboured annexationist ideas and the young Dominion faced not only the danger of a Fenian invasion but also internal difficulties with the part-Indian *métis* – appeared to support the assertion that such a heartless policy could not be 'the act of men friendly to the colonial connexion'.[2]

The actions of Granville, who was thought to be a disciple of the Manchester School, coming at a time when anti-empire sentiments were receiving widespread publicity, were bound to create further apprehension as to the future connection of Great Britain with her colonies. Doubtless this apprehension was increased by the fact that Gladstone was now Prime Minister and both Bright and Lowe were members of the new Cabinet. Had not Goldwin Smith prophesied that Palmerston would be succeeded 'by statesmen more imbued with the ideas, and more alive to the exigencies of our own age . . . disposed to retrench our Empire in order to add to our security and greatness'?[3] If the members of the new administration were not attempting to initiate a new departure in public policy, why did they persist in such apparently controversial actions?

The ineptitude of the Liberal ministers and their servants, or plain lack of interest on their part, served to heighten the controversy. The offer of the K.C.M.G. to Alexander Tilloch Galt, a prominent Canadian denigrator of the imperial connection, and Granville's subsequent refusal to publish the full correspondence for Parliament, also aroused suspicions about the government's views on colonial policy. Speeches by the Canadian Governor-General, Sir John Young, a former Liberal M.P., and by Sir Philip Wodehouse, Governor of the Cape Colony, created further doubts among colonial zealots in Parliament, and Granville's own evasive speeches did little to ease the tension. Not until criticism of the government's conduct of colonial affairs had reached a crescendo early in 1870 – with organised protest meetings, public petitions, a scathing press campaign and attacks on Granville, by Carnarvon in the Lords and by several Liberal back-benchers in the Commons – did the government attempt to

---

[2] *Weekly Globe* (Toronto), 14 Oct. 1870.
[3] Smith, *The Empire*, p. 10.

explain the basis of its policy. Gladstone and Granville then publicly disavowed any intention to dissolve the empire : withdrawal of the imperial military presence from self-governing colonies did not imply a refusal to protect the colonies in cases of foreign aggression. After these assurances and a forthright speech in 1871 by Edward Knatchbull-Hugessen, Parliamentary Under-Secretary at the Colonial Office, emphatically denying that the Liberal government had any intention of cutting the colonies adrift, the recent interest shown by Parliament in the direction of colonial policy rapidly declined. But were the fears expressed in 1869 and the mammoth attack subsequently mounted by the critics of the government justified? What in fact was the basis of the Gladstone government's colonial policy?

I

The Liberal administration was committed to a programme of peace, retrenchment and reform, and the colonies were not to escape the reappraisal of Great Britain's affairs. Indeed, many observers feared that Gladstone's belief in colonial autonomy and free trade and his determination to reduce defence expenditure would lead to a radical colonial policy. Shortly before Russell's government resigned in 1866, Lord Clarendon, the Liberal Foreign Secretary, had complained : 'in the present state of Ireland, and the menacing aspect of our relations with the United States, the military and pecuniary resources of England must be husbanded with the utmost care'.[4] Gladstone's election pledge for economy in 1868 seemed to augur ill for the existing imperial relationship. Indeed, when the Liberals won the general election, Charles Dilke, the new M.P. for Chelsea, noted :

> Of the two colonists who are members of the Ministry, Mr Lowe has used the strongest and plainest language about colonial military expenditure that ever statesman has resorted to; and the robust mind of Mr Childers is not likely to be imposed upon by interested representations, while we certainly need not fear opposition from Mr Gladstone or Mr Bright.[5]

Gladstone returned to office determined to attack what Disraeli

[4] Clarendon to the Queen, 31 Mar. 1866, quoted in G. E. Buckle (ed.), *The Letters of Queen Victoria*, 2nd ser. (London, 1926) I 314–15.
[5] C. W. Dilke, *Mr Dilke M.P. on 'Colonies'* (London, 1869) p. 17.

had called 'bloated armaments'. The defence estimates were
ready for the axe.

The withdrawal of the garrisons from the self-governing
colonies played an essential part in the new government's reform
programme. Edward Cardwell, the Secretary of State for War,
advised the Prime Minister :

> The withdrawal of Troops from distant stations is at the
> bottom of the whole question of Army Reform. As long as the
> period of Foreign service bears so large a proportion to that at
> home, the discouragement to enlisting among the more respect-
> able portions of the population must be great : – & it will be
> difficult if not impossible to reduce the period of enlistment.[6]

Cardwell proposed to reduce the imperial troops stationed in the
colonies from 50,000 to 26,000. In Parliament he resolutely
defended this policy. The greatest protection for the colonies was
'the aegis of the name of England'. 'You are', he asserted,

> strengthening and defending your colonies, and increasing the
> power of England, when you generate in every one of the
> settlements where the British name is known a spirit of British
> energy, and self-reliance; for you consolidate and concentrate
> the strength of the mother country for their defence in time
> of need.[7]

With Parliament's acquiescence, the phased withdrawal of
British garrisons begun by Cardwell in 1864 was now hurried
through to completion.

As the year 1870 progressed, developments on the continent
of Europe made reform of Great Britain's defensive strategy more
urgent. Lord Clarendon confessed to Queen Victoria :

> It is the unfriendly state of our relations with America that
> to a great extent paralyses our action in Europe. There is not
> the smallest doubt that if we were engaged in a Continental .
> quarrel, we should immediately find ourselves at war with the
> United States.[8]

[6] Cardwell to Gladstone, 9 Jan. 1869, *Cardwell Papers*, P.R.O. 30/48/2/6,
pp. 29–31.

[7] 3 *Hansard*, 11 Mar. 1869, cxciv 1111–39.

[8] Clarendon to the Queen, 1 May 1869, quoted in Buckle, *Letters of
Queen Victoria*, i 594–5.

The alarm generated by the Franco-Prussian war led Kimberley, the Lord Privy Seal, to view the future pessimistically : 'We are only at the end of the first act of the tragedy, & we shall be fortunate if the next acts are not more gloomy & horrible still.' H. C. E. Childers, the First Lord of the Admiralty, feared Russian aggression : 'however unprepared they may be just now, sooner or later we shall have them on our hands.'[9] Thus new international complications required Great Britain to reorganise and strengthen her defences. The withdrawal of the garrisons became increasingly more urgent. The process had to be speeded up to enable army reform to be carried out. The protracted dispute with New Zealand would have to be brought to an abrupt end. This was the backcloth against which the Gladstone government entered upon its task. The policy adopted by the administration was by no means new : it was the existing policy, pursued for over a decade, hurriedly pushed to its logical conclusion.

Granville, the Colonial Secretary, worked closely with Cardwell. He agreed with the Secretary of State for War that colonial susceptibilities could not be allowed to stand in the way of paramount British interests. The novelty of the situation, however, was the unusually open indifference of the Colonial Secretary, the even harsher than usual tone of Colonial Office despatches, and the rather peremptory manner in which the decisions were conveyed to the colonists. Granville took the bit between his teeth. The treatment of New Zealand aroused a great deal of protest from colonists in England and was certainly the foundation of the charge that Granville was intent on following a separatist policy. But was this really the case?

II

Throughout the 1860s relations between the various New Zealand ministries and the Colonial Office had rapidly deteriorated. Even the liberal Duke of Newcastle, who had conveyed reinforcements to New Zealand in 1860 when war broke out in Taranaki, and again in 1863 for the invasion of the Waikato, talked of withdrawing 'Regiment by Regiment as

---

[9] Kimberley to Cardwell, 7 Sept. 1870, *Cardwell Papers*, P.R.O. 30/48/5/31, and S. Childers, *Life and Correspondence of the Rt Hon. H. C. E. Childers, 1827–96* (London, 1901) I 173–4.

the Local Government fails to fulfil each of the fair requirements placed upon them from home'.[10] He had eventually decided to assist the colonists through their existing difficulties, on the understanding that the British troops would then be withdrawn. Cardwell, Newcastle's successor as Colonial Secretary, had begun the withdrawals in November 1865 and the Conservative ministers, Carnarvon and Buckingham, had adhered to his decisions. But the New Zealanders stubbornly refused to alter their policy towards the Maori resisters or to contribute towards Great Britain's expenses, and they continually protested at the withdrawal of British troops. Governor Sir George Grey remonstrated with the Colonial Office and argued with the local military commander. Such were the circumstances in July 1867, in which the Duke of Buckingham and Chandos decided to withdraw the last regiment from New Zealand. Even the massacre, shortly afterwards, of some thirty colonists at Poverty Bay on the east coast of North Island did not affect the Colonial Secretary's stand.

Granville set about implementing Buckingham's decision. Negotiations with New Zealand had been allowed to drift on too long; it was now in British interests to bring the matter to a speedy conclusion. The publication, in February 1869, of a pamphlet by F. A. Weld, a former Premier of New Zealand, no doubt fortified Granville's resolution. On the use of British troops Weld was adamant :

> Their employment would only be a signal for a long and expensive war, expensive to England, unjust to the British taxpayer, because unnecessary, ruinous financially to New Zealand, destructive to the spirit of self-reliance in the Colony, and productive of all the old evils of divided command and distracted councils. Do not send troops, I repeat – The Colony has learnt much under this disaster, it will not forget the success of its forces in 1865, and I doubt not that we shall soon hear that those successes had been renewed.[11]

Granville now became determined to make the colonists stand on their own feet. He refused all requests for delay in withdrawing the one remaining regiment and rejected a plea for an

[10] Min., 3 Sept., on W.O. to C.O., 22 Aug. 1863, C.O. 209/177.
[11] F. A. Weld, *Notes on New Zealand Affairs* (London, 1869) pp. 69–70.

imperial guarantee for a loan of £1.5 million to enable them to provide for internal security. Instead Granville treated the colonists to 'a lecture' for their 'information and guidance'. The acid pen of Sir Frederic Rogers, the Permanent Under-Secretary, who had long ago seen the necessity for some plain language, was now used against the unsuspecting New Zealanders.[12]

The government's refusal to contemplate an imperial guarantee for a loan was conveyed to the colonists in a strongly worded despatch dated 21 March 1869. The New Zealanders were reminded that colonisation had started without encouragement from the British government and that the Maori wars had largely arisen through the greed of the settlers for Maori lands. Far from the colony having a moral claim on the mother country, Great Britain, having spent large sums for the benefit of the colonists, possessed 'a claim, and a very heavy claim, if we thought proper to urge it . . . against the colony'.[13] Granville's refusal of a guarantee was heartily endorsed by both Gladstone and Cardwell.[14]

The Liberal leaders were well aware that such brusque treatment of New Zealand would arouse opposition, but the risk was a calculated one. Granville informed a rather dubious Cardwell:

I took the stern line, but as you say we can reverse it at the next Cabinet if desired.

I quite agree about the obloquy to which we may expose ourselves, but on the other hand even a short delay may have entangling consequences.

You are probably right in supposing that for the future it will be a war of Banditti, but if so what chance is there of matters improving much in three months? As long as the troops remain the Colonists will never decide on what is to be their final policy, whether arrogant or conciliatory.[15]

[12] Min. by Granville, 17 Feb., on Fitzherbert to Granville, 5 Feb. 1869, C.O. 209/215. For Rogers's position, see Rogers to Newcastle, 4 Jan. 1863, *Newcastle Papers*, NeC 10,908a.

[13] Granville to Bowen, 21 Mar. 1869 (printed copy), C.O. 209/212.

[14] Granville to Cardwell, 19 May 1869 (telegram), *Cardwell Papers*, P.R.O. 30/48/5/28, p. 42; Cardwell to Granville, and Gladstone to Granville, 20 May 1869 (telegrams), C.O. 209/210; Gladstone to Granville, 21 May 1869, *Granville Papers*, P.R.O. 30/29/57.

[15] Granville to Cardwell, 22 May 1869, private, *Cardwell Papers*, P.R.O. 30/48/5/28, p. 43.

Cardwell's fears were not unwarranted. The publication of the despatch caused a storm both in the colonies and at home. The *New Zealand Advertiser* thought the despatch

> a production doubtless of some *sour doctrinaire* of the Colonial Office, ruling from behind his official screen [which] must be read as conveying in ungracious terms the resolve of the new Ministry, that among its economies one of the first and least debatable is the repudiation of all liability for the defence of the Colonies. Language could not be plainer or more ungracious.

Equally, the *Sydney Morning Herald* and the Melbourne *Argus* were shocked by the 'heartless hypothesis' of this 'cold contemptuous greeting'.[16]

In London, Sir George Grey and four prominent New Zealanders addressed a letter to *The Times*, protesting that the government's actions were calculated to drive New Zealand out of the empire :

> We regard the allegations, expressed and implied in Lord Granville's despatch, as calculated deeply to injure the European population of New Zealand in the estimation of their fellow countrymen in Great Britain, to inflame the passions of natives already in arms against the Government, to produce disaffection among those who are friendly, to drive those who are neutral or wavering into the hostile ranks, and at the same time to create a bitter feeling of hostility on the part of the colonists towards the Government of the mother country, which it is to be feared may become a national tradition.

And in the House of Commons, Lord Bury, recently elected president of the new Colonial Society, declared that this was not the time to convey to the settlers the news that 'it mattered not to this country whether they were eaten up by the savages'.[17]

New Zealand's plight was now taken up by certain sections of the press. The *Spectator* and the *Standard* attacked the govern-

[16] *New Zealand Advertiser*, 26 May 1869; *The Argus* (Melbourne) and *Sydney Morning Herald*, 14 Aug. 1869.

[17] *The Times*, 18 June 1869; speech by Bury, 3 *Hansard*, 22 July 1869, CXCVIII 457.

ment's policy. The *Spectator* described Granville's despatch as 'from end to end a repertory of carefully worded contempt' and concluded that the snub would only irritate the colonists and drive them 'into enmity as a condition of continued self-respect. It is clear that Mr Goldwin Smith's colonial "policy", the policy, that is, of shaking off the colonies . . . has not only been accepted by the existing Government, but they are acting on it.' The government remained unmoved, however, as protest meetings were held in the rooms of the Colonial Society. A conference was canvassed to discuss colonial affairs and suggestions were made that New Zealand should reconsider the benefits of empire. 'Even this Government powerful as it is', declared the *Spectator*, 'will wince under the question "What have you done with the British Empire?" '[18]

Granville, for one usually so susceptible to political pressure, remained strangely immune. His only reaction to the controversy was : 'I think we must harden our hearts.'[19] He now insisted that British troops could not remain in New Zealand under *any* conditions. Cardwell urged caution :

The wind has changed in N.Z. since my responsibility at the C.O. ceased. Three years ago it was easy for me to offer them the troops on condition of paying – for they would not hear of that condition : I therefore easily threw upon them the responsibility for the withdrawal. . . . The responsibility under which you could now act is different. Northbrook, Lugard & Stubs urge upon me so far as they feel at liberty to do so, their opinion that, if any serious calamity recur in N.Z., there will be a great revulsion of feeling in this country; pretty much what I said to you at Whitsuntide.

On the other hand, to leave a single Regiment for a long period is a course full of difficulty – both on the grounds of which you are the exclusive judge; & also on military grounds for the soldiers will not like to play a subordinate part to the Colonial forces, if real hostilities begin.

Granville replied : 'Gladstone has agreed with me, that we should insist upon the immediate withdrawal of the regiment.'[20]

[18] *Spectator*, 24 July 1869.
[19] Granville to Rogers, 28 Sept. 1869, C.O. 209/212.
[20] Cardwell to Granville, 5 Oct., private (copy), and Granville to Cardwell, 6 Oct. 1869, *Cardwell Papers*, P.R.O. 30/48/5/28, pp. 70, 74.

The following day the Colonial Secretary outlined to the Governor of New Zealand his reasons for refusing to allow the retention of British troops under any circumstances. The presence of imperial troops raised the whole problem of divided authority which led to constant disagreements between the civil and military leaders. British troops must always remain under British command. The British government could not transfer troops, maintained at its own expense, to the control of the colonial government; nor could it assume responsibility for any lack of military success – which would raise the expectation of a continuance of the war at imperial expense. If disasters did occur while British troops were stationed in New Zealand, the troops would undoubtedly be called upon and all these problems would be raised once again. The worst aspect of the case, however, was that the presence of imperial troops encouraged a responsibly governed colony in a policy 'pregnant with danger'. The present difficulties – the discontent of the Maoris with regard to the settlers' confiscation policy and the failure of the colony to raise its own military force – could only be combated by distasteful remedies which would not be considered while British troops remained. Granville concluded that Great Britain was not acting as a friend to New Zealand in providing a 'delusive shadow of support'.[21]

The Colonial Secretary had made an important decision. It could not be reversed without great loss of face. In the privacy of the Colonial Office, the Permanent Under-Secretary admitted that the government had 'changed its mind' and felt compelled to acknowledge that the Liberal administration's action 'was no doubt in advance of the policy adopted by previous governments'. Rogers, in fact, had become increasingly concerned with the reputation the office was acquiring for 'snubbing N. Zealand'.[22]

Granville was equally well aware of the public outcry his policy was causing. He knew his actions were under constant supervision. Privately he admitted to Cardwell:

[21] Granville to Bowen, 7 Oct. 1869 (draft), C.O. 209/212.
[22] Min. by Rogers, 22 Mar., and in margin of Bowen to Granville, 13 Jan. 1870, C.O. 209/216. See also mins., 24 Sept. and 1 Oct., on drafts of Granville to Bowen, 4 and 6 Oct. 1869, C.O. 209/212. Also min., 14 Jan., on Granville to Bowen, 28 Jan. 1870, C.O. 209/213.

any great disaster immediately after the withdrawal of the Regiment will influence public opinion, but I shall have something to say for myself in the House of Lords, and if you, Gladstone, Lowe, Bright & Childers cannot defend me in the Commons, you deserve to be sent to New Zealand yourselves.[23]

As Granville anticipated, the latest information on the British government's position conveyed in the despatch was not without its repercussions. The colonial ministers immediately protested at this sudden change in the imperial government's policy: previously it had been maintained that the withdrawals sprang from a colonial refusal to pay for the troops, but now that the situation had deteriorated and the colonists were prepared to meet the demands of the British government, troops could not be retained at any price. The only conclusion to be drawn, declared the New Zealand ministry, was that the imperial government wished to sever the colony's connection with the empire.[24] As a result, annexation to the United States was mooted in the New Zealand press, and in the British House of Lords Carnarvon questioned the government's latest declaration: 'Heavily pressed as we are in the race of international competition, are our fortunes so well assured that we can afford to throw away the affection, the loyalty and the warm feeling of the colonists as if they were merely so much idle lumber?'[25] He begged Granville to think again. Nevertheless, the last detachment of British troops left New Zealand in February 1870.

At last, now that all imperial troops had left New Zealand's soil, Granville was prepared to make a concession. He reassured the colony in March 1870:

Her Majesty's Government disavow any wish to abandon New Zealand or to bring about the separation between this Country & the Colony. The refusal to retain the troops in N.Z. did not proceed from any indifference to the true welfare of the Colony but from a conviction that . . . the employment of British troops in a Colony possessed of responsible Government was objectionable in principle except in the case of foreign War, and . . . it is not for the interest of the Colony itself that

[23] Granville to Cardwell, 9 Oct. 1869, *Cardwell Papers*, P.R.O. 30/48/5/28, p. 78.
[24] Bowen to Granville, 13 Jan. 1870, C.O. 209/216.
[25] 3 *Hansard*, 7 Mar. 1870, cxcix 1324.

New Zealand should be made an Exception from that rule, which, with due consideration for circumstances, is in course of application to other colonies.[26]

Granville then conceded an imperial guarantee for a reduced New Zealand loan of £1 million. Harmony in relations between mother country and colony was finally restored. All talk of secession from the empire was promptly forgotten. And Granville even went so far as to declare his 'deep interest' in the 'welfare and prosperity of this great possession of the Crown'.[27]

Clearly, the British government had followed a rigid and uncompromising policy towards New Zealand – uncompromising, that is, until its principal concern had been accomplished. With dogged determination, and despite vocal opposition, Granville had carried through the decision of his Tory predecessor to withdraw the British garrisons from New Zealand, a policy made more pressing by the urgent need to reform Great Britain's armed forces. But Granville's stubborn disregard for colonial susceptibilities did not amount to an attempt at separation. It did aim at removing one of the anomalies of responsible government and was intended to force the New Zealand ministry to face the consequences of its own internal policy. In the process, British troops were withdrawn from a difficult position and a reasonable chance was secured to reorganise the British army.

Granville regarded his policy, planned in close consultation with Gladstone and Cardwell, as 'just though now generous'.[28] When Robert Lowe, the Chancellor of the Exchequer, objected to the proposed imperial guarantee for a New Zealand loan, the Colonial Secretary urged the Chancellor not to mar his good judgement by desiring to push every principle to its logical conclusion : 'Let us struggle against our virtues.'[29] In fact Granville, by bringing his great powers of statesmanship to bear on colonial affairs – by his tactful handling of certain New Zealand approaches to the United States[30] and timely concession of an

26 Granville to Bowen, 25 Mar. 1870 (draft), C.O. 209/216.
27 Granville to Bowen, 20 May 1870 (draft), C.O. 209/216.
28 Note 21 on Lowe to Granville, 9 May 1870, *Granville Papers*, P.R.O. 30/29/25.
29 Ibid. note 26.
30 See A. J. Harrop, *England and the Maori Wars* (London, 1937) pp. 379–80. Granville became Foreign Secretary at this time and handled the matter with Kimberley.

imperial guarantee – was able finally to restore harmonious relations with the colony. New Zealand's resentment soon gave way to protestations of loyalty based on financial dependence.

It seems obvious that the motives of the government's policy towards New Zealand were misinterpreted. Granville may have been preoccupied with British interests and the Defence Review of the 1860s, but he was by no means intent on forcing the colonies to separate. In the last resort he was prepared to conciliate them. If, then, the government's policy towards New Zealand, which according to C. A. Bodelsen gave rise to the 'empire scare' of 1869–70, was misunderstood, could it be that Granville's somewhat tarnished reputation as a Colonial Secretary is undeserved? Is it possible that the government's policies in other parts of the world were equally misinterpreted?

III

During Granville's tenure of office relations with British North America also became strained. Withdrawal of the garrisons had a similar effect in Canada, faced by the Fenian menace and the uncertain attitude of the United States.[31] Cardwell's plans for military reduction, conveyed to the Canadian government in April 1869, were received as a 'manifestation of indifference, tempered by timidity in the face of responsibility'.[32] Only 6,000 British troops were for the moment to remain in British North America. But in this case an imperial guarantee for a loan was offered – should the Canadians wish to carry out further fortifications. The Toronto *Globe* noted the 'entire change of views on the part of the Imperial authorities':[33] Great Britain was no longer urging the Canadian government to complete Canada's defences. As in New Zealand, concern for colonial security had been replaced by a concern for purely British interests. Even a rejection by the Senate of the United States, after an inflammatory speech by Charles Sumner, chairman of the Senate's Committee on Foreign Relations, of the Johnson–Clarendon Convention arranging a settlement of the *Alabama* question, failed to alter the British government's resolve to implement the

[31] C. P. Stacey, *Canada and the British Army, 1846–71* (London, 1936) pp. 204–29.
[32] Ibid. p. 217.
[33] *The Globe* (Toronto), 16 June 1869.

second stage in its plan – the complete and unconditional withdrawal of the imperial garrison. Accordingly, the Dominion was informed in February 1870 that all British troops were to be withdrawn, apart from the garrison at Halifax, and that only one battalion of infantry and one battery of garrison artillery would be retained in Canada for a further year. As in the case of New Zealand, the British government appeared determined to sever most of the connections between the colonial and British military systems. The British taxpayer was no longer to be burdened with expenditure for Canadian defence.

Granville, doubtless with the New Zealand agitation in mind, did not think that this withdrawal would be so difficult to implement. 'What will be the more so', he informed Cardwell, 'is the language to be held in debate about our future relations with the Dominion. I do not think it would be wise to be abrupt on the subject.'[34] His belief that the government's policy towards Canada would now come in for attack was soon realised. But an injudicious speech by the Governor-General of Canada, in which Sir John Young had declared that the Dominion was now 'in reality independent', gave unexpected authority to the accusations of Granville's critics.

Granville had no one but himself to blame for the embarrassing situation in which he now found himself. In May 1869 Gladstone, the Prime Minister, had reminded Granville, 'for the chance of being useful at a future stage when we resume the discussion', of his view when he was Colonial Secretary, distinctly enough laid down in a despatch to the Canadian Governor-General in 1846, 'that we did not *impose* British connection upon the colony, but regarded its good will and desire as an essential condition of the connection'.[35] The following month Granville had decided to repeat the Gladstonian doctrine of 'freedom and voluntaryism' to Sir John Young, and to sound out the Canadian position :

It has been more and more felt on both sides that Canada is part of the British Empire because she desires to be so; and under the influence of this conviction the attachment of the

[34] Granville to Cardwell, 9 Sept. 1869, *Cardwell Papers,* P.R.O. 30/48/5/28, p. 60.
[35] Gladstone to Granville, 29 May 1869, *Granville Papers*, P.R.O. 30/29/57.

Colonists to Great Britain has grown with the growth of their independence. H.M. Government value the existing relation as the symbol and support of that attachment. . . . They have no desire to maintain it for a single year after it has become injurious or distasteful to them. . . . The greatness of England consists not in the geographical extent of her Empire, but in the spirit which animates those who inhabit it, and the traditional regard of her allies. It will be far more truly consulted by retaining Canada as an ancient, prosperous and cordial friend, than as a half-hearted Dependency. H.M. Government believe that hereditary cordiality is best secured by not only treating the continuance of the imperial authority as dependent on the interest of Canada, but by holding the statesmen and people of the Dominion to be the proper judges of that interest.[36]

Granville directed Young not to communicate these thoughts to his advisers as 'such an overture might be liable to misconstruction'. Young was, however, to encourage them to speak unreservedly to him. Granville then added to Rogers's draft in his own hand :

You will also be good enough to bring to my notice any line of policy, or any measures which without implying on the part of H.M. Government any wish to change abruptly our relations, would gradually prepare both countries for a friendly relaxation of them.[37]

Undoubtedly this injunction led Sir John Young, in July 1869, to remind his listeners in a speech at Quebec replying to the critics of the imperial government's evacuation policy, that Canada's destiny lay in their own hands. It was for Canadians to decide whether to maintain the existing link 'or in due time of the maturity of the Dominion to change it for some other form of alliance'.[38]

This ambiguous statement, widely reported in Canada and Great Britain, was interpreted by some sections of the press as a reference to union with the United States. Two months later Young found it necessary to explain his remarks in a further

[36] Granville to Young, 14 June 1869, confidential (draft), C.O. 42/678.
[37] Ibid.
[38] *The Globe* (Toronto), 16 July 1869.

speech at Halifax. Privately he reported to the Colonial Secretary that Canadians were 'averse to any change either of alliance or allegiance' and were 'simply anxious to remain as they are'. Granville received this declaration of Canadian affection as remarkable proof of the wisdom of the Liberal policy of separation by consent: whether the present connection 'continues in precisely the same form, or whether at some future time the strong but elastic bond between them should be further relaxed . . . feelings of the strongest attachment and mutual respect' would endure.[39]

But Granville's colonial policy was still under suspicion. The withdrawal of the garrisons from Canada was regarded by the government's critics as an attempt to show that Canada could, and ought to, stand on her own feet, which in the light of Young's speech amounted to nothing less than an invitation to declare herself independent. This belief was increased by Granville's tough despatches pushing British Columbia into the new Dominion.[40]

After the Maritimes had been successfully pressurised into joining the original confederation, the Hudson's Bay Company's territory had been acquired for the Dominion and the new province of Manitoba created in the Red River region. British Columbia thus remained the final link in the unbroken Dominion from the Atlantic to the Pacific. Because British Columbia was still very much a dependency lacking responsible government, Granville felt it justified for the British Government to give 'a more unreserved expression of their wishes and judgment' than might have been fitting elsewhere. In despatches dated June and August 1869 Granville ordered the specially appointed governor, Sir Anthony Musgrave, to take such steps as he 'properly and constitutionally' could to ensure the colony's entry into the confederation. Carnarvon felt Granville's words and actions would be interpreted as a desire to be rid of British Columbia.[41]

The government's determination to confer the Order of St Michael and St George on Alexander Tilloch Galt, the Canadian

[39] Young to Granville, 11 Nov., confidential, and Granville's min. dated 30 Nov. 1869, C.O. 42/678. For Young's speech at Halifax, see *Standard*, 7 Sept. 1869.

[40] Granville to Seymour, 17 June, and Granville to Musgrave, 14 Aug. 1869, C.O. 60/36.

[41] 3 *Hansard*, 14 Feb. 1870, cxcix 209–10.

Finance Minister, seemed to confirm the uneasy feeling about the government's colonial policy. At this time Galt held strongly separatist views and had informed the British government of his opinion that confederation was but a preliminary to complete independence.[42] When his views were characterised as disloyal in the Canadian Parliament in February 1870, however, Galt retorted that 'so far as his loyalty to the Crown was concerned, he stood on the same ground as the Ministers of the Crown of England'. He asserted that a 'policy of independence had been arrived at by the Imperial Government'.[43] Thus Granville's subsequent refusal to publish all his correspondence with Galt seemed to endorse the conclusion that the Gladstone government and Galt were in complete agreement as to the most desirable political future for Canada.

In South Africa, where Granville's scorn at the slow progress of the colony towards responsible government had been felt, a similar view was also expressed before the Legislative Assembly by the Governor of the Cape, Sir Philip Wodehouse:

In Northern America we have unmistakable indications of the rapid establishment of a powerful independent State. In Australia it is probable that its several settlements with their great wealth and homogeneous population will see their way to a similar coalition. In New Zealand, the severance is being accomplished under very painful circumstances.[44]

Such feelings were widespread.

Besides the fears expressed in the Canadian and New Zealand Parliaments and at the Cape, concern about the apparent trend of the government's policy was expressed in New South Wales and Victoria. Annexation to the United States was openly being advocated in New Zealand and British Columbia; a separatist movement had begun in Victoria; and Hamilton Fish, the American Secretary of State, apparently believed that the whole of Canada favoured union with the United States. That the American government could interpret Great Britain's actions in

---

[42] O. D. Skelton, *The Life and Times of Sir Alexander Tilloch Galt* (Toronto, 1920) pp. 451–2.

[43] Quoted by R. R. Torrens, 3 *Hansard*, 26 Apr. 1870, cc 1820.

[44] Ibid. 1823.

North America as a prelude to a 'hemispheric flag-withdrawal'[45] increased the alarm felt in the mother country.

The genuine misgivings of many observers, and the suspicions of political opponents inclined to believe the worst of the government, provided ammunition for a parliamentary attack and for an extended press campaign against the colonial policy of Gladstone's administration. The radical *Spectator* deplored the fact that

> It is not only New Zealand which is going to be dismissed, but Australia, not only Australia, but the Canadian Dominion, all that ring of Anglo-Saxon States which, with a little trouble, a little patience and a little consideration . . . might be converted into a chain of faithful and most powerful allies.[46]

The Conservative *Standard* roundly declared:

> Solely on his own responsibility, and without any sanction from any of the recognised depositories of public opinion, the Ministry of Mr Gladstone has resolved to dismember the Empire. By a minute of Lord Granville it has been ordered that there shall be no colonies.[47]

The feared dissolution of the empire appeared to be at hand:

> any politician of ordinary sagacity will draw the inference that a deliberate colonial policy of no insignificant moment has been, at all events, *provisionally* adopted by the present Cabinet, which they are not willing to confide to Parliament. . . .[48]

The Gladstone government, it was alleged, was responsible for the 'boldest and most startling innovation in modern statesmanship'. In the Lords, Carnarvon rose melodramatically to inform the Colonial Secretary: 'There are whispers abroad that there is a policy on foot to dismember the Empire. . . . If there is such a policy in God's name let us know it; if there is not, let it be disavowed.'[49] For many, the government's proposal to abandon the Gambia to France, admitted in the Commons in June 1870,

[45] Schuyler, *Fall of the Old Colonial System*, pp. 270–1. See also C. F. Adams, *Lee at Appomattox and Other Papers* (New York, 1902) p. 158.
[46] *Spectator*, 24 July 1869.
[47] *Standard*, 13 Oct. 1869.
[48] *Spectator*, 26 Mar. 1870.
[49] 3 *Hansard*, 14 Feb. 1870, cxcix 209.

was a surer indication of the government's intentions than the feeble denials of Granville in the Lords.

IV

Was there smoke without fire? The Gladstone government was clearly intent on making the self-governing colonies assume the burdens attached to responsible government. It was determined to withdraw the imperial military presence : internal security was a corollary of self-government and a necessity if 'free' communities were to be established. Cardwell had followed these Liberal doctrines during his own tenure of the Colonial Office from 1864 to 1866. Yet his actions had led to no public outcry. In 1869, however, the urgent need to economise, to withdraw the garrisons, to reorganise Great Britain's defences and reform the army, caused the British government to force the pace. Unfortunately the steps taken occurred at difficult moments in New Zealand and Canadian history and such spartan treatment not unnaturally led to controversy. A policy followed throughout the 1860s reached its climax at the turn of the decade.

But the policy pursued was not a separatist one. Granville both publicly and privately declared, quite genuinely, that he had no wish to dismember the empire. In reply to Lowe's assertion that separation from New Zealand would 'do us no harm', Granville stated positively : 'I don't wish them to separate, and if they do, it will do us politically a little harm – but they will not separate.'[50] And Granville's Canadian despatch of 14 June 1869 was probably little more than a gentle reminder that no obstacle would be placed in the path of complete independence should the Canadians desire it. The Governor-General's strongly negative reply convinced Granville that the time for separation was not yet ripe and seems to have dismissed all such thoughts from the Colonial Secretary's mind. Whatever might be thought in some quarters of the possibility of Canada joining the United States, it was not the object of Granville's policy to promote this end. Indeed, he specifically urged the incorporation of British Columbia into the Canadian confederation so forcefully in order to strengthen the independent position of the existing Dominion.

[50] Granville's remarks on Lowe to Granville, 9 May 1870, *Granville Papers*, P.R.O. 30/29/25. See also Granville to Gladstone, 30 June 1870, *Gladstone Papers*, B.M., Add. MSS. 44,167, p. 62.

Perhaps Granville's own views are most accurately summed up in a minute he wrote in the privacy of the Colonial Office :

The friendly separation of Canada from this country, and a declaration of its independence would relieve Great Britain and the Dominion from some present embarrassment, and from future risks. But I should regret that this country should appear to adopt any abrupt proceeding which may alienate the Canadians.[51]

His own views coincided with traditional Liberal ideas of separation by consent, but with one extremely important reservation. He did not believe that the mother country should forgo her right to introduce a 'friendly separation' in the future. He enquired of the Prime Minister : 'May not circumstances arise, in which it would be politic for this country to say "You are now so rich and so strong that we must take the initiative and ask you to agree to a friendly separation"?'[52] The 'climax of anti-imperialism' in British policy has certainly been more correctly defined as a 'crisis of opinion'.[53]

What were the views of the other members of the Cabinet? If the Gladstone government did not inaugurate any abrupt change in the direction of Great Britain's colonial policy, its members certainly professed stronger separatist sentiments than any of their predecessors. Indeed, J. A. Froude, the historian, was convinced that 'Gladstone & Co. deliberately intend to shake off the colonies. They are privately using their command of the situation in order to make the separation inevitable.'[54] To his mind, certain members of the Cabinet were using their position to press their private views on public policy.

Granville did indeed receive a wealth of conflicting advice from Cardwell, Gladstone, Bright, Lowe and from the ageing Liberal statesman, Earl Russell. But if it was Granville's treatment of New Zealand that hit the headlines, sparked off the controversy in Parliament and the press, produced the Youl Circular and proposals for a colonial conference, and provoked

---

[51] Min., 30 Nov., on Young to Granville, 11 Nov. 1869, C.O. 42/678.
[52] Granville's remarks on a secret memo. by Gladstone, 19 Jan. 1870, *Gladstone Papers*, Add. MSS. 44,759.
[53] McIntyre, *Imperial Frontier*, p. 50.
[54] J. Skelton, *The Table Talk of Shirley* (London, 1895) I 142.

the Cannon Street meetings,[55] it was the position of Canada which caused the Cabinet most concern.

Canada had long been the *bête noire* of the separatists and was to loom large in Cabinet discussions. After a Cabinet meeting on 8 May 1869 the Earl of Kimberley, Lord Privy Seal, noted in his journal :

> We have had a gloomy discussion on the relations between this country & the United States. Nearly all the Ministers were of the opinion that it would be impossible to defend Canada successfully against the Americans, and it is much to be desired that Canada should become independent. It would be for the interest both of England and Canada. We should be relieved from a continual source of weakness and danger, and the Canadians would then have nothing to fear from the United States whose ill will to Canada arises from a desire to injure us, and would cease when Canada no longer formed a part of the British Empire. There is no reason why an independent Canada should not be on equally good terms with both nations.[56]

Bright apparently openly told the Canadians that they 'ought to join the U.S.'; Lowe was certainly against all concessions to the colonies; and Cardwell often advocated the most spartan treatment.[57] According to Granville, 'Our relations with North America are of a very delicate character. The best solution of them would probably be that in the course of time and in the most friendly spirit the Dominion should find itself strong enough to proclaim her independence.' But unfortunately the time was not yet ripe. As Lord Clarendon, the Foreign Secretary, noted : 'We cannot throw them off, and it is very desirable that we should part as friends.'[58]

Gladstone remained convinced that Canada should retain the

---

[55] For the agitation against Granville's policy, see below, Chapter 4.

[56] Kimberley, 'Journal', 8 May 1869, p. 4.

[57] Cardwell to Granville, 21 June 1869, *Granville Papers,* P.R.O. 30/29/53; Lowe to Granville, 9 May 1870, *Granville Papers,* P.R.O. 30/29/25; Granville to Cardwell, 27 Dec. 1869, *Cardwell Papers,* P.R.O. 30/48/5/28, p. 8.

[58] Granville to Russell, 28 Aug. 1869, quoted in Lord. E. Fitzmaurice, *The Life of Granville George Leveson Gower, Second Earl Granville, K.G.* (London, 1905) II 22; Clarendon to Lyons, 1 June 1870, quoted in Lord Newton, *Lord Lyons: A Record of British Diplomacy* (London, 1913) I 292.

threads of her political destiny in her own hands – with the assurance that Britain would maintain the political connection as long as Canada desired it. The Dominion should assume the responsibility for internal defence in the knowledge that in times of crisis 'whether Canada were independent of us or not, such assistance would be freely accorded & would only be limited by our means.'[59] Granville was not in entire agreement. But Kimberley probably summed up best the attitude of the majority of the Cabinet when he wrote that severance of the colonial link would

> give a shock to our influence and reputation. It is difficult to see in what way their connexion with us can be permanently maintained. But it will be a gain for both us and them, if we can keep up the connexion till they become stronger. Separation would then seem more natural, and would bring with it less annoyance.

After Kimberley had become Colonial Secretary in July 1870, the more radical views expressed in the Cabinet seem to have become less influential. Shortly after his appointment Kimberley recorded in his journal:

> Those who know Canada best are convinced that Canada would fall into the hands of the Americans if she were to cease to be British, unless she had become much stronger and more populous than she can be for some time to come . . . the question of independence ought not to be regarded as a practical one in our time. It is reduced to a mere speculation as to the future.[60]

As time progressed, the actions of the Gladstone government became more circumspect. Had the public outcry against Granville's policy at last had some effect?

V

The strength of the opposition to the apparent trend of Granville's policy in 1870 does seem to have surprised and shaken the government. At the same time, moreover, the position of the

[59] Memo., 19 Jan. 1870, secret, *Gladstone Papers*, Add. MSS. 44,759.
[60] Kimberley, 'Journal', May 1870, p. 13; 22 July 1870, pp. 17–18.

Liberal administration had become less secure after a series of unpopular domestic measures. Further controversial decisions were certainly not desirable. And when, in the opening months of 1870, most of the leading periodicals carried disparaging articles about the government's colonial policy, and *Fraser's Magazine*, the *Quarterly Review*, *Blackwood's Magazine* and the *Westminster Review* joined ranks with the *Spectator* and the *Standard* in attacking the government, Granville, Gladstone and, later, Knatchbull-Hugessen each found it necessary to disavow separatist tendencies. The Prime Minister and his colleagues now set about explaining the basis of their policy. Gladstone warned Granville: 'I have no doubt your Colonial Policy will be discussed and attacked, in Parliament. I hope we shall all claim it as *ours*, & give it no half hearted defence. And it so happens we are very strong in Colonial men of different kinds: Cardwell, Childers, Lowe, Fortescue, Forster.'[61]

Gladstone's expectations were correct. In February 1870 Carnarvon rose in the House of Lords to accuse the government of following a policy 'cheeseparing in point of economy and spendthrift in point of national character' and 'a course fatal to the highest and best interests of the country'. He hoped Her Majesty's Government were serious in the belief that their policy would not lead to dismemberment of the empire, but he warned them, 'as anyone who stands calmly and impartially by must warn them, that, whatever may be their meaning, they are doing the very acts, they are taking the very steps which must accomplish that result'. Granville appeared to be somewhat perplexed: 'the noble Earl's argument seemed to be an attack against some policy of mine, without in any way defining what that policy seemed to him to be'. The withdrawal of 2,000–3,000 troops would surely not lead to the severance of all links with the colonies. A policy of separation would never meet with general consent at the present time. On the other hand, no colony would ever be retained by force.

Viscount Monck, former Governor-General of Canada, was less evasive. Colonies were useless. The most substantial link he wished to see was one of 'sentiment and affection'. The present ministry had his whole-hearted support. Another Liberal peer failed to see what all the fuss was about. Lord Lyveden declared

61 Gladstone to Granville, 1 Oct. 1869, *Granville Papers*, P.R.O. 30/29/57.

that 'there never was a time when there was less colonial controversy than at present, in fact, there was absolutely none'.[62]

Carnarvon's speech did, however, earn the gratitude of one colonial politician, J. A. Macdonald. The Canadian Prime Minister wrote to Carnarvon:

We are glad to know that we have in you a friend. I may almost say a friend in need for we greatly distrust the men at the helm in England who cannot, I fear, be considered as appreciating the importance of maintaining the empire as it is, intact.

We indulge the belief here, however, that Messrs. Bright, Lowe and Gladstone (shall I add Lord Granville?) are not the true exponents of the public opinion of England. We may perhaps be obliged to appeal from the Government to the people of England.[63]

Many Liberal back-benchers were also dissatisfied with the government's conduct of colonial affairs. In April 1870 R. R. Torrens, a former Premier of South Australia, called for a select committee on colonial policy, asserting that some colonies were being 'encouraged by significant suggestions to ask for independence, whilst others were being incited and goaded on to the same end by an unequal and inconsistent course of difficulties, by misrepresentations and bitter taunts'. He drew attention to the widespread feeling of uneasiness and uncertainty and called for an indulgent and sympathetic consideration of colonial difficulties.[64] There then followed a long debate before a thin house in which, according to *The Times*, 'men spoke as if it were incumbent on them to occupy a certain number of minutes in the utterance of articulate words, without any obligation to connect sound and meaning'.[65]

The government planned its response well. The first member to reply from the government benches was 'that exemplary colonial champion', past critic of the government's New Zealand policy and present president of the Colonial Society, Lord Bury, whose 'perfervid ardour in behalf of the colonies', it was noted in

[62] 3 *Hansard*, 14 Feb. 1870, cxcix 193 ff.
[63] Macdonald to Carnarvon, 14 Apr. 1870, private, quoted in Sir J. Pope, *The Correspondence of Sir John Macdonald* (Toronto, 1921) pp. 132–4.
[64] 3 *Hansard*, 26 Apr. 1870, cc 1820.
[65] *The Times*, 27 Apr. 1870.

the *Evening Standard*, 'has of late undergone a suspicious miti-
gation, which has diluted it into cold aversion or even active
hostility'.[66] And Bury's speech supporting the principles assailed
by Torrens was ably seconded by C. B. Adderley, the Conservative Colonial Reformer. The Conservative opposition in fact
did not care for an enquiry into colonial policy. Disraeli and the
Conservative leaders did not vote in favour of the motion for a
select committee.[67]

Despite Conservative lack of interest, however, Gladstone did
attempt a vindication of the government's policy, for the benefit
of his own sceptical back-benchers:

> Assumptions have been made that the present Government has
> aspired to be the heralds and inaugurators of a new policy and
> a new era in regard to the colonies. . . . There is no question
> of any new policy at all; but there is a question of the succes-
> sive development and application of admitted principles to one
> colony after another, according as circumstances allow and
> invite their application.

But Gladstone's interpretation of those principles – the necessity
of ensuring a peaceful separation 'should it occur', which had
formed 'the sense, the principle and the secret of our policy' –
must have done little to allay the fears of those back-benchers
who were apprehensive about the future of the imperial connection. 'Freedom and voluntaryism' may have formed 'the
character of the connection', but many observers would not have
accepted Gladstone's assertions that his policy was 'the truest and
best, if not the only means, of fulfilling our obligations' to the
colonies. Gladstone concluded his sermon by reminding his
wayward disciples:

> It is impossible to establish a free community unless you have
> along with the enjoyment of the privileges of freedom, a fair
> distribution of the burdens which they entailed. Unless men

---

[66] *Evening Standard*, 27 Apr. 1870. In his speech Bury made use of a
memo. drawn up by Sir John Rose for the Colonial Office (to be found in
C.O. 42/694). This would seem to indicate that Bury had been deliberately
chosen by the government to reply to the motion.
[67] *The Times*, 28 Apr. 1870. The resolution was defeated by 110 votes
to 67.

are taught to rely upon themselves, they can never be truly
worthy of the name of freemen.[68]

Had, therefore, the New Zealand loan been refused, the imperial
garrisons withdrawn, and the criticism voiced in parliament, the
press and at public meetings withstood, simply in order to teach
the colonists to stand on their own feet, to become 'truly worthy
of the name of freemen'? If this was the case, the distinction
between moral concern for ensuring a colony's 'independence'
and a policy aimed at provoking a unilateral declaration of
independence seemed blurred to many of Gladstone's critics. It
was not the whole-hearted disavowal of separatism that many
Liberal back-benchers had hoped for.

However 'moral' the government's policy may have been,
events were soon to force a change of policy – or at least a
divergence from declared principles. The Riel rebellion led to a
British expedition leaving British shores to fight on Canadian
soil. International complications necessitated an increase in the
military estimates and even Gladstone was forced to instruct
Cardwell 'to study the means of sending 20,000 men to Antwerp
with as much promptitude as at the *Trent* affair we sent 10,000
to Canada'.[69] The animosity aroused by the government's conduct of relations with New Zealand also required some gesture
of conciliation. It was at this juncture that Granville 'modified'[70]
his policy and carried through an imperial guarantee for a
reduced loan of £1 million to New Zealand. Similarly, conciliatory gestures were later made in the direction of Canada,
which suffered a Fenian incursion in May 1870 and was expected
to become a signatory to the Treaty of Washington in 1871. In
return for co-operation in this settlement the final withdrawal of
British troops from Canada was postponed until August 1871
and an imperial guarantee for a loan of £3.6 million for the
building of canals and the Pacific railway was eventually
arranged in 1872 by Granville's successor.

The *Standard* not unnaturally poured scorn on the logic and
morality of the government's policy. The *Spectator* was jubilant:

[68] 3 *Hansard*, 26 Apr. 1870, cc 1899–1903.
[69] J. Morley, *The Life of William Ewart Gladstone* (London, 1906) ii 339.
[70] Granville to Gladstone, 30 June 1870, *Gladstone Papers*, Add. MSS.
44,167, p. 62.

Ministers have changed their policy, have changed it very abruptly and have changed it for the best of all reasons – because they had begun to discover that their line was not the line of the people of England, and would, if pushed to its logical results, end in events which would bring down the bitter displeasure of the people of England.[71]

But the government still had not given a convincing denial of separatist aspirations. Earls Russell and Grey continued to attack the government's colonial policy. And even after Granville's removal to the Foreign Office, on the death of Clarendon, doubts about the government's intentions towards the colonies persisted. The feeble denials of William Monsell, Parliamentary Under-Secretary at the Colonial Office, counted for little. Not until a select committee on colonial policy was requested for the second year in succession, this time by the Liberal, R. A. Macfie, did Monsell's successor, Edward Knatchbull-Hugessen, at last come forward with an emphatic rejection of separatism. Self-reliance, he declared,

did not mean separate existence, for a Colony might be great and self-reliant, and still maintain an intimate connection with the mother country. The government wished to retain the colonies; but they wished to retain them bound to this country by ties of kindred and affection. . . . Let them feel that there was nothing to be gained by separation; let them have nothing to complain of; let them see that we regard them as brethren, made their interests our own, and viewed their increasing power and prosperity not only without jealousy, but with real and cordial satisfaction, and he believed that their hearts would be more and more closely knit to us. . . . This was the policy of the Government, it was no new policy; it was no party policy. It had been endorsed by successive Governments, confirmed by the votes of Parliament, ratified by the opinion of the Colonists themselves and approved by the intelligence of the people of this country.[72]

This was much more to the liking of the Liberal back-benchers.

[71] *Spectator*, 21 May 1870; see also *Standard*, 24 May, 20 June 1870.
[72] 3 *Hansard*, 12 May 1871, ccvi 761–8.

But the tone of the speech was not fully approved by the Prime Minister. He dubbed it 'an excellent bit of *Bunkum*'.[73]

Kimberley, at odds with his Prime Minister, could still record in his journal in March 1872 : 'Gladstone, Lowe and Cardwell make no secret of their opinion that we should be well rid of the colonies.'[74] But with Disraeli's speech at Manchester on 3 April 1872 and his accusations at the Crystal Palace banquet in June 1872, the Liberals trod warily and were careful not to give the opposition any grounds for further attack.

By 1872 the Gladstone government was rapidly declining in popularity. The Cardwell army reforms, Forster's Education Act and the Ballot Act of 1870, the University Tests Act, 1871, and the 1872 Licensing Act had all succeeded in alienating influential interests. Great Britain had also cut a poor figure on the world's stage : the *Alabama* arbitration, Russia's tearing-up of the Black Sea clauses in the Treaty of Paris of 1856 and Britain's failure to prevent the annexation of Alsace–Lorraine by Germany had combined with the publication of an anonymous magazine article, 'The Battle of Dorking', depicting a German invasion of England, to cause discomfort among the British electorate. The early 1870s had also seen a general rise in prices, strikes by the Metropolitan Police and gas company stokers, a budget failure in 1871 and an uninspired budget for 1872. Two recent government appointments – the Collier and Ewelme cases – had brought the government into additional disrepute.[75] The Liberal administration just could not afford to allow the Conservatives to make further political capital out of the government's colonial policy.

The day after Disraeli's Crystal Palace speech, Knatchbull-Hugessen returned to the attack in the Commons. He had sometimes heard of the party who desired the disintegration of the empire, but he had never met them :

> If they existed he believed that their number was infinitesimally small and they might be practically ignored. In fact he was inclined to think that they only existed in the fertile brains of imaginative statesmen who, in order to create a new political

[73] *The Political Diary of Lord Brabourne, 1858–88*, unpublished MS., IV 558, quoted in McIntyre, *Imperial Frontier*, p. 63.

[74] Kimberley, 'Journal', 2 Mar. 1872, p. 29.

[75] R. C. K. Ensor, *England, 1870–1914* (Oxford, 1936) p. 20.

THE LANCASHIRE LIONS.

"SO HAVE I HEARD ON INKY IRWELL'S SHORE,
ANOTHER LION GIVE A LOUDER ROAR,
AND THE FIRST LION THOUGHT THE LAST A BORE."

Bombastes Furioso.

programme for their own party, found it necessary to mis-represent the policy of their opponents.[76]

As the Gladstone government tottered on throughout 1873, Liberal speeches advocating the desirability of colonial independence and the need to prepare for such a contingency became less frequent. Kimberley soon came to believe that in Great Britain's relations with her colonies

> our interests as a rule clash so little on account of their immense distance from England, that unless the Home Govt. is very wrong headed collisions may be avoided. For this reason I think the connexion may be maintained indefinitely in time of peace – that is a connexion which is based on absolute independence of the colonies in all their local affairs.[77]

Indeed, by the time the Gladstone government fell in February 1874 the Cabinet was actually considering enlarging British obligations in West Africa, the Malay States and the Pacific. The criticism voiced in the House and the activities of several Liberal back-benchers, as well as pressure from the men on the spot, at last appeared to be having some effect on the Cabinet, if not on Gladstone himself.

The *tone* of the government had definitely altered, if not its policy. All signs of separatist tendencies in policy had disappeared and similar sentiments among the Liberals in Parliament had been largely suppressed. In 1875 W. E. Forster in a speech at Edinburgh could ask: 'who talks now of casting off the colonies?'[78] Truly by that date such ideas had become unfashionable. Greater attention was now given to consolidating imperial ties, rather than smoothing the pathways towards independence. And the Liberals were as responsible as the Conservatives for this revived imperialist spirit, if not more so. The 'empire scare' during the years 1869–70 appears to have given a death-blow to many almost universally accepted sentiments, after certain defenders of the imperial connection had gathered their forces in the mistaken belief that Granville was about to cut the colonies adrift.

[76] 3 *Hansard*, 25 June 1872, ccxii 210.
[77] Kimberley, 'Journal', 24 May 1873, pp. 38–9.
[78] W. E. Forster, *Our Colonial Empire: An Address* (Edinburgh, 1875), an address before the Philosophical Institution, Edinburgh, 5 Nov. 1875.

VI

In what light, then, should we view the colonial policy of Gladstone's first administration? How can Granville's controversial conduct of colonial affairs be explained? Does he deserve his rather unenviable reputation as a Colonial Secretary? Or was he merely unfortunate in having to preside over the Colonial Office at a particularly difficult period in British domestic history and in the evolution of the empire?

Granville was obviously uninterested in colonial affairs. Colonial problems were rarely discussed in his correspondence with Gladstone. In fact much of Granville's time was taken up in acting as an arbitrator between the Liberal government and the Queen and within the Cabinet itself. He also possessed heavy responsibilities managing government business in the House of Lords. As a result he left much of the work of his department to the Permanent Under-Secretary. Rogers, not surprisingly, found Granville 'the pleasantest and most satisfactory' of all the Secretaries of State; he was not inclined to 'meddle beyond what is required'.[79] Consequently, colonial interests frequently possessed no official champion in the Cabinet: while Granville remained at the Colonial Office, colonial interests were more consistently subordinated to the requirements of British domestic politics and foreign policy than usual. And when Granville did choose to stand up for the interests of an individual colony – as over the question of free emigration to Western Australia in 1869 – he was overruled by his colleagues.[80]

There was little agreement on the conduct of colonial affairs in the Cabinet. Such men as Bright, Gladstone, Fortescue and Forster could hardly be expected to agree on a united approach to empire. As a result the future of the colonies was left an open question; each issue was discussed on its own merits. And more often than not this attitude resulted in colonial policy being entirely dictated to the Colonial Office by other departments in Whitehall. The Chancellor of the Exchequer, the Foreign Secretary, the Secretary of State for War and the Prime Minister

[79] G. E. Marindin, *Letters of Frederic, Lord Blachford, Under-Secretary of State for the Colonies, 1860–71* (London, 1896) p. 264. Also Rogers to Miss Rogers, 20 Dec. 1868, ibid. p. 275.

[80] See Granville's memo. to the Cabinet, 18 June, on Treas. to C.O., 11 June 1869, C.O. 18/164.

all intervened in colonial affairs, without much resistance from the Colonial Secretary, when colonial developments affected British interests. Gladstone was intent on making responsible government work; Clarendon wished to maintain friendly relations with foreign powers, especially the United States; Cardwell was busy withdrawing imperial garrisons; and Lowe wanted to reduce British expenditure. To such men the crisis in relations with New Zealand was merely tiresome and the possession of Canada an awkward embarrassment.

Most of the influential members of the Cabinet would probably have agreed with Gladstone's emphasis on the desirability and inevitability of colonial devolution. The government's purpose was to ensure that the transfer of power was carried out amicably. Granville, who relied heavily on advice from Cardwell, took a slightly more *avant-garde* position than his leader, since he did not believe that the mother country should herself forgo the right to inaugurate a peaceful separation – at the right moment. But even Granville was not prepared to accept the more radical outbursts of Bright and Lowe. Kimberley, on the other hand, was more sanguine than the Prime Minister. He did not see any need for a separation to take place in the foreseeable future. But he agreed with Gladstone that all the 'frothy talk' about cementing imperial bonds was totally misguided.

It was precisely this refusal of Gladstone to associate himself with the growing agitation for 'consolidation', the cause Disraeli so neatly adopted, that allowed rumours concerning the intentions of the government towards the colonies to persist, even within the Liberal party. The aged Russell was concerned lest the government's attitude should 'allow the horses to run away with the carriage, tho down hill & tho the road ends in a precipice',[81] thus promoting a premature separation. This was also Carnarvon's fear. Yet such ideas were furthest from the Prime Minister's thoughts. Gladstone argued against Kimberley's request to allow the Australians to introduce preferential tariffs, for the very reason that it would open up another road to independence.

Ever since the disallowance of a request from New South Wales in 1866 asking for the repeal of a clause in the Australian Colonies Government Act which forbade the levying of differ-

[81] Russell to Granville, 31 Aug. 1869, *Granville Papers*, P.R.O. 30/29/79.

ential duties, the Australian colonies had persistently pleaded for more freedom in dealing with local customs tariffs. Kimberley, under pressure from Robert Herbert and Knatchbull-Hugessen, was prepared to make such a concession, but the Prime Minister, fearing foreign complications, consistently opposed such a course. In the *Alabama* affair and Russia's violation of the Black Sea clauses in the Treaty of Paris, Great Britain had made a stand on the literal interpretation of international law and had sought to uphold the sanctity of treaties. Gladstone feared the Australasian demands might violate the terms of some of Great Britain's commercial treaties and thus lay her open to the charge of taking her own obligations lightly. Kimberley was required, therefore, to write several circular despatches in an attempt to dissuade the Australians. But the colonists would not be dissuaded and remained unmoved by homilies on free trade. Instead, at an intercolonial conference in September 1871, they proceeded to demand an end to all imperial interference with colonial legislation. The Premier of Victoria penned a memorandum professing an inability to 'understand how any treaty obligations with foreign countries can now or hereafter pretend to regulate the relations of two British Colonies any more than the relations between two Countries of the United Kingdom'. As these remarks coincided with a memorandum from Julius Vogel, the Treasurer of New Zealand, which bluntly stated that the choice of the British government lay between granting full fiscal independence, an imperial preferential system or imperial federation, Gladstone was incensed by this attack on imperial supremacy. Was this a deliberate attempt to destroy the unity of the British empire? Gladstone shrank from doing anything that might have dangerous and far-reaching consequences: 'I really do not see upon what foundation any duty of military & naval protection on our part is to rest, if the foreign relations of Colonies are to pass out of our hands into theirs.'[82]

Kimberley was equally worried and left 'colonies & Parliament in no doubt as to my apprehensions of the separatist tendency of the measure'. But in spite of his chief's moral problems, he recorded in his journal: 'I think it is far better to give way. The question is not vital: the practical effects of the concession will

[82] Gladstone to Kimberley, 29 Dec. 1871, quoted in Knaplund, *Gladstone and Britain's Imperial Policy*, pp. 247–50.

probably be very small, as it is unlikely that the colonies will
be able to agree upon a common tariff.'[83] The battle from
Gladstone's point of view was finally lost, however, when the
Governor-General of Canada, oblivious of political repercussions,
assented to a Canadian tariff bill discriminating against American
coffee and tea. Disallowance was not in the realm of practical
politics and so the demands of the Australasian group could no
longer be denied. Consequently, by the Australian Colonies
Duties Act of 1873, the colonies of Australasia were allowed to
give preferential treatment to each other's produce. Kimberley
fended off an attack in the Lords by the doctrinaire third Earl
Grey with the statement: 'the principle of self-government was
even more important than the principle of free-trade'.[84]

It is clear then that the Liberal government's attitude towards
colonial policy must be viewed in the context of traditional
Liberal doctrines: responsible government, free trade and self-
reliance. It must also be viewed against the background of
immediate needs: the commitment to economy; the need to
withdraw the garrisons to permit army reform and the reorganisation of Great Britain's defences; the need to foster good relations
with the United States and to provide the means for meeting
European engagements. These were the concerns of Gladstone,
Cardwell, Clarendon and Lowe. Against this background
Granville's colonial policy appears less inexplicable and also
less sinister.

In these circumstances the Colonial Secretary was prepared to
force the pace of colonial development. Economy had to be
achieved and the garrisons withdrawn. But even so, Cardwell's
plan for the reduction of British troops in South Africa was never
carried out in full. By 1873, however, Knatchbull-Hugessen
could boast that the only British troops remaining in self-
governing colonies secured imperial interests.[85] British Columbia
had been jostled into the Canadian confederation and the Cape
Colony hurried towards self-government. Such spartan treatment,
regardless of all mitigating circumstances, was bound to arouse
opposition, especially at a time when anti-empire sentiments were
receiving widespread publicity. Yet the policies Granville pursued,

[83] Kimberley, 'Journal', 24 May 1873, p. 38.
[84] See Knaplund, *Gladstone and Britain's Imperial Policy*, pp. 103–21.
[85] 3 *Hansard*, 7 March 1873, ccxiv 1528.

including that of troop withdrawals, had all been inaugurated many years earlier and had been approved by the Conservative party. Even the proposal to exchange the Gambia, for example, had been raised in 1866 and eagerly endorsed by Adderley, the Conservative Parliamentary Under-Secretary. Granville was doubly unfortunate that so many issues should have come to a head at a time when the British government was intent on reducing its overseas commitments. Later Kimberley was able to make a partial concession to South Africa concerning troop withdrawals in return for the acceptance of self-government.[86]

Must Granville, therefore, be dubbed merely unfortunate and his numerous colonial difficulties regarded as coincidences? The answer is 'no'. Not only did the government underestimate the opposition to their policy, but in failing to explain adequately the basis of that policy they completely bungled their own case. Granville's reply to the charges made in the House of Lords was evasive and Gladstone's phrases in the Commons were equally ambiguous. Gladstone's assertion, for example, that he did not regard the unity of the British empire 'as bound up essentially in the maintenance of any administrative function whatever',[87] sounded too close to the doctrines of Goldwin Smith for the comfort of many back-benchers. The government allowed a ripple of discontent over the treatment of New Zealand, expressed by a few sympathisers in London, to erupt into a full-scale parliamentary and press campaign. The ministers continued to equivocate. Granville's statement to a deputation from the Colonial Society and the Cannon Street meetings that 'he would be exceedingly sorry to see England deprived of all her colonies, but England would never attempt to retain them by brute force',[88] was taken as an avowal that he would not be sorry to see the emancipation of some colonies.

Even the most commendable acts of the government were not publicised. Granville's instructions in July 1869 that every possible demonstration by naval forces should be made in support of the colonists as the imperial troops withdrew from New Zealand was not made public until eight months later. A disavowal of any intention to cut the colonies adrift, given to

---

[86] Kimberley to Barkly, 17 Oct., 17 Nov. 1870, *Parl. P.* (1871) XLVII, C. 459.

[87] 3 *Hansard*, 26 Apr. 1870, cc 1905.

[88] *The Times*, 17 Dec. 1869.

commissioners from New Zealand in January 1870, seems to have received no publicity in England. Not until March 1870 were the New Zealanders publicly reassured that the government's policy was not an attempt to abandon New Zealand but proceeded from 'a conviction that . . . the employment of British troops in a Colony possessed of responsible Government was objectionable in principle except in the case of foreign War'.[89] There was indeed some truth in Carnarvon's criticism of Granville's actions :

> To reduce the garrisons, or even in some cases to withdraw them altogether, might not in itself be wrong but the ostentatious manner in which it was done, and the language which unfortunately was held, was I think calculated to do mischief by spreading abroad the belief that it was the intention of the Imperial Government to loosen the ties between us and the Colonies.[90]

In his dealings with the colonies Granville made no attempt to employ the charm and tact for which he was so renowned.

It would seem that Granville's poor reputation as Colonial Secretary was to a large extent of his own making. He placed greater emphasis on the firmness of his actions than on the justice of his case. Even his concessions to the colonists were misinterpreted. His decision to offer an imperial guarantee to New Zealand, for example, came after a year's implacable resistance to the pleas of the New Zealanders and after opposition to the government's policy, particularly in Liberal circles, had clearly manifested itself. The concession appeared as an act of capitulation. Similarly, the decision to send an expedition to quell the Red River rebellion was also seen in the press as a defeat for government policy.

Amid such clamour, the positive aspects of Granville's term of office – his settlement of the terms for the transfer of the Hudson's Bay Company's territories to the Dominion of Canada in 1869;[91]

---

[89] Granville to Bowen, 25 Mar. 1870 (draft), C.O. 209/216.

[90] Carnarvon to Dufferin, 31 Oct. 1874, quoted in A. Hardinge, *Life of Henry Howard Molyneaux Herbert, Fourth Earl of Carnarvon, 1831–90* (London, 1925), II 96–8.

[91] J. S. Galbraith, *The Hudson's Bay Company as an Imperial Factor* (Berkeley, 1957) pp. 422–8; E. E. Rich, *The History of the Hudson's Bay Company, 1670–1870* (London, 1959), II 850–936.

the establishment of the Order of St Michael and St George as a colonial decoration; his tactful handling of the New Zealand approaches to the United States; his loosening of the hold of the Treasury over the Crown colonies and the improvements in the Crown Agents' department[92] – were ignored. There can have been few clearer cases of a government's need for a lesson in good public relations. The actions of the government, the attitude of the Colonial Secretary and the known beliefs of certain members of the ministry all contributed to the fear that the government had embraced separatist sentiments. These fears seemed to be all too clearly based in apparently undeniable fact. For this the government had no one but itself to blame.

It has often been asserted, however, that the government's unpopularity was largely due to the permanent officials in the Colonial Office. Granville, who possessed the social graces of an earlier age, was certainly lax in his official habits. He took his colonial duties lightly and like most Colonial Secretaries left the writing of despatches to the Permanent Under-Secretary. But he left a number of important decisions to his discretion as well. Granville's love of pleasure and dislike of work is notorious. Kimberley thought him slipshod and 'an indifferent departmental Minister'. He criticised his way of existing 'from hand to mouth' and suggested that Granville was 'singularly ignorant of the details of the questions he has to deal with'.[93] Rogers's impression was, of course, entirely laudatory : Granville's term of office formed 'so large and so bright a space' in his recollections of the Colonial Office.[94] But perhaps it is as well to record the recollection of another senior Colonial Office official, Sir Robert Meade :

It is the fashion to speak of him as a pleasure-loving man who sacrificed business to pleasure. Never was a greater mistake. He enjoyed amusements, but never neglected business. He was an excellent administrator, because when he had a good man under him, he trusted him while holding all the threads in his

---

[92] See B. Blakely, *The Colonial Office, 1868–92* (Durham, N.C., 1972) pp. 21, 149.

[93] Kimberley, 'Journal', 1 June 1872, p. 31.

[94] Blachford to Granville, 2 Feb. 1886, *Granville Papers*, P.R.O. 30/29/213.

hands. His judgment was sounder than that of any other man I ever came across.[95]

Granville certainly knew what he was doing at the Colonial Office and was well aware of the issues involved. Rogers may have written the despatches but Granville often toned them down, even cancelling whole paragraphs, and he fully approved of everything sent from the Colonial Office in his name. Indeed, the most controversial sentence written during the years 1868–70 was penned by Granville's own hand. He had written to the Canadian Governor-General :

> You will . . . be good enough to bring to my notice any line of policy, or any measures which without implying on the part of H.M. Government any wish to change abruptly our relations, would gradually prepare both countries for a friendly relaxation of them.[96]

These words, almost certainly unseen by the Prime Minister,[97] were the most separatist in sentiment to emerge from the Colonial Office during Granville's term of office. The Colonial Secretary, unlike the Prime Minister, did not believe Great Britain should relinquish the right to inaugurate a friendly separation. This should be done at the most propitious moment, not forced on the colonists too soon, nor exacted from the imperial government under pressure, too late. His sounding of the Canadian Governor-General's views was his only attempt to put this philosophy into practice. If Canada was not yet sufficiently mature, no part of the empire was yet ready for independence.

Thus there does seem to be some basis for the arguments of Bodelsen and Schuyler concerning the years 1868–70. If there was no 'climax of anti-imperialism' as such, there was certainly an important 'crisis of opinion'. Extreme separatist sentiments do appear to have figured to some extent in the pressures exerted on actual policy-making, despite earlier assertions that 'no responsible statesman' adopted separatist beliefs and that British interests were always safeguarded.[98] Not all British statesmen

---

[95] Fitzmaurice, *Life of Granville*, II 500.

[96] Granville to Young, 14 June 1869, confidential (draft), C.O. 42/678.

[97] Granville to Gladstone, 25 Jan. 1870, *Gladstone Papers*, Add. MSS. 44,167, p. 10, indicates that the Prime Minister had not seen Granville's despatch of 14 June 1869.

[98] Galbraith, *A.H.R.*, LXVII 35.

viewed British interests in the same light, as the debate over foreign policy during the years 1877–80 was to show. It cannot be denied that the years 1868–70 witnessed an increased interest in colonial affairs among normally disinterested observers and that colonial affairs figured more prominently in the prolonged press campaign against the government than they had ever done before.

If the government had no intention of adopting a separatist policy, there was certainly sufficient evidence abroad (because of government ineptitude and bungling) to allow this interpretation to be placed on their actions. Even Granville's departure from the Colonial Office failed to calm the nervous. The gradually mounting opposition in Parliament, the press, at protest meetings and in public petitions sprang from a sincere belief that the government was about to set the colonies adrift. Gladstone had never intended to adopt such a policy, but the Conservatives constantly returned to the charge in the House of Commons and the suspicion persisted even among Liberal back-benchers. Not until Knatchbull-Hugessen's speech in 1871 did a whole-hearted and convincing denial of separatism come from the government benches. In sheer exasperation, Knatchbull-Hugessen had taken it upon himself to scotch once and for all the unjust cry that 'the Liberals would like to give up the Colonies'.[99] Although the Prime Minister did not choose to disclaim this statement, the phantom of 'anti-imperialism' stalked Gladstone throughout the remainder of his career. In 1870, however, 'anti-imperialism' amounted to nothing more than a drab anticlimax.

[99] *Political Diary of Lord Brabourne*, unpublished MS., IV 558, quoted in McIntyre, *Imperial Frontier*, p. 63.

4

Granville's Critics:
The Empire Enthusiasts

SEPARATISM had been disavowed. Even if it did not intend to dismember the empire, the Gladstone government had been forced to repudiate this idea and to declare publicly the basis of its policy. The opposition of a small number of vocal groups – the genuine misgivings of many observers, the apprehension voiced in certain sections of the press and the Conservative attack in the Lords – had been strong enough to cause concern in official Liberal circles. Indeed, 'public opinion' (in reality the views of a few enthusiasts antagonised by the apparent confirmation of separatist tendencies) for once proved sufficiently vehement to influence the thinking of the government. It was a significant victory for a small pressure group. But what was the significance of this revival of the imperialist spirit? How was this opposition organised and who were behind the protests? Was the agitation politically inspired and the attack, at first sight heartily backed by the Conservative press, no more than a clever political manoeuvre?

The continuing debate concerning the value of overseas possessions, repeated crises in colonial affairs, the American Civil War, the fear of foreign entanglements and the consequent expense, certainly focused increasing attention on to the colonies during the late 1860s. In fact Great Britain's apparent impotence in Europe gradually led to a revived concern with and pride in empire, especially when the Defence Review of the sixties was nearing completion and the economic and military situation was improving in India. And so, in 1869, mistaken fears about

Granville's colonial policy finally led the defenders of the imperial connection to gather their forces. By the end of the first year of Gladstone's administration some sort of semi-coherent organisation had indeed begun to emerge.

I

The need for an association to promote colonial interests had been constantly felt by colonists in London throughout the 1860s. The General Association for the Australian Colonies had functioned well from 1855, but this venture collapsed in 1862 through lack of funds.[1] The establishment of a colonial club had subsequently been canvassed but the project never materialised. In March 1867, however, the idea of a Central Institute suggested by Sir Charles Nicholson, an influential businessman and former colonial politician who had lived in New South Wales and Queensland for thirty years, was discussed and approved by Canadian delegates then in London on business concerning Canadian confederation. Further discussion occurred among interested Australian colonists at gatherings in the Scottish deer forests organised by the explorer Sir George Macleay, who had played an important part in promoting the foundation of South Australia. But contrary to popular belief, the initiative for founding a 'Colonial Society' in 1868 did not come from these men.[2] Another group was assembling in London to promote colonial interests and, in a public advertisement, they announced a preliminary meeting for this purpose to be held in Willis' Rooms, King Street, St James's, on 26 June 1868. The Australian colonists attended this meeting in force.

The meeting was chaired by Viscount Bury, author of *The Exodus of the Western Nations*, who had apparently tempered his earlier separatist views. In opening the discussion, Lord Bury advocated the need for a meeting-place where gentlemen arriving from the colonies 'might obtain the latest intelligence from their own part of the world, and place themselves in communication with other gentlemen connected with their own and other

[1] Min. Book 1855–62, *G.A.A.C. Papers*, R.C.S., London.

[2] D. S. Macmillan, 'The Australians in London, 1857–88', *J.P.R.A.H.S.*, XLIV (1958) 162, asserts that these men were responsible for founding the Colonial Society. But Edward Wilson noted at the preliminary meeting: 'it is only by mere accident that any of us who represent the Australian Colonies have heard of this meeting at all', *P.R.C.I.*, I (1869–70) 12.

colonies, and with them concert such measures as should tend to the interest of all'.[3] He suggested that papers on colonial subjects could be read and discussed at society meetings and that information of a scientific, literary and statistical character should be gathered from all parts of the empire into a central library. He felt such a society could occupy much the same position with regard to the colonies as the Royal Geographical Society did with regard to geography.

When the discussion was thrown open to the assembled multitude of M.P.s, colonials and ex-settlers, the project received general applause. The Marquis of Normanby, former Lieutenant-Governor of Nova Scotia, spoke of the need to bring the colonies together and Chichester Fortescue, Chief Secretary for Ireland and a former Under-Secretary of State at the Colonial Office, referred to the prevailing ignorance among colonies concerning each other. He also stressed the need for a colonial library: that at the Colonial Office was not available to the general public and was virtually unavailable to the permanent staff, as it was required to shore up the ramshackle structure of the Colonial Office building.[4] Several Members of Parliament present, including Baillie-Cochrane, urged the necessity to combat 'the erroneous notion that pervades some minds that England would be as great without her colonies as with them', and M. Marsh, M.P., concluded:

> In conveying a more accurate idea of our colonies to the people of this country, and as affording a means for the interchange of knowledge amongst the colonies themselves, I think the association is calculated to do great good, and that it would tend to bind more firmly together those links by which the colonies are united to the mother country.[5]

The society was also warmly welcomed by ex-settlers and

---

[3] Ibid. p. 2. For the foundation of the society, see T. R. Reese, *The History of the Royal Commonwealth Society, 1868–1968* (London, 1968) pp. 13–28.

[4] The Colonial Office had been condemned in 1839 but had received a reprieve on the condition that its library was kept in the basement and on the ground floor to give additional support to the structure. Report of the Select Committee on Public Offices, *Parl. P.* (1839) XIII 245, quoted in E. Trevor Williams, 'The Colonial Office in the 1830', *H.S.A.N.Z.*, II (1943) 141.

[5] *P.R.C.I.*, I (1869–70) 10, 14–15.

colonists present, including Leonard Wray from the West Indies, Sir Charles Nicholson, H. E. Blaine of the Cape of Good Hope and Edward Wilson, the wealthy proprietor of the Melbourne *Argus*.

At the close of the meeting it was formally agreed to establish a non-political 'Colonial Society' in order to promote knowledge of and interest in the problems of the colonies. A provisional committee consisting of twenty-eight persons was nominated to draw up the rules and to receive the names of gentlemen willing to serve on the Council of the society.

The provisional committee met four times during the ensuing two months. Most of the detailed work was done by Chichester Fortescue, Edward Wilson, Leonard Wray and James Youl, a Tasmanian who had settled in England in 1854 and who had acted as honorary secretary and treasurer to the Australian Association during the brief period of its existence. The experience gained by the governing body of that association was now placed at the service of the organisers of the new society. Indeed, many members of the earlier body became active supporters of the Colonial Society.[6]

At the second general meeting on 12 August 1868 the rules of the society were amended and finally adopted and the officers of the society appointed. The nominal founder, Lord Bury,[7] became the first president. The vice-presidents elected were all leading politicians. They included the existing Secretary of State for the Colonies, the Duke of Buckingham and Chandos, and three of

[6] J. Youl, E. Wilson, Sir C. Nicholson, Sir C. Clifford, W. Westgarth, Ald. W. M'Arthur, Lord A. Churchill and F. P. de Labilliere were all members of the association. Min. Book, *G.A.A.C. Papers*.

[7] A. Folsom, *The Royal Empire Society* (London, 1933) pp. 36–7, and Bodelsen, p. 94, n. 2, suggest that the first honorary secretary, A. R. Roche, was the real founder of the society. Goodliffe's evidence, cited by Folsom, however, appears to be no more than a recollection of Bury's speech at the inaugural meeting in 1869 (*P.R.C.I.*, I 72) on which Bodelsen bases his assertion. Undoubtedly, Roche was the organising genius of the society during the first four years of its existence, after his appointment in 1868. But the initial suggestion for a public meeting seems to have sprung from Bury, apart from any separate plans by Roche or the Australians. At the preliminary meeting Bury stated: 'I need not say that I have not canvassed the matter and I may observe that only on one occasion, and that was at a social gathering, have I mentioned it to anyone' (*P.R.C.I.*, I 1). In fact most of the correspondence prior to the foundation seems to have been conducted by Bury. Later Bury did claim to be the founder of the society, in 'The Unity of the Empire', *The Nineteenth Century*, XVII (Mar. 1885) 384.

his predecessors, Edward Cardwell, the Earl of Carnarvon and
Bulwer-Lytton; the existing Parliamentary Under-Secretary at the
Colonial Office, C. B. Adderley, and a former holder of that
office, Chichester Fortescue; the Secretary of State for India, Sir
Stafford Northcote; and three noblemen interested in the colonies,
the Duke of Manchester, the Marquis of Normanby and Viscount
Milton. The names of Earl Granville and the Duke of Argyll
were subsequently added when Gladstone's government came
into office. Also appointed at the second general meeting were
the honorary secretary, the treasurer and the trustees who
included among their number three M.P.s – T. Baring, G. G.
Glynn and Arthur Kinnaird. A. N. Birch of the Colonial Office
was co-opted on to the Council, and during the succeeding
months the names of Henry Blaine, H. E. Montgomerie, Herman
Merivale (Permanent Under-Secretary at the India Office and
formerly Under-Secretary at the Colonial Office), Major-General
Sir William Denison (ex-Governor of New South Wales and of
Madras), J. E. Gorst, Sir Charles Nicholson and Sir E. H.
Drummond Wolff were appended to the list.

By the spring of the following year the society was ready for
its public launching. An inaugural dinner was held on 10 March
1869 and was attended, like all gala nights, by a company
liberally sprinkled with the names of the great and the politically
influential. A glittering array of noblemen, Secretaries of State
and Members of Parliament dined at the same tables as a
number of delighted but less well-known colonials. Earl Granville
sat down with the society's honorary secretary, A. R. Roche, and
before an assembly of humble colonists Gladstone partook of his
repast with the Duke of Manchester, Sir Stafford Northcote
chatted with the Rt Hon. H. C. E. Childers and Sir John
Pakington exchanged table talk with Lord Alfred Churchill. The
back-benchers present, Arthur Kinnaird, Colonel Maude and
R. A. Macfie, mixed with the colonial elite, the Nicholsons, the
Cliffords and the Cartiers; the representatives of the India and
Colonial Offices, Sir Bartle Frere, Gordon Gairdner and Arthur
Blackwood, mingled with the Youls and the Wilsons, while the
unfortunate unknowns, the Montgomeries, the Blaines, the Wrays
and their friends, looked on. The only notable absentees from the
august company were the Conservative leaders, Disraeli and
Carnarvon.

Viscount Bury presided over a seemingly interminable series of toast and response as Gladstone declaimed on the 'noble tradition of the unity of the British race' and the American ambassador, Reverdy Johnson, tactlessly envisaged Her Majesty's subjects falling under the sway of the Stars and Stripes.[8] Earl Granville found the whole occasion a 'very great encouragement to do one's best'. Speech followed speech. The Marquis of Normanby referred to the future possibility of colonial independence; Sir Charles Clifford, a former Speaker of the New Zealand House of Representatives, denied that the occasion need ever arise. And finally, in the early hours of the morning, Viscount Bury addressed those diners still remaining and closed the proceedings with a glowing tribute to his political superior, Earl Granville :

> the terms in which he has spoken of . . . the trust which has been conveyed to him by the Queen must convince the colonists, if they needed to be convinced, that in the whole of that empire upon which, quoting Daniel Webster, 'the sun never sets', there is but one wish that universal brotherhood should unite us all together and that that tie should be strengthened day by day.[9]

With more than one bottle of champagne that night, the Colonial Society had been finally and properly launched.

At the inaugural meeting five days later, enthusiastic after-dinner speeches were replaced by a more sober air of reality. In his address Lord Bury outlined the aims and aspirations of the society and referred to the many obstacles to be surmounted. One of the most important duties of the newly founded society would be to combat the anti-colonial sentiments expressed by many of the leading adherents of the Manchester group of economists,

> whose leading idea appears to be that colonies are an excrescence of our empire rather than an important element of its prosperity; an encumbrance, rather than a material element of its strength; a source of commercial and political loss, rather than a national wealth. . . . Their doctrines attack not only the root of our colonial system, which would of itself be serious

[8] Dinner speeches, *P.R.C.I.*, I: Gladstone, p. 28; Johnson, pp. 21–2; Granville and Normanby, p. 36; Clifford, pp. 49–50.
[9] Ibid. p. 60.

and well worthy of attention, but the very existence of our
colonial empire, which is of infinitely more importance. A
faulty system may be reconstructed; an empire thrown away
can never be recovered.

Bury reminded his listeners that 'while it has been nobody's
business to defend, the writers who attack and would dismember
our empire have grown into a regular school of politicians – keen,
ready and able' and it was 'not one of the least important facts
that the doctrines of that school have been enunciated from a
professorial chair in our oldest university'.[10] This attack on
Goldwin Smith provoked an immediate rejoinder from one of the
professor's former Oxford colleagues. J. E. Thorold Rogers
denied that Goldwin Smith had ever used his professorial chair
as a means of inculcating his own views on questions of controversial politics. He stated that Professor Smith had merely
enunciated the simple fact 'uncontested by all but the ignorant
and self-interested' that attempts to govern and defend colonies
were 'a transparent absurdity and a real source of weakness'
which 'induced serious political evils in the colonies themselves
and . . . a heavy additional burden on the overladen taxpayers
of the United Kingdom'.[11]

The hearty endorsement which the members of the society
gave to their president's condemnation of the views of the
Manchester Radicals, however, demonstrated that no longer
would the enunciation of such ideas be accepted passively. No
longer would suggestions for imperial dissolution or immediate
separation by consent go unchallenged through lack of organisation among those who held contrary opinions. A forum had
been constructed whose influence might well be of vital significance in ensuring the continued existence of the empire.

II

But during this initial period the Colonial Society did not fulfil
any such function. The non-political society, presided over by a
Liberal supporter of the Gladstone government, took no official
part in the agitation of 1869–70 opposing the apparent trend of

[10] Ibid. pp. 52–3.
[11] *The Star*, 18 Mar. 1869.

Granville's colonial policy. Instead the first overt protest at Granville's treatment of New Zealand appeared in the press following the publication of the Colonial Office's despatch of 21 March 1869. In a letter to *The Times* signed by Sir George Grey and four prominent New Zealanders, Sir Charles Clifford, Henry Sewell, Harry Atkinson and J. Logan Campbell, Grey and his associates affirmed 'that the policy which is being pursued towards New Zealand would have the effect of alienating the affections of Her Majesty's loyal subjects in that country, and was calculated to drive the colony out of the Empire'.[12] This letter added to the fuel already provided by the attacks of the Radical *Spectator* on the government's colonial policy and initiated an extended newspaper campaign against Granville's conduct of colonial affairs. Arthur Kinnaird felt that the Colonial Secretary was insufficiently 'aware of the gravity of the present "crisis" in New Zealand' and warned Gladstone that a meeting was going to be held in London to discuss the situation.[13]

If the prominent politicians connected with the Colonial Society were determined that the society should remain strictly non-political, some of the more militant colonists among its members were determined to make good use of the recently provided facilities. A meeting of 'influential colonists' was held in the Colonial Society's rooms on 4 August 1869 to protest against the government's New Zealand policy which 'seemed to point as an ulterior result to a severance of the connection between the colonies and the mother country, perhaps hurriedly and in an unfriendly spirit'.[14] The outcome was a resolution to appoint a committee to communicate with the different colonial governments. A circular dated 13 August was subsequently addressed to the various self-governing colonies proposing that a conference of colonial representatives should assemble in London in 1870 to discuss the administration of colonial affairs. The circular was signed by three fellows of the Colonial Society: James Youl, Henry Blaine and Henry Sewell, one of the signatories to Grey's letter of protest to *The Times*. For his part,

[12] *The Times*, 18 June 1869. All the signatories were men prominent in New Zealand affairs (see Biographical Notes).
[13] Kinnaird to Gladstone, 31 July, encl. in Gladstone to Granville, 2 Aug. 1869, *Granville Papers*, P.R.O. 30/29/57.
[14] *The Times*, 26 Aug. 1869.

Viscount Bury hurriedly wrote to Earl Granville dissociating the Colonial Society from the proposals.[15]

The Youl Circular was published in the press on 26 August 1869. The idea of a colonial conference was generally welcomed. *The Times* thought the circular 'marked an epoch' and the proposal was also applauded by the *Morning Post*, the *Daily Telegraph*, the *Pall Mall Gazette*, the Conservative *Standard* and the Radical *Spectator*.[16] Earl Granville, however, was not so pleased. The proposed conference had been suggested without the approval of the Colonial Office and without any prior consultation. Consequently, in September 1869, he addressed a despatch to the self-governing colonies outlining his objections to the scheme. While Her Majesty's Government were always ready to consider the wishes and interests of the colonies and the Colonial Office had in fact often encouraged combined colonial action, he felt little useful purpose could be served by arranging a colonial conference in London. The interests of the colonies were so diverse, their problems so individual, that there seemed little common ground on which to base a general conference. The present system of communication between governments had always proved satisfactory in the past and was certainly better than communicating through a group of private gentlemen resident in London 'acting in pursuance of their own interests or of mere written instructions; under influences not always identical with those which are paramount in the Colony'.[17]

In response to this despatch, all the self-governing colonies, together with the Cape of Good Hope and Natal, rejected the idea of a conference. The Canadian government was particularly emphatic in its rejection, and in Australia the proposal was thought to be thoroughly objectionable. The *Sydney Examiner* found the meeting 'almost too ridiculous for words' and was amazed at the 'cool impudence' of 'a few holiday-makers' in London. The newspaper deplored 'the mischievous tendencies of this inter-meddling on the part of our busybody absentees' who were 'almost entirely unknown in these colonies'. In the

---

[15] Folsom, *Royal Empire Society*, p. 197; Reese, *History of the R.C.S.*, p. 34.

[16] See *The Times, Daily Telegraph, Standard,* 26 Aug. 1869; *Morning Post,* 27 Aug. 1869.

[17] Circular to Governors of Colonies with Responsible Government, 8 Sept. 1869, *Parl. P.* (1870) XLIX, C. 24, pp. 1–2.

Legislative Assembly of Victoria the promoters were designated 'presumptuous busybodies'[18] and the Attorney-General, George Higinbotham, deprecated the 'either very lamentable ignorance, or something which I cannot help designating as very gross presumption' of those who presumed to ask the government and the legislature of Victoria to 'send a delegate to London, invested with plenipotentiary powers, to alter or arrange, at his discretion, and in concert with the Colonial Office, the basis of government in this colony'. Higinbotham had no sympathy with the 'self-constituted and irresponsible body of absentee colonists' behind the Youl Circular and the Colonial Society:

> I do not envy those persons who have deserted the sphere of their natural duties . . . who conceive that they achieve the proudest moment of their lives when they are permitted to sit down to a subscription dinner at the London Tavern in company with half a dozen English noblemen; and yet I cannot help fearing that the persons who have sent this invitation are persons, many of whom, at least can be actuated by no other motives and no other ambitions in life.[19]

Before these decided colonial views became known in London, however, the Youl Circular received the blessing of one veteran statesman and former Colonial Secretary, the third Earl Grey. Grey disowned the British government's policy, which he believed would undoubtedly lead to the loss of the colonies, but remarked that it was a policy which 'had been practically acted upon by their predecessors, and is no doubt in accordance with what is now the prevailing opinion in Parliament'. However, he was not in total agreement with Youl. In his view the only reason for discontinuing the policy would be acceptance by the colonists of 'a larger measure of authority over them by the Imperial Government than they have of late been willing to submit to'. The Conservative *Standard* agreed with much of Grey's letter and throughout the month of September continued its attack on the government's colonial policy: 'England allows the few . . . to speak for the many . . . and drifts towards a separation quite as unwelcome to her heart as disastrous to her greatness, simply for

[18] *Sydney Examiner*, 5 Nov. 1869; *The Argus* (Melbourne), 8 Nov. 1869.
[19] E. E. Morris, *A Memoir of George Higinbotham, Australian Politician and Chief Justice of Victoria* (London, 1895) p. 160.

want of resolution to consider whither she is tending.'[20] The promoters of the Youl Circular continued their attempts to provide the necessary resolution for tackling the subject.

In October 1869 Viscount Bury informed Lord Granville that he had accepted the chairmanship of a much-enlarged committee that was pursuing the object laid down in the Youl Circular. The committee was seeking

> as far as possible in concert with Her Majesty's Ministers . . . to prepare the way for the assembly of the proposed Colonial Conference, by concerting with the delegates . . . by giving them a place of meeting and an organised body with whom to communicate on all preliminary arrangements.

It was proposed that the conference should be held in the rooms and under the sanction of the Colonial Society.

The proposal was not received enthusiastically. Granville immediately objected to the suggestion and Lord Carnarvon also deprecated the idea :

> It appears to me moreover to be at the least a very irregular proceeding for any committee of gentlemen in London – however well informed on Colonial matters – to open a formal correspondence with the various Colonial Legislatures and Governments without the consent of the Crown or Parliament.[21]

The new committee, which besides Youl, Sewell and Blaine included the Duke of Manchester, Lord Alfred Churchill, Sir William Denison, Colonel Maude, M.P., E. Wilson, J. E. Gorst and H. A. Atkinson, then met on 11 November 1869 to consider the position.

In view of Granville's decided opposition to the conference, Viscount Bury was against taking any further action. The Duke of Manchester, on the other hand, was sure the policy of the Colonial Office was viewed with disapproval by the public, especially by working men. Perhaps it would be impolitic to involve the Colonial Society, but the Circular had his hearty

[20] Grey to Youl, 4 Sept., printed in *The Times*, 26 Oct. 1869; *Standard*, 11 Sept. 1869.

[21] Folsom, *Royal Empire Society*, p. 199; letters of Granville, 17 Oct., and Carnarvon, 25 Oct., printed in *European Mail*, 3 Dec. 1869.

support. He stood for rebellion against the Colonial Secretary. Sir William Denison was more practical. He reminded the committee that 'in England, the colonists and their friends were an isolated body, without the weight and status to give adequate effect to their efforts'. Lord Alfred Churchill agreed that it was best not to appear antagonistic to the government. Instead it was resolved to appoint a deputation to wait on Lord Granville with the intention of removing any misconceptions as to the purpose of the committee and to urge him to 'recognise the necessity of providing without delay for the free expression of colonial opinion upon colonial affairs'.[22] But when the Duke of Manchester declared it would be 'the best thing possible to abolish Sir James Murdoch and others like him at the Colonial Office'[23] and Henry Sewell called for drastic reform of the Colonial Office machinery, Sir William Denison withdrew his name from the deputation. It was finally decided that the deputation would consist of Lord Bury, the Duke of Manchester, Lord Alfred Churchill, Sir Charles Nicholson and Messrs. Sewell, Youl, Blaine, Gorst, Westgarth, Montgomerie, Roche and Wilson.

At the same time a subcommittee appointed to examine Lord Granville's despatch relating to the Circular, reported :

The tone assumed by Lord Granville in recent despatches is the expression of a sentiment widely prevalent among the people of England. There is a vague idea afloat in men's minds that the colonies are an undue burden upon the taxpayers of England, and that their tariffs are framed to inflict an injustice upon her industry; it is also believed that the Colonists, with all their professions of allegiance to the Queen, are impatient of everything like Imperial control. Colonists, on the other hands, are aggrieved by the system of administration at the Colonial Office. The prevalence of these feelings (however erroneous they may be) prevents the cordiality which should exist between Her Majesty's subjects at home and abroad.

Your committee thinks that if the points upon which differences exist were clearly defined, and were brought under the consideration of the Colonial Governments and the people

---

[22] Folsom, *Royal Empire Society*, p. 199.
[23] Presumably Sir T. W. C. Murdoch, Colonial Land and Emigration Commissioner.

of this country, error might be dissipated and harmony restored.[24]

It was probably this report which inspired one of the committee's number to take more active steps than a harmless deputation to wait on Lord Granville. Recent successes of some of the fellows of the Colonial Society and their associates in popularising the colonial cause at the September meeting of the National Association for the Promotion of Social Science and in stirring up interest in state-aided emigration once again, probably led Edward Wilson, the proprietor of the Melbourne *Argus*, to call for a series of public meetings to air the 'colonial question'. Earlier, Wilson had written to *The Times* as a colonist, Englishman and supporter of the Liberal ministry, deploring the poor treatment meted out to New Zealand and fearing that, because of public ignorance and indifference, a premature separation would occur in which Britain would lose 'three-quarters of its prestige and half of its trade'.[25] He now hired, from his own pocket, rooms in the Cannon Street Hotel in which to hold his meetings for enlightening the British public about the advantages of empire.

III

The 'Cannon Street meetings' lasted from 24 November 1869 until 5 January 1870. They attracted a large crowd of colonists and ex-settlers and received a great deal of attention in the press.[26] The small group of Colonial Society members, reinforced by the promoters of the Youl Circular and colonial conference, were now joined by several workers interested in preserving the empire: Sir George Grey, who had written the protest letter to *The Times* concerning New Zealand and addressed numerous meetings on the subject of emigration, but who had so far not associated himself with the Colonial Society or the Youl Circular; Frederick Young, chairman of the National, Colonial and Emigration League who was later to become honorary secretary

[24] Folsom, *Royal Empire Society*, p. 201.
[25] *The Times*, 10 Nov. 1869.
[26] For a discussion of the Cannon Street meetings, see C. S. Blackton, 'The Cannon Street Episode: An Aspect of Anglo-Australian Relations', *H.S.*, XIII (1969) 520–32.

of the Royal Colonial Institute; and another important recruit, the Victorian F. P. de Labilliere.

The meetings convened by Edward Wilson were chaired by James Youl. In his opening address Wilson intimated that a crisis in imperial relations had been reached : the Colonial Secretary was intent on disbanding the empire. The voice of the people must be heard and the attention of the public directed to this dangerous policy. A powerful speech by Sir George Grey followed, envisaging a united empire as a future preserver of world peace. Resolutions drafted by W. Westgarth, a colonial broker who had lived in Melbourne for seventeen years, were then passed deprecating the government's colonial policy, criticising Granville's despatches to New Zealand and emphasising the advantages of empire to both mother country and colonies.[27]

The Conservative *Standard* welcomed the meeting and insisted that the government had no right to cast off the colonies without prior discussion. While Granville always maintained that Parliament and the country supported his policy, no opinion had ever been explicitly asked for. All the public meetings had opposed what the *Evening Standard* called 'the suicidal freak of which Lord Granville is either the author or the exponent'. This abuse of the Colonial Secretary caused the *Pall Mall Gazette* to examine the credentials of the critics. It concluded :

If the promoters of these weekly meetings wish to do real service to the unity of the empire, they will devote themselves to ascertaining what are the genuine wishes of the colonies with regard to it; what the methods by which they would propose to put these wishes into effect; and above all, what the sacrifices they are prepared to make in order to ensure that these methods shall be efficacious.[28]

Support for the meetings, however, came from a rather surprising direction. The Liberal *Daily Telegraph* was much impressed by Grey's speech. Wise use of the empire could well prove a panacea for Great Britain's future difficulties concerning lack of resources and fields for emigration. As regards Australia, a future mighty Anglo-Saxon nation, 'it rests with us to determine whether she shall be an *alter ego* of ourselves – a sea-girt Britain of the

[27] *The Times*, 25 Nov., 1869; *European Mail*, 3 Dec. 1869.
[28] *Standard, Evening Standard, Pall Mall Gazette*, 26 Nov. 1869.

southern hemisphere – or an estranged and indifferent observer of our future fortunes'.[29]

Granville found this change in the sentiments of the paper disturbing. He protested that the *Daily Telegraph* had always supported the government's New Zealand policy and he was unaware of any differences with other colonies. In his opinion, 'Sir George Grey, who is boiling over with personal discontent, is the principal mover in this matter. He has long complained that he could get at none of the Press, excepting the *Standard*. It now looks as if he has got hold of the *Telegraph*.'[30] But after the second meeting of the Cannon Street agitators at which further resolutions were passed condemning the government's policy, criticising discourteous despatches to New Zealand and urging the need for drastic reform of the Colonial Office, the *Telegraph* fell into line :

> The loyalty of some of these gentlemen is so demonstrative as to be almost unpleasant. They may be as affectionately disposed towards the mother country as they claim to be; but it is hardly a filial way of showing fondness to 'square up' to the venerable creature with clenched fists and say in almost as many words that they will fight her if she does not lavish on them new displays of her maternal guardianship.

The Conservative *Standard*, however, continued to support the meetings and hoped they would have a salutary effect.[31]

But the third meeting at the Cannon Street Hotel, on 8 December 1869, clearly showed that the discussions were getting out of hand. Futile, fiery and formless speeches merely drew the questions discussed into 'ridicule, contempt and disgrace'. The London-based *Australian and New Zealand Gazette* felt that the Cannon Street forum, with its uncertain aims and abstract resolutions, was declining into a mere debating club for ex-colonial governors and judges to air their grievances against

---

[29] *Daily Telegraph*, 26 Nov. 1869.

[30] Granville to Glynn, 27 Nov. 1869, private, *Granville Papers*, P.R.O. 30/29/37. Grey was regarded with distrust by the Liberal ministry after his activities in New Zealand and his pronouncements during the 1868 election campaign in Ireland. He was also a critic of the Manchester School, an advocate of state-aided emigration and a known 'imperialist'.

[31] *Daily Telegraph*, 3 Dec. 1869; *Standard*, 4 Dec. 1869.

the Colonial Office.[32] So far had the meetings fallen into disrepute that Viscount Bury feared some of the ignominy might be transferred to the Colonial Society. On 8 December 1869 he resigned the chairmanship of the Youl Committee and dissociated the society from the plans to hold a colonial conference. He did, however, consent to remain the leader of the deputation which was still hoping for an interview with Lord Granville. This was now to be a joint deputation with the Cannon Street colonists.

The Youl Committee deputation – Bury, Manchester, Viscount Milton, Arthur Kinnaird, Youl, Sewell and Wilson – now supplemented by Frederick Young, de Labilliere, C. W. Eddy, Colonel Synge, and Leonard Wray, finally obtained an interview with Lord Granville on 15 December 1869. The Colonial Secretary did not prove to be very accommodating. Granville repudiated the Youl Circular's description of his colonial policy and vehemently denied the need for a conference to improve relations with the colonies. Such a course had been shown to be unacceptable to the colonists and could never serve its purpose. The Circular had been issued without prior consultation with the Colonial Office and the whole spirit of the Cannon Street meetings had been hostile and uncooperative. He was not against the imperial connection and felt that 'the bonds which unite us, though slender are elastic and much stronger than some suppose'.[33]

The news of the deputation to the Colonial Secretary was treated with scorn by the Liberal *Daily News*. It was tired of the 'army of martyrs' who

> have been holding conferences, forming deputations, writing long and exciting letters, making a prodigious noise about the grievances of a vast variety of people whom they cannot, except by a polite fiction, be held to represent, and airing their own importance on behalf of the integrity of the empire.

Both the *Morning Post* and the *Daily Telegraph* felt that the agitation had been carried too far, and *The Times* scorned the 'flagrant puerilities' of 'the Cannon Street Colonists and their

---

[32] *European Mail*, 31 Dec. 1869; *Australian and New Zealand Gazette*, 11 Dec. 1869.
[33] *Daily News*, 17 Dec. 1869; Reese, *History of the R.C.S.*, pp. 34–5.

noble patrons'. Even the *Standard* was forced to admit that the deputation had been a 'tactical blunder'.[34]

At the fifth Cannon Street meeting, on 22 December 1869, James Youl, the chairman, complained that newspaper reports of the deputation had been grossly unfair. The work of a single Downing Street reporter, revised by the Colonial Office and subsequently issued to the press, was not only inaccurate but also contained omissions. There followed sharp personal criticism of Lord Granville and a renewed attack on the government's New Zealand policy.

Such noisy demonstrations were not only in bad taste; they were utterly futile. The *European Mail* contained fair comment on the 'haste, indecision and want of preparation' shown at the meetings in a letter to the paper signed 'Spectator'. According to the writer, the convener of the meetings, Edward Wilson, was known to be high-minded and patriotic but he had called to his aid lesser spirits. The meetings had been conducted with the barest order, little procedure, and speakers remained undisciplined. Sir George Grey had never really associated himself with the agitators and Westgarth's resolutions had been lost from sight. The only hope for the future of the empire when real tangible difficulties arose, wrote 'Spectator', would be that there was 'head and heart enough among the good men of all parties at home and in every settlement to adjust difficulties, to heal differences, and to preserve long and peaceful relations with mutual advantage'. The *Montreal Gazette* agreed that imperial relations were best left alone by agitators on both sides of the ocean.[35]

The *Daily News* hoped, rather maliciously, that the Christmas festivities would not interrupt the Cannon Street meetings, for it wished to know what the participants thought their intervention as oracles had accomplished during the last four months. New South Wales had openly laughed at their efforts and the Victorian Legislative Assembly had protested at their impudence. The editorial concluded: 'We may hope that these gentlemen will henceforth occupy their leisure in some other way and leave the Colonial Office and the Colonies alone. At any rate, thus ends the most factitious agitation ever adventured in England.'[36]

---

[34] *Daily News, Daily Telegraph, Morning Post*, 17 Dec. 1869; *The Times*, 18 Dec. 1869; *Standard*, 22 Dec. 1869.

[35] *European Mail*, 31 Dec. 1869; *Montreal Gazette*, 5 Jan. 1870.

[36] *Daily News*, 28 Dec. 1869.

To the participants the verdict appeared entirely different. Frederick Young recalled a few years later :

The success of these meetings was most remarkable. They seemed at once to touch the springs of national feeling, and elicited in an unmistakeable manner from a most influential and powerful section of English society a thoroughly sympathetic colonial sentiment.[37]

And even *The Times*, which had declared the meetings an abject failure, was forced to admit that the agitators could boast that

they have set politicians talking everywhere about the colonies and their relations with England. Reviewers and pamphleteers at home have taken up the subject. Every colonial mail adds something to its discussion. Our columns furnish abundant evidence of the attention it has excited.[38]

The colonies were no longer a neglected subject.

Indeed, the Cannon Street forum was but one place where the colonies had excited attention. In September 1869 'The Legal and Constitutional Relations between England and her Colonies' had appeared on the agenda of the meeting of the National Association for the Promotion of Social Science. Sir Stafford Northcote, the Conservative ex-minister, presided over the conference and made a tentative speech in favour of the imperial connection.[39] This was in marked contrast to the enthusiastic paper delivered to the conference by F. P. de Labilliere, who declared that 'the union of the Empire is a sentiment or rather a sacred principle, in devoted loyalty to which we should vie with one another'.[40] Papers were also contributed by J. E. Gorst, Thomas Hare, R. A. Macfie, M.P., and by John Noble, the only speaker to argue against the advantages of the imperial connection. R. A. Macfie in his paper, 'The United Kingdom and the Colonies : One Autonomic Empire', pressed for government support for a programme of state-aided emigration. This was yet

[37] F. Young, *Imperial Federation of Great Britain and her Colonies* (London, 1876) p. xiv.
[38] *The Times*, 18 Jan. 1870.
[39] *Standard*, 2 Oct. 1869.
[40] Labilliere, 30 Sept. 1869, 'What Ought to be the Legal and Constitutional Relations between England and her Colonies?' *T.N.A.P.S.S.* (1869) 114.

another aspect of colonial policy debated by the agitators of 1868–70.

IV

The revived agitation in favour of government-assisted schemes for emigration was closely connected with the movement to preserve the empire. The new participants were all either fellows of the Colonial Society or had been connected with the Cannon Street meetings. In 1869 Edward Wilson read a paper entitled 'A Scheme for Emigration on a National Scale' before the Society of Arts, Frederick Young wrote a long article on 'Transportation' and C. W. Eddy contributed a pamphlet in 1870 on *Assisted Colonisation*. Edward Jenkins, a young Radical barrister, who had campaigned for a scheme of state-subsidised emigration at the Birmingham meeting of the National Association for the Promotion of Social Science in 1868, issued a pamphlet entitled *State Emigration* the following summer. James Youl, J. E. Gorst and Sir George Grey joined the agitation in company with a number of M.P.s, including R. A. Macfie, R. R. Torrens and the Radical W. T. McCullagh Torrens. Sir William Denison's paper on 'Colonisation', read to the Colonial Society shortly before his death, earned the active support of Lord Alfred Churchill and Arthur Kinnaird.

One of the most active campaigners promoting emigration was Sir George Grey. He wrote numerous articles to the press and addressed public meetings in Liverpool, Manchester, Birmingham and London, campaigning for 'a policy of emigration by which . . . our colonies would be regarded as a natural outlet for our excessive population . . . a home and a heritage for the people of England'.[41] In publicising the views of the working classes Grey found a valuable ally in the Duke of Manchester, chairman of one of the many emigration leagues. Manchester, in fact, in company with Jenkins, Young, Youl, Sir William Denison and Edward Wilson, secured an interview with the Prime Minister in February 1870, in order to urge the desirability of government assistance to working men emigrating to the colonies.[42]

[41] J. Rutherford, *Sir George Grey, 1812–98: A Study in Colonial Government* (London, 1961) p. 583.
[42] *The Times*, 4 Feb. 1870.

Public petitions were also drawn up. In November 1869 the *Standard* revealed the existence of one gigantic petition to the Queen, officially organised by a Working Men's Association, to enable 'those who are willing to work to go to those parts of Your Majesty's dominions where their labour is required, and where they may prosper, and may increase the prosperity of the whole Empire'. The petitioners had 'heard with alarm that Your Majesty has been advised to give up the colonies', containing 'millions of acres which might be employed profitably both to the Colonies and to ourselves as fields of emigration'. Thomas Carlyle, Alfred Tennyson and J. A. Froude, the historian, had each claimed the right along with certain M.P.s to sign the petition as working men. The *Standard* declared :

> It is to the working class that we must make our last appeal, not to permit the surrender of our common heritage – not to consent to the destruction of their own empire – not to suffer that those who are now hungering for the friendship and sympathy of England, who are only too anxious to remain in union with us upon any terms, should be cast off with insult and contumely, to become the bitter enemies for all time to come, of the name of England.[43]

Sir George Grey presided over a meeting patronised by the Lord Mayor of London and held under the auspices of the National Emigration League in the Egyptian Hall of the Mansion House, to appoint a deputation to present the petition to the Home Secretary. Among those who attended were Messrs Wilson, Youl, Young and Jenkins, Colonel Maude, M.P., E. B. Eastwick, M.P., Sir Charles Nicholson and McCullagh Torrens, M.P.[44] It was decided that a deputation consisting of such 'working men' as Sir George Grey, Viscount Milton, J. A. Froude, F. W. Chesson (secretary to the Aborigines Protection Society), J. E. Gorst, J. Youl and C. W. Eddy should wait on the Home Secretary on 15 February 1870.

The deputation was introduced by R. R. Torrens, M.P., and the Home Secretary was addressed by the honorary secretary to the Working Men's Association, C. W. Eddy, a fellow of the Colonial Society and its future honorary secretary, member of

---

[43] *Standard*, 4 Nov. 1869.
[44] *The Times*, 27 Jan. 1870.

the Youl Committee and participator in the Cannon Street meetings. Eddy clearly linked the agitation for state-aided emigration and all the movements for preserving the empire. His address was an attack on the government's colonial policy:

> The resolutions passed at the late meeting of the petitioners state that they regard the colonists as fellow countrymen whose rights are as sacred as their own, and, viewing them in that light they are strongly of the opinion that they are entitled to such aid from the Imperial forces as may be necessary for the purposes of defence, and that when any colony evinces its need of British troops by offering to contribute the established colonial rate for the maintenance of such troops, the Home Government will have incurred a most serious responsibility if it refuses to comply with their request, without previously obtaining the sanction of Parliament to such a refusal.

Eddy also called for reform of the Colonial Office.[45]

The deputation, not surprisingly, did not achieve anything tangible. The agitation for state-subsidised emigration continued before the September meeting of the Social Science Congress with papers entitled 'Colonies as Fields of Experiment in Government' and 'Imperial and Colonial Policy' read by Wilson and Macfie respectively. Further papers were presented at the Westminster Palace Hotel conference in 1871. But the idea was considered too fanciful to receive general support. One supposed result of the movement, however, was noted by the Melbourne *Argus*: 'Whatever statesmen may feel and think upon the subject, the working men of England, to whom the colonies are a land of promise, have entered their vigorous protests against the dismemberment of the Empire.'[46] It sounded very good, but who the 'working-class' organisers of the petition were remains a mystery!

One important result of the emigration controversy was the intervention of the historian J. A. Froude on behalf of the agitators. In a rectorial address delivered in the University of St Andrews on 16 March 1869, Froude had looked forward with enthusiasm to the peopling of new lands: 'Britain may yet have a future before it grander than its past; instead of a country

[45] *Morning Post*, 16 Feb. 1870.
[46] *The Argus* (Melbourne), 23 Apr. 1870.

standing alone, complete in itself, it may become the metropolis of an enormous and coherent empire.'[47] Froude now proceeded in a series of articles, published in *Fraser's Magazine* in 1870, to criticise the policy of the Liberal government, to denounce the 'cess-pit civilisation' of *laissez-faire* and to stress the importance of the empire. He castigated the government for its attitude of indifference towards the colonies and pleaded for a scheme of state-assisted emigration to lessen overcrowding at home, improve the living conditions of the working classes and to maintain a healthy country-bred stock throughout the empire. England was becoming a land of rich industrialists, merchants and bankers living off the sweat of the poor. 'Disease and demoralisation go hand in hand undermining and debilitating the physical strength, and over-civilisation creates in its own breast the sores which will one day kill it.' The mettle of the country was being undermined. Froude appealed to Disraeli and the Conservatives to take up the cause of colonisation. England could remain a great power only by retaining her colonial empire : 'These are not days for small states.' If England lets her colonies drift apart, 'we shall sink as Holland has sunk into a community of harmless traders, and leave to others the place which once we held and have lost the energy to keep'.[48] To Froude's mind, 'That separation is, or has been, the drift of the colonial policy of the present Ministers there is no occasion to argue'.[49]

Froude's articles were an important contribution to the debate on Granville's colonial policy. They were also a scathing attack on the principles of the Liberal administration. Many critics of the government must have enjoyed turning to the pages of *Fraser's Magazine* to watch Gladstone's government sinking in an orgy of drugged beer, poisoned gin and infanticide. The year 1870 saw several more eminent men joining the small band which aimed as disseminating empire sentiment. John Ruskin, the new Professor of Fine Art at Oxford, who on 14 January

[47] W. A. Knight (ed.), *Rectorial Addresses delivered in the University of St Andrews, 1863–93* (London, 1894) p. 102.

[48] J. A. Froude, *Short Studies on Great Subjects* (London, 1891), II 205, 211, 214. Froude collected together the articles attacking the Gladstone government in vol. II of this work. The most important of these, entitled 'England and her Colonies', 'Reciprocal Duties of State and Subject', 'On Progress', 'The Colonies Once More' and 'England's War', were first published in *Fraser's Magazine* from Jan. 1870 to Feb. 1871.

[49] Froude, *Short Studies*, II 504.

1870 had written to the *Daily Telegraph* calling on country gentlemen to become 'Captains of Emigration', urged his students during his inaugural lecture to become colonists, so as to make England 'a royal throne of Kings, a sceptred isle, for all the world a source of light, a centre of peace . . . this is what she must either do, or perish : she must found colonies as fast and as far as she is able, formed of her most energetic and worthiest men'.[50] In Ruskin's eyes the art of any country was 'the exponent of its social and political virtues'.

W. E. Forster also became an adherent of the movement. In a speech at Bradford in January 1870 he affirmed his belief that

> neither in England nor in the colonies do we intend that the English Empire shall be broken up. It may be a dream, but I still believe in its fulfilment. I believe that the time will come when, by some means or another, statesmen will be able to weld a bond together which will unite the English speaking people in our colonies at present – unite them with the mother country in one great federation.[51]

It was an important speech, coming from a leading member of the Liberal government.

The participation of such prominent statesmen and men of letters in the movement to popularise the colonies marked a significant development in the personnel of the small band which had hitherto been involved. With the attack in Parliament on the government's colonial policy, led by Carnarvon in the House of Lords and R. R. Torrens and R. A. Macfie in the Commons, more public men entered the discussion. This turn of events was clearly reflected in a conference held at the Westminster Palace Hotel in 1871. Gone was the abuse and poor organisation of the Cannon Street meetings; instead a series of polished papers was presented followed by serious discussion among a body of men prominent in British political circles and in the colonies.

The conference was organised by Edward Jenkins, F. P. de Labilliere, Edward Wilson and R. R. Torrens. Jenkins read the inaugural address and prepared the report; de Labilliere acted as honorary secretary. The guarantors of the expenses of the conference included Viscount Sandon, M.P., Lord George

[50] J. Ruskin, *Lectures on Art* (London, 1894) pp. 36–7.
[51] *The Times*, 18 Jan. 1870.

Hamilton, M.P., Sir Charles Nicholson, Alexander M'Arthur, C. W. Eddy and W. Westgarth. Several of the meetings were chaired by the Duke of Manchester and the Earl of Shaftesbury.

The company, assembled to hear papers by R. R. Torrens, de Labilliere, Professor Sheldon Amos, F. W. Chesson, McCullagh Torrens and Sir E. H. Drummond Wolff, was a distinguished one. Besides the long-established supporters of the cause – Frederick Young, Sir Charles Clifford, R. A. Macfie and Henry Blaine – the Earls of Airlie and Lichfield, and Sir Benjamin Pine, Governor-in-Chief of the Leeward Islands, attended together with a host of M.P.s : Lord Alfred Churchill, Lord Eustace Cecil, Sir John Bowring, Arthur Kinnaird, R. N. Fowler, William M'Arthur, S. Aytoun, Baillie-Cochrane and E. B. Eastwick. Clearly, a movement begun by a few unknown colonials in the opening months of 1868 had by 1871 attracted the attention and support, through their various agitations, of an increasing number of well-known public figures. How then should we regard these men whom Bodelsen dubbed the pioneers of a revived interest in empire, and what were their real reasons for creating such a rumpus?

v

The people behind the agitation of 1869–70 can be divided into three categories according to the extent of their participation. The nucleus of the group can easily be traced and conforms roughly to the members of the original General Association for the Australian Colonies : four English-born former colonial residents, Edward Wilson, Sir Charles Nicholson, W. Westgarth and Sir Charles Clifford, and two Australians, James Youl and F. P. de Labilliere. These men, joined by Henry Blaine of the Cape of Good Hope and C. W. Eddy, who had lived both in Canada and Australia, were ably assisted by four parliamentarians, R. A. Macfie, Lord Alfred Churchill, the Duke of Manchester and J. E. Gorst, who had lived in New Zealand and written the classic account of *The Maori King*. Between them this group formed the core of most of the movements designed to promote the interests of the empire during the years 1868–70 – the foundation of the Colonial Society; the Youl Committee; the Cannon Street meetings; the agitation for state-aided emigration, especially among working men – and they were also largely

responsible for arranging the Westminster Palace Hotel conference in 1871.

The activities of these men were supported in various
spheres by a large number of interested M.P.s – Arthur Kinnaird,
Viscount Milton, Colonel Maude, McCullagh Torrens, Drummond Wolff – including some who had a particular interest in
certain parts of the empire, such as Viscount Bury, who had
served in Canada, William M'Arthur, who had close connections
with New South Wales, and R. R. Torrens, who had been
Premier of South Australia. Outside Parliament, support was
received from two former colonial governors, Sir William Denison
and Sir George Grey, and from the historian J. A. Froude. An
important contribution was also made by Henry Sewell, former
Premier of New Zealand, and by three men with Canadian connections, A. R. Roche, Frederick Young and Edward Jenkins.
The latter two were to play an increasingly important role after
1870.

Behind these men who organised the various agitations or
played leading roles in individual fields there stood a third group
of M.P.s and less easily identified colonists. Among the parliamentarians numbered M. Marsh, Stephen Cave, Chichester
Fortescue, Baillie-Cochrane, Lord William Hay, Lord Elcho,
Viscount Sandon, Lord George Hamilton, Colonel Synge and
the Marquis of Normanby. The colonists included Harry Atkinson, Leonard Wray, H. E. Montgomerie, H. Goodliffe, C.
McGarel and W. Walker.

Thus there seems to emerge a new body of men – colonists,
pushing ex-settlers and journalists – who, in conjunction with a
group of back-benchers who had always professed an interest in
colonial affairs, were determined to generate interest in the
empire. These form a distinct group, as opposed to the more
'traditional' champions of the colonies, Lord Carnarvon, Earls
Russell and Grey and C. B. Adderley. None of these men
associated themselves with the popular agitation and they confined their opposition to the political arena. Earl Russell remained
aloof; C. B. Adderley resigned from the Colonial Society of
which he was a vice-president; and even Earl Grey, who
approved of the Youl Circular, refused to aid the agitators. Lord
Carnarvon also insisted that the Colonial Society should steer
clear of political matters.

Yet the popular agitation against Granville's colonial policy during the year 1869–70 was certainly not based on political motives. Few Conservative M.P.s joined the critics of the government's policy, and in the House of Commons the Conservative leaders usually supported the government in the lobbies. When, for example, in April 1870 a select committee was called for to examine Great Britain's relations with her colonies, not only did C. B. Adderley firmly sustain the principles assailed by R. R. Torrens and his supporters, but Disraeli and Gathorne Hardy sided with the government. Lord Robert Montagu, the eccentric brother of the Duke of Manchester, and John Mowbray alone represented the Conservative front benches in the opposition lobby. Such was the interest manifested in the colonies by the Conservatives at this debate that when Adderley addressed the chamber in the early evening only two M.P.s were to be found sitting on the Conservative side of the House.[52]

In the House of Lords, Granville was able to argue convincingly that he was merely carrying out a policy approved by his Conservative predecessor, the Duke of Buckingham and Chandos, and he was able to quote Carnarvon's own despatches and actions in support of this policy. Obviously the Conservatives had no clear alternative policy. Not until 1872 did Disraeli, who had remained strangely silent throughout 1869–70, try to make political capital out of the agitation.

In the newspaper controversy during these years the *Standard* was alone in censuring the government on what may be suspected were purely party grounds. The Conservative *Morning Post* supported the government's policy towards New Zealand and the Liberal *Daily Telegraph*, which welcomed the idea of a colonial conference, was not averse to attacking the anti-colonial sentiments of certain members of the Manchester group of economists. The ablest and most persistent attack on the government's supposed separatist policy came not from a Conservative newspaper but from the Radical but anti-Manchester *Spectator*. In January 1869 the *Spectator* had printed a eulogy on Lord Granville and as late as May 1869 had opposed financial assistance to New Zealand. The anti-government campaign it launched in June 1869 seems to have sprung from a sincere conviction that the government was about to cut the colonies adrift. Thus the news-

52 *Evening Standard*, 27 Apr. 1870; *The Times*, 28 Apr. 1870.

paper controversy of 1869–70 was not predetermined by political allegiance. There was no general agreement among the Conservative press to make political capital out of an attack on the government's colonial policy.

Indeed, the more closely the agitation of 1869–70 is studied, the clearer it becomes that this agitation was not based on party motives at all. Not only did the majority of the participants whose political affiliations can be determined have Liberal sympathies, but the majority of the moves opposing the government's colonial policy in the House of Commons were initiated by Liberals: Viscount Bury, R. R. Torrens, R. A. Macfie and McCullagh Torrens, an Independent Liberal. Evidently the opposition in the Commons did not spring from political manoeuvring. The agitators of 1869–70 were not concerned with political propaganda against a government which many of them supported. Their opposition, like that of the *Spectator*, sprang from genuine fears about the apparent trend of the government's colonial policy and apprehension lest sympathy with the teachings of the Manchester Radicals should lead Granville into a separatist policy.

The campaign in support of the agitation among these Liberal sympathisers remained completely unorganised. Apart from certain general basic assumptions, there was no attempt at concerted strategy inside or outside Parliament. Viscount Bury resigned the chairmanship of the Youl Committee, answered the Torrens motion for a select committee in the House of Commons and objected to R. A. Macfie raising a similar matter at a later date; Sir William Denison deliberately dissociated himself from a deputation to the Colonial Secretary; Sir George Grey never became a member of the Colonial Society and Edward Jenkins resigned in disgust from its membership in April 1870.[53] The more respected members of the movement, the Duke of Manchester, Lord Alfred Churchill, Arthur Kinnaird, Sir Charles Nicholson and the Marquis of Normanby, had nothing to do with the Cannon Street meetings. Clearly, this was a paradoxical situation. There were obvious disagreements. Yet points of contact remained numerous. The chief promoters of the various agitations still met regularly. A core of resistance to the ideas

[53] Jenkins to Roche, 26 Apr. 1870, quoted in Folsom, *Royal Empire Society*, pp. 179–80.

of separation by consent and general public indifference had
come into being. A definite springboard for more positive action
had been formed.

There were more obvious paradoxes, however. The initiators
of the agitation were not only unknown in British political circles
but, the New Zealanders apart, they were often unheard of in
the colonies, which they could in no way be held to represent. In
many cases they were disowned by those whose interests they
were supposed to be seeking to promote. Not only did the
agitators seriously misinterpret government policy, they were
more often than not completely out of step with representative
colonial opinion. Consequently it is not surprising if few of their
names are remembered today. It is surprising, however, that the
most successful part of the agitation in attracting attention to the
loyalty and benefits of the colonies were the Cannon Street
meetings. In themselves these meetings were a fiasco and the
participants became objects of derision.

Nevertheless, a group of men had come into existence who
were seriously trying to inaugurate a change in British outlook
on the prospects of empire. Whether this constituted the 'turn of
the tide' outlined by C. A. Bodelsen and R. L. Schuyler, however, remains obscure. Was there really such a change in public
attitude towards the empire in the 1870s or even, for that matter,
in the 1880s? Popular support for 'overseas imperialism' arose in
later decades, it is true, but the unusually active interest in
colonial affairs shown during the years 1868–71 faded abruptly.
The negative, separatist attitude declined, but it was not replaced
by anything constructive. If, then, these men cannot be classed
as the pioneers of a 'New Imperialism', what did their subsequent
activities in campaigning for the empire amount to?

5

The Future of the Empire: Federation or Disintegration?

THE 'crisis of opinion' precipitated by Earl Granville and made into an issue by the small group of agitators in 1869–70 had caused the question of empire to be discussed at length in Parliament, the daily press and in the better-class periodicals. The noisy meetings at the Cannon Street Hotel and the miscellaneous activities of various fellows of the Colonial Society (renamed the Royal Colonial Institute in March 1870) finally forced people to consider seriously whether they wished to see the empire disintegrate without any attempt being made by the mother country to secure the existing relationship.

The debate concerning the value of overseas possessions became more intense. Need the British empire disappear, as the prophets of the so-called Manchester School so vociferously claimed? After all, it was the colonists who had protested at a policy apparently aimed at bringing the day of separation nearer. Moreover, was it really in Great Britain's interest that such a separation should occur? Much had recently been made of the value of colonies as fields for emigration. Had the contribution of the colonies to the British economy been correctly assessed by the Manchester Radicals? And, more important, was the vision of peace, of free trade, and of a world dominated by the commerce of Great Britain, on which their assumptions were based, a plausible one? An industrial depression in the late 1860s, recent European developments, and the manner in which the views of Great Britain on international affairs had been largely ignored throughout the 1860s, raised doubts in the minds of many observers concerning Great Britain's future economic strength, political primacy and military security. In such circumstances the existence of colonies assumed a new importance.

I

In some respects 1870 may conveniently be regarded as a significant year in the development of British political attitudes (if not yet in the attitude of the general public) towards the colonies. A new set of circumstances were, to some extent, forging a new outlook on empire.[1] The protests emanating from several colonies against the supposedly separatist policy of Granville led to the discovery of colonial 'loyalty'. Many colonists clearly did not wish to separate from the mother country. Labilliere dubbed such an attitude a 'sacred principle'. There were obvious ties of kinship. In the House of Lords, Carnarvon wondered whether British fortunes were so secure that we could afford to treat the friendship offered by the colonists with such disdain.[2]

Moreover, these loyal colonies were no longer insignificant and worthless possessions. Much play was made of the population explosion in the settlement colonies. The population of British North America had increased from 1,282,000 in 1838 to 3,689,000 in 1871; that of Australia from 52,000 in 1825 to 1,647,000 in 1870; that of New Zealand from 59,000 in 1858 to 256,000 in 1871. This tremendous growth rate was expected to be maintained in the future.[3] R. A. Macfie thought the lesson to be drawn from the recent Franco-Prussian war was that 'a nation's strength depended in no small degree upon its numbers. Strip away the Colonies, what are we, where are we, in comparison with populous and growing nations like the United States, Russia and Germany?'[4] According to his reasoning, the colonies were such a potential source of strength to Great Britain that it would be madness to sacrifice them.

[1] For a brief assessment of the new forces at work, see Bodelsen, pp. 79–87, and J. E. Tyler, *The Struggle for Imperial Unity, 1868–95* (London, 1938) pp. 7–20.

[2] 3 *Hansard*, 7 Mar. 1870, cxcix 1324.

[3] Bodelsen, p. 83, n. 2; see Forster, *Our Colonial Empire*, and J. Vogel, 'Greater or Lesser Britain', *The Nineteenth Century*, i (July 1877) 809–31, for some wildly exaggerated estimates.

[4] R. A. Macfie, *Letter to a Prominent Member of the Cabinet* (London, 1870) p. 43.

The defenders of the imperial connection also maintained that the burdens of empire were fast disappearing. The progressive development of responsible government and the maintenance of internal security, together with the withdrawal of British garrisons from self-governing colonies, had reduced the specifically colonial burden on the defence estimates considerably, and the Manchester Radicals' loudest objection to the possession of colonies had largely been removed. In July 1870 the *Westminster Review* calculated that the colonial empire cost Great Britain £1 million per annum – approximately 9d. per head![5] F. P. de Labilliere asserted that Australia, New Zealand and the Cape of Good Hope were safe from foreign aggression and that Canada alone was open to foreign attack. But relations with the United States had so improved recently that Canada had little to fear from this direction. The establishment of the Dominion of Canada in 1867 and the withdrawal of British troops during the years 1870–71 had also removed the fear of continual British entanglements with the United States. All this helped to show the colonies in a more favourable light. Labilliere concluded, rather magnanimously on the behalf of colonies he could not claim to represent:

We have, hitherto, only seen England nursing infant nations. I believe and ardently hope, and I am certain I express the feelings of all the colonies in saying that she is destined to retain under her mild sway her colonial children, long after they shall attain the maturity and strength of manhood. I am convinced that the existence of such a relation will not only be of vast moral and material advantage both to the parent nation and to the offspring nations, but will constitute an Empire more splendid than any the world has yet seen.[6]

Such a confident prophecy was to appeal more and more to empire enthusiasts in Britain as the 1870s progressed.

The recent upheavals on the continent of Europe – the Franco-Prussian war and the unification of Germany reinforced by the textiles of Alsace and the minerals of Lorraine – revealed a significant tilt in the balance of power in Europe. And it was not

[5] J. Spedding, 'The Future of the British Empire', *Westminster Review*, xxxviii (July 1870) 59.
[6] Labilliere, 30 Sept. 1869, *T.N.A.P.S.S.* (1869) 114–19.

the face of Europe alone that was changing. The emergence of the United States from the throes of her Civil War as a united country, coupled with Russian encroachments in Asia, led Disraeli to inform the House of Commons in 1871 :

Not a single principle in the management of our foreign affairs, accepted by all statesmen for guidance up to six months ago, any longer exists. . . . You have a new world, new influences at work, new and unknown objects and dangers with which to cope at present involved in that obscurity incident to novelty in such affairs.[7]

In such a period of doubt the Manchester School's vision of a world of peace and British commercial prosperity seemed highly questionable. Both Great Britain's position as a world power and her industrial supremacy appeared to be challenged.

Indeed, even in 1870 fears were being expressed about Great Britain's continued existence as the leading industrial nation. D. Grant, in his *Home Policies or the Growth of Trade* (London, 1870), maintained that the workshop of the world was 'already a dream of the past'; R. R. Torrens referred to the growth of European trade competition; and J. A. Froude in articles in *Fraser's Magazine* concluded that 'there are symptoms which suggest, if not fear, yet at least misgiving as to the permanency of English industrial supremacy'.[8] These misgivings were reinforced by a trade depression which had set in, after a decade of prosperity, in 1868. A cry for reciprocity was soon raised, from Manchester of all places, by the Revivers (of Trade) Association.[9] And in 1872 one colonial writer, Jehu Mathews, claimed that 'the possibility of England being obliged to abandon free trade and return to her old commercial policy constitutes, we believe, a valid and practical argument in favour of the colonies'.[10]

[7] W. F. Monypenny and G. E. Buckle, *The Life of Benjamin Disraeli, Earl of Beaconsfield*, 6 vols. (London, 1910–20) ɪɪ 473–4, henceforth cited as Buckle.

[8] Froude, *Short Studies*, ɪɪ 195.

[9] C. J. Fuchs, *The Trade Policy of Great Britain and her Colonies since 1860* (London, 1905) pp. 188 ff.

[10] J. Mathews, *A Colonist on the Colonial Question* (London, 1872) pp. 52–3.

Attention was once again riveted on the benefits of colonies as markets for British goods. But no satisfactory figures could be obtained. Froude asserted that the colonies purchased per capita an amount several times larger than that purchased by foreign nations. He calculated that the United States spent 10s. a head per annum on British goods while Australian colonists spent £10. The *Standard* attempted to show that the colonies, with their population of 12 million, purchased £65 million worth of British goods, while France with a population three times as great imported only £57 million of British wares. Thus the colonies spent £12 5s. per capita while France spent £1 12s. per capita on British goods. Similarly, according to their figures, the United States purchased goods valued at £1 17s. per capita while Canada bought at the rate of £4 a head.[11] It was by no means clear how these (often ridiculous) figures had been arrived at. But while adherents of the Manchester group of economists might argue that the discrepancy arose from the specific circumstances of the colonies and not from the simple fact that they were colonies – colonists bought in the cheapest and sold in the dearest markets like everybody else – the vague belief that 'by some mysterious process trade has a great tendency to follow the flag'[12] began to assume a new importance.

Vast improvements in communication had also brought the colonies much nearer to the mother country. Steam transport enabled the traveller from London to reach Toronto in eleven days, and after the completion of the Suez Canal in 1869 communication between England and Australia was reduced to seven weeks. An Atlantic telegraph cable had been laid in 1866 and that to Australia completed in 1872. Between them steam and electricity, it seemed, had, as Froude optimistically claimed, 'abolished distance'.[13]

Reference has already been made to the continuing demand for schemes of state-aided emigration. Froude, always interested in social problems, made a powerful plea for the removal of British pauperism in his articles in *Fraser's Magazine* : 'We have land, we have capital, we have labour. Yet we seem to have neither the ability nor the desire to bring them together, and

[11] Froude, *Short Studies*, II 187; *Standard*, 11 Dec. 1869.
[12] E. Wilson, 'National Disintegration', letter to *The Times*, 10 Nov. 1869.
[13] Froude, *Short Studies*, II 210.

develop their results.'[14] Torrens raised the matter in the House
of Commons in March 1870, and though it was generally agreed
that the colonies were useful as fields for emigration, for relieving
Great Britain's difficulties while still allowing the emigrants to
remain within the British family, the Gladstone government
refused to subsidise British emigration. Froude roundly declared
that if Great Britain persistently refused to aid the colonies and
eventually allowed them to drift from her, the mother country
would degenerate into a community of harmless traders, leaving
to others the greatness which was once her own.[15]

The feeling that strength in numbers and extent of territory
was essential if Great Britain were to maintain her position in
the world was frequently expressed in Parliament. Viscount
Sandon declared in 1870 that 'the tendency of the day was in
favour of large nationalities and the day of small nations was
past'. And R. A. Macfie explained that 'other empires were
growing in extent and population. Germany, Russia and the
United States had increased in territory and in the number of
inhabitants, and this country could not maintain its relative
position if it did not retain its population as members of this
noble empire.'[16] As the *Standard* remarked :

If we do not value our colonial Empire ourselves, at least we
know those who do, who are striving by all their might to do
precisely that which we are called upon to undo. While we
are cutting off our arms and legs and loosening our members,
every other nation on earth is actively engaged in consolidating
its possessions.[17]

At a meeting of the Royal Colonial Institute, Labilliere enquired:

Is there a German who loves his country, from Prince
Bismarck down to the most insignificant politician, who would
not give much and strive hard to make the German Empire

[14] Ibid. p. 187. See also 'Reciprocal Duties of State and Subject' and
'The Colonies Once More', II 308–47, 397–438.
[15] Ibid. p. 214.
[16] Sandon, 3 *Hansard*, 26 Apr. 1870, cc 1893; Macfie, 3 *Hansard*, 12 May
1871, ccvi 753.
[17] *Standard*, 13 Sept. 1869.

like our British Empire which some Englishmen think should
be allowed to fall to pieces?[18]

No longer was it a simple matter of allowing the colonists to
separate and go their own way. There was now a very real
possibility that they might be annexed by a foreign power. Earl
Russell lamented at the prospect of colonies trying 'each its little
spasm of independence', while France, the United States and
Russia would be looking on, 'each and all willing to annex one
or more of the broken fragments to the nearest portion of their
dominions'. The *Westminster Review* declared that 'should
America, Prussia or any other rising power take a helpless but
abandoned colony under its protection, England's loss will be the
other nation's gain'.[19]

The significance of such possibilities led to a gradual reassessment in the 1870s of British political and commercial attitudes
towards colonies. Once doubt had been cast on the Manchester
School's prophecy of an era of universal peace and free trade,
dominated industrially by Great Britain, the value of overseas
possessions once again became a completely open question.
Attempts by the defenders of the imperial connection to illustrate
the potential value of the empire to Great Britain during the
coming decades – 'at present the Colonies are a potentiality that
is not called into play'[20] – received a more sympathetic reception
than at any time during the 1860s. The benefits of empire were
outlined before Parliament by Carnarvon, Russell, Knatchbull-
Hugessen, R. R. Torrens and R. A. Macfie; and the same views
were expressed equally cogently for the reading public by J. A.
Froude, F. P. de Labilliere, Edward Jenkins, Edward Wilson and
Jehu Mathews. The difficult subject of Canada was dealt with,
most ably, by 'A Colonist' in three letters to *The Times* in
January 1870.[21]

[18] F. P. de Labilliere, 'The Permanent Unity of the Empire', *P.R.C.I.*, vi
(1875) 36–85.
[19] Earl Russell, *Selection from Speeches of Earl Russell, 1817–41, and
from Despatches, 1859–65* (London, 1870) i 152–3; Spedding, *Westminster
Review*, xxxviii 47–74.
[20] R. A. Macfie, *A Glance at the Position and Prospects of the Empire*
(London, 1872) p. 25.
[21] *The Times*, 18–20 Jan. 1870. The correspondent was later identified
as Sir John Rose in M. H. Long, 'Sir John Rose and the Informal Beginnings
of the Canadian High Commissionership', *C.H.R.*, xii (1931) 23–43.

By 1872 even *The Times* was forced to agree that 'the call for a severance of the connexion between England and her off-spring . . . has for the present died away'. Similarly, Anthony Trollope revised his opinions in 1873 and admitted

> that some of us in England have been a little too forward in our assurances to the colonies that they have only to speak the word themselves, and they shall be free. . . . Separation, though it may be ultimately certain is, I think, too distant to have a place as yet in the official or parliamentary vocabulary of a Colonial Minister.[22]

Alfred Tennyson felt sufficiently constrained in 1872 to admonish the separatists in his 'Epilogue to the Queen' added to a new edition of *Idylls of the King*:

> And that true North, whereof we lately heard
> A strain to shame us 'keep you to yourselves,
> So loyal is too costly! friends – your love
> Is but a burthen : loose the bond and go'.
> Is this the tone of Empire? here the faith
> That made us rulers?

The *Westminster Review* probably summed up the new outlook for a new age when it calculated, in July 1870, the penalties of separation : loss of trade, raw materials and profitable fields of investment; loss of lands for emigration, of strategic bases on Great Britain's trade routes, of depots and ports for naval rendezvous and refuge; a loss in military experience and training openings for the young; the loss of national prestige and a debase-ment of national aspirations.[23] The points made in this reappraisal achieved increasing acceptance during the 1870s. They heralded the beginning of a significant change in outlook which did not become evident, or general, until two decades had passed. In the 1870s the negative, separatist attitude lost popularity; separatism was disavowed by the government and the way was eventually laid open for a more constructive approach to empire.

[22] *The Times*, 25 Oct. 1872; A. Trollope, *Australia and New Zealand* (London, 1873) I 8. Cf. his earlier statements in *The West Indies and the Spanish Main* (London, 1859) I 129, and *North America* (London, 1862) I 130-1.

[23] Spedding, *Westminster Review*, xxxviii 47–74.

II

In Great Britain the most significant and immediate change probably concerned the small group of enthusiasts who had fought to maintain the empire. Now that all aspirations of separation were disavowed, they changed from the defensive to the offensive. Each put forward his own scheme to consolidate the remaining links of empire. Throughout the 1870s innumerable schemes for imperial federation and colonial representation were launched in books, pamphlets, articles, letters to the press, speeches, debates in Parliament and in discussions in the Royal Colonial Institute, each with this object in mind.[24]

The proposals now put forward for regulating relations between mother country and colony emanated from a belief that the existing imperial relationship was too precarious to endure. But the new critics of a policy of 'drift' were not concerned with ideas for planned separation (as most had been at the end of the previous decade). Imperial consolidation was the new cry. 'A Colonist' declared in *Fraser's Magazine* in December 1872 :

> I am sure that if we could arouse the mass of the people in England to a lively sense of what was going on, the Government would be speedily forced to do something to avert the threatened disruption instead of standing by in an irritating inactivity, distilling honeyed words from mocking lips.[25]

Without constitutional reform the empire would disintegrate. Some symbol of empire unity was required. The colonies must be allowed some say in the running of the empire and must bear their share of the burden of imperial defence. The need for closer political unity seemed obvious.

The policy of 'drift' was attacked in two articles in the *Contemporary Review* for 1871 entitled 'Imperial Federalism' and 'An Imperial Confederation', written by Edward Jenkins, the young Radical barrister who had attained some notoriety with his social satire, *Ginx's Baby*. Jenkins thought the alterna-

---

[24] What follows is but a mere summary of the most important proposals made during the 1870s. For a detailed survey of the schemes, see S. C. Y. Cheng, *Schemes for the Federation of the British Empire* (New York, 1931); also Bodelsen, pp. 130–45.

[25] A Colonist, 'Empire or No Empire?', *Fraser's Magazine*, vi (Dec. 1872) 667–85. The writer was apparently the Australian, W. Jardine Smith.

tives lay between 'Confederation or confusion . . . we cannot go back, we cannot remain where we are; our only chance of unity is Federation'. The possibilities of imperial federation were immense: it would improve the prospects for imperial defence, trade, investment and emigration, remove hostile colonial tariffs and unequal burdens of imperial expenditure, promote efficiency in legislation and remove the anomaly of existing relations between the colonies and the Colonial Office. It might even solve the Irish question. To Jenkins, imperial federation was the solution for most of Great Britain's outstanding problems. In the second of his articles he proposed the formation of 'a Senate or Parliament of representatives from every province' and concluded that 'all other schemes dwindle before the practical simplicity of a federal union'.[26]

These articles attracted a great deal of attention and helped to popularise once again a federal solution to the colonial question. In 1871 schemes for what was loosely termed 'imperial federation' were enunciated before the Westminster Palace Hotel conference, mentioned in Parliament, formulated in magazine articles and debated by the Royal Colonial Institute. All those colonists and writers who had so ably defended the benefits of empire – Labilliere, Young, Froude, Westgarth, Eddy, Youl – and all those who had espoused the same cause in Parliament – Macfie, Torrens, Wolff, the Duke of Manchester and Earl Russell – had their own ideas on imperial consolidation. There were as many schemes as there were individuals.

The proposals put forward concerned schemes as varied as inviting colonial representatives to Westminster, extending the Privy Council, establishing a Council of Advice and creating a supreme federal parliament. Each scheme had its attractions; each had its drawbacks. Few found favour with the more practical men of affairs accustomed to dealing with the colonies.

The proposal to admit colonial representatives to the British Parliament – suggested before the American War of Independence to overcome the slogan 'No taxation without representation' – found least favour among the advocates of closer political unity. The drawbacks were obvious. No colony in the 1870s would be prepared to give up some of its financial powers merely because

[26] *Contemporary Review*, xvi (Jan. 1871) 176–86; xvii (Apr. 1871) 60–77.

it had sent a representative to Westminster. Neither was the suggestion acceptable to the British. Nobody wanted a small number of colonial M.P.s voting on United Kingdom matters or allying themselves with a British political party. Similar proposals to secure colonial representation in the British Cabinet, by the appointment of colonial ministers as 'Secretaries of State' for each colony, and a proposal to extend the British Privy Council to include ex-colonial governors, were also received unenthusiastically. A project for reviving the Trade and Plantations Committee of the Privy Council to include colonial Agents-General was proposed by C. W. Eddy in 1874 and backed by Earl Grey in his article 'How Shall We Retain the Colonies?' in *The Nineteenth Century* for June 1879. But the scheme was dubbed impracticable by Labilliere and the Duke of Manchester, and R. R. Torrens maintained that it had been rendered obsolete by the telegraph.

The idea of constituting some sort of 'Board of Advice' presided over by the Colonial Secretary was, however, a popular one. It was suggested at length by Sir E. H. Drummond Wolff, M.P., and received conditional support from Macfie, the Duke of Manchester, Labilliere and Westgarth. But most of the support for this scheme came from those who possessed a much grander conception. In their view a 'Board of Advice' was merely an intermediate step towards what was variously termed an Imperial Assembly, a Council of State or a Federal Parliament – a new body to be constituted after imperial federation. The Duke of Manchester, for example, who was a keen supporter of an advisory council in the mid-1870s, looked to the future for 'some central body in the Constitution of the Empire, with effective legislative power'.[27] He confided to Young:

I am more and more convinced, the more I think about it, that Emigration as well as other matters of Colonial, or rather Imperial, importance should be managed, not by a minister depending on the success of political parties in England, but by a Council elected by the several independent Legislatures of the United Kingdom and of the Colonies, and, being so

[27] Speech, inaugural dinner, 10 Mar. 1869, *P.R.C.I.*, I (1869) 31. For a further expression of his views, see the discussion on Labilliere, *P.R.C.I.*, VI (1875) 119, and a letter to *The Colonies*, 27 Dec. 1875.

elected, superior to each of them. It is a dream I have had for many years – and it seems at last to be sprouting in public opinion.[28]

Federation was easily the most popular solution to the problem of closer unity in the 1870s: 'union is strength'. It was by no means a new idea. Arthur Mills referred to it as 'a popular and fashionable idea' in his review of 'Our Colonial Policy' in 1869,[29] and the proposal had recently been canvassed on numerous occasions by Labilliere, Macfie and Froude. A plan for federal union was outlined by James Spedding in the January 1870 edition of the *Westminster Review*, and at the same time Earl Russell called for 'a Congress or Assembly, representing Great Britain and her dependencies'.[30] But not until Jenkins's articles had been published by the *Contemporary Review* in January and April 1871 did detailed plans for imperial federation become numerous. Then *Fraser's Magazine*, under the editorship of Froude, carried articles on federation in its numbers for July, August and September; and Labilliere put forward his proposals in a paper on 'Imperial and Colonial Federalism' delivered before the Westminster Palace Hotel conference in July 1871. In 1872 Jenkins and Labilliere continued their campaign with papers at the Social Science Congress; *Fraser's Magazine* contributed an article on 'Empire or No Empire?'; and a Canadian, Jehu Mathews, outlined his own ideas on a federal parliament in *A Colonist on the Colonial Question* (London, 1872).

By 1873 the debate was well under way. Macfie pestered Parliament with his scheme for an Imperial Council and the question was taken up in a small newspaper, *The Colonies*, owned by S. W. Silver, a member of the Royal Colonial Institute who had participated in the Westminster Palace Hotel conference of 1871. The initial debate between two correspondents signing themselves 'Philo-Colonus' and 'H. de B.H.' was extended in 1875 to include letters from Frederick Young, Labilliere and the Duke of Manchester. This correspondence was published

[28] Manchester to Young, 29 Sept. 1869, *Young Papers*, R.C.S., file 1, A.38/1.
[29] *Contemporary Review*, xi (June 1869) 216–39. See Bodelsen, pp. 133–42.
[30] Spedding, *Westminster Review*, xxxvii 1–37, xxxviii 47–74; Russell, *Selection from Speeches*, i 152–3.

separately by Young in 1876 in a work posing the stark alternatives of federation or disintegration.[31]

Further notable schemes for an imperial parliament were put
forward by a 'British Subject' in *The Great Game: A Plea for
a British Imperial Policy* (London, 1875); by W. Bousfield, *The
Government of the Empire* (London, 1877); and in three articles
entitled 'The Federation of the English Empire' in the April,
July and October issues of the *Westminster Review* for 1879.
The debate was continued throughout 1879.[32] There then appears
to have been a short respite from books and pamphlets proposing
yet more schemes for a federal parliament. But the foundation
in 1884 of the Imperial Federation League led to another flood
of publications. There was no shortage of would-be constitutional
reformers, cranks and political commentators; there was a multi-
plicity of ideas, some serious, some fanciful, none achieving anything approaching general acceptance. If there was unanimity of
sentiment, there was no agreement on practicalities.

The term 'federation' was used extremely loosely and generally
included any scheme securing closer co-operation with the
colonies. Even when a federal union was proposed, however,
there existed no agreement as to the most practical form of
federation : whether it should be a loose confederation of states
retaining a large amount of local autonomy or a tighter federation with a central body possessing legislative and executive
power for the whole empire. The constitution of the central body
caused much disagreement. Some writers like Jenkins and Young
preferred not to go into details; others such as Labilliere, Macfie,
Mathews, Staveley Hill and Hollis True delighted in propound-
ing their own solutions. Some writers wished to see the British
Parliament moulded into a federal parliament, while others
proposed the establishment of an entirely new body, a super-
parliament, the Westminster Parliament becoming the local legislature for the United Kingdom. There was at least some
agreement that the central body should deal with matters of
peace and war, imperial defence and foreign policy. But there
the agreement ended. Opinions on issues concerning tariffs, land

[31] F. Young, *Imperial Federation* (London, 1876).

[32] G. C. Cuningham, 'The Federation of the English Empire', *Westminster
Review*, LVI (Oct. 1879) 313–34; J. S. Little, *A World Empire* (London,
1879); Hollis True, *Victoria Britannia* (London, 1879); A. Staveley Hill, 'An
Empire's Parliament', *P.R.C.I.*, XI (1880) 136–77.

policy and the raising of imperial revenue remained diametrically opposed.

By the end of the 1870s no acceptable formula for imperial federation had been found. No agreement had been reached and no ground gained. The proponents of the various schemes argued among themselves both privately and publicly. Nor did the creation of the Imperial Federation League under the auspices of Labilliere, Westgarth and Young, along with Dennistoun Wood, Sir George Baden-Powell and Captain Colomb, who had read several papers on imperial defence to the Royal Colonial Institute in the 1870s, heal the breach; it only enhanced it. The League itself was destined to become a victim of the same dissension and to break up in confusion in 1893.

III

Internal dissension was not the only reason for the failure of the exponents of imperial federation to achieve any effective influence in British political circles. Many empire-minded observers disagreed with the basic assumptions of the movement and were not prepared to accept Jenkins's prophecy of 'Confederation or confusion' or Young's alternatives of federation or disintegration. Men of the calibre of Gladstone, Kimberley, Viscount Bury, Blachford and Adderley, exponents of the 'voluntary tie' school of thought, publicly attacked the movement and maintained that such schemes contradicted existing tendencies and would not, in the long run, extend the life of the empire. In fact, federation might shorten it.

Gladstone, Kimberley, Carnarvon, Blachford and Adderley were all practical men, experienced in dealing with the colonies. Their suppositions were correct. It is hard to envisage any of the proposed schemes receiving endorsement from the various self-governing colonies in the 1870s.

No greater exponent of the 'voluntary tie' school could be found than Gladstone. To him all talk of imperial reconstruction was anathema. He constantly expounded his beliefs in Parliament and repeatedly refused to consider suggestions concerning imperial consolidation. Disraeli, on the other hand, flirted with the idea in his Crystal Palace speech of 'some representative council in the metropolis' which would have brought the colonies into

'constant and continuous relations with the Home Government'.[33]
But little more was heard from him on this subject once he had
climbed the greasy pole again in 1874.

The Colonial Secretaries of the period were equally contemptuous of the various schemes. Granville laughed at Russell's
proposals for a 'Colonial Representative Assembly' in London
and asked Gladstone : 'Shall we immortalise your Administration
by proposing this?' In more serious vein, he pointed out to a
joint deputation from the Colonial Society and the Cannon
Street meetings that colonists, who were jealous of anyone except
their own accredited representative, would never accept advice
from any 'imperial council'.[34]

Similarly, Kimberley, before he took over the Colonial Office,
thought imperial confederacy 'a vain dream' and after greater
experience in administering the empire remarked :

One cannot help asking oneself how many of these enthusiasts
have ever reflected on the real difficulties of keeping great
self-governing communities such as Canada & Australia
permanently united with us. Possibly tho' not probably, these
difficulties may not prove to be insuperable, but the contrast
is striking & not encouraging between the 'tall' talk about the
integrity of the Empire & the action of the colonial governments especially the Australian, whenever home & colonial
interests come or seem to come into conflict.[35]

He concluded with Gladstone that the imperial connection could
be maintained only by 'the absolute independence of the colonists
in all their local affairs'.[36] Even Carnarvon, with his tendency to
be attracted by 'showy schemes', did not at this time back the
proposals for imperial federation. According to him federation
was impossible and the idea of a council impracticable. It would
be attended by 'inferior men', while under the existing system

---

[33] Buckle, II 535. Probably the most concise and balanced summary of
the imperial ideas of Gladstone and Disraeli is to be found in McIntyre,
Imperial Frontier, pp. 17–26.

[34] Granville to Gladstone, 2 Sept. 1869, quoted in Fitzmaurice, *Life of
Granville*, II 22; *Daily News*, 17 Dec. 1869.

[35] Kimberley, 'Journal', 14 Nov. 1872, pp. 34–5.

[36] Ibid., 25 Apr. 1873, pp. 38–9.

Britain could always acquire the services of the most distinguished representatives whenever they were needed. His own solution was all sweetness and light : 'a greater sympathy, a greater heartiness of expression, a greater affection, a more sincere pride in this great Empire, are all circumstances which would tend to promote the object in view'.[37]

The comments of former Colonial Office civil servants on the possibilities of imperial federation were equally discouraging. In 1870 Herman Merivale thought that the remaining ties with the self-governing colonies were entirely voluntary, 'arising partly from the nature of things, partly from a policy, which it is mere idle assertion to call recent, or to attribute to this or that party in the State, since it has been deliberately adopted and persevered in by the Home Government for nearly thirty years'.[38] A reversal of this trend would never be accepted by the colonists without compulsion or promises of greater imperial expenditure. But schemes for colonial representation at Westminster and federal union were impracticable. A Council of Advice was anachronistic: a Committee of the Privy Council for Trade and Foreign Plantations which discussed the constitutions for the Australian colonies and the Cape of Good Hope plus some minor matters in 1849 had fallen into disuse. The interests of the colonies were too divergent. And comparison with the Council of India was misguided since in India Great Britain actually ruled. As regards the repeated proposals of R. R. Torrens to allow the colonies *chargés d'affaires* to put them on the 'same footing as Belgium', Merivale could think of no more open road for hastening complete colonial independence.

Lord Blachford (Sir Frederic Rogers) reiterated the same point of view in 1877. He thought all proposals for closer political unity 'hollow and impracticable'. Any attempt to tamper with responsible government would be a standing complaint among the colonists. What common interests did the colonies have? There was certainly none in foreign policy. How, asked Rogers, could you expect the colonies to be interested in an invasion of Belgium? On the other hand, colonial aspirations in the Pacific might well disturb relations with Great Britain. Such friction could only lead

---

[37] 3 *Hansard*, 14 Feb. 1870, cxcix 199.
[38] H. Merivale, 'The Colonial Question in 1870', *Fortnightly Review*, vii (Feb. 1870) 154.

to a more immediate separation and possibly a parting in anger. The colonies were best left as they were.[39]

H. C. E. Childers, the First Lord of the Admiralty in the Gladstone administration, who had been a member of the first Cabinet in Victoria under the new constitution of 1856, was equally explicit:

> I deprecate and reject all those fanciful notions of bringing the United Kingdom and her Colonies and dependencies into a Bund, or Zollverein, or some such combination, with a Federal Parliament, which have caught so many well-meaning people of late years, and at which Lord Beaconsfield hinted himself in one of his speeches in the North. If you want to find a good cause of quarrel with your Colonies this would be the method and I speak with some little knowledge of colonial politics.[40]

Similarly, Viscount Bury, the first president of the Royal Colonial Institute, dissociated the Institute in 1873 from Macfie's call for a select committee to enquire into colonial relations and the establishment of an Imperial Council. Bury retorted that

> the new system was based on mutual interest and the influence of a common language and religion, a tie the very elasticity and slightness of which constituted its strength. To be constantly probing what the hon. Gentleman wrongly deemed a wound, to be constantly investigating the strength of the claim and raking up grievances would be the very way to lose our colonies.[41]

Arthur Mills, Lord Alfred Churchill, Sir William Denison and Arthur Kinnaird all agreed with this point of view. The colonies were best left alone.

C. B. Adderley, the Conservative Colonial Reformer, continued to maintain that the real secret of a lasting connection lay 'between the alternatives of dependence and separation . . . – that

[39] Lord Blachford, 'The Integrity of the British Empire', *The Nineteenth Century*, II (Oct. 1877) 355–65.

[40] Childers, speech at Pontefract, 16 Oct. 1879, quoted in F. P. de Labilliere, *Federal Britain; or, Unity and Federation of the Empire* (London, 1894) pp. 92–3.

[41] 3 *Hansard*, 28 Feb. 1873, CCXIV 1109. See also Folsom, *Royal Empire Society*, pp. 180–1; Viscount Bury, *The Nineteenth Century*, XVII 381–96.

of common partnership'.[42] In April 1870 *The Times* advanced a similar ideal :

> it is for the glory and the renown, and for the safety and the dignity, of the United Kingdom that we should recognise a confraternity of English-speaking nations as a better ideal than the maintenance of a nominal dominion which would fall to pieces under any serious agitation through the mere weight of its separate parts.[43]

But it was in November 1875 that a leader in *The Colonies*, the newspaper which had carried the fullest examination of the possibility of imperial federation, explained the simple truth, so obvious to all those used to dealing with the colonies, yet completely overlooked by all those who proposed schemes for imperial federation : 'The more completely [the colonies] manage their own affairs, the less England interferes with their own administration the stronger, the more ardent, has become the imperial feeling.'[44] Was not the concept of partnership, of scattered Britains united in the closest friendship, more acceptable to the colonies themselves and more applicable to the imperial future than the extremes of federation and disintegration?

Thus the men who had most experience in administering the empire, or who had taken a deep interest in the development of the colonies, often opposed the movement for imperial federation. They did not accept the assumptions upon which the demand for closer union was based and did not think that federation was the solution to the problem of maintaining the imperial connection. In fact these men, the 'traditional' defenders of colonial interests who had stood aloof from the 'popular' agitation of 1869–70, virtually became the opponents of the small group, principally consisting of ex-colonists, who advocated imperial federation in the 1870s. It was not that Adderley, Gladstone, Carnarvon, Kimberley, Childers, Blachford and Merivale lacked

---

[42] Adderley, *Review of 'The Colonial Policy of Lord John Russell's Administration'*, p. 420. For further statements by Adderley, see his articles in *The Nineteenth Century*, 'How Not to Retain the Colonies', vi (July 1879) 170–8, and 'Imperial Federation: Its Impossibility', xvi (Sept. 1884) 505–16.

[43] *The Times*, 27 Apr. 1870. See also the copy for 10 Sept. 1869.

[44] *The Colonies*, 27 Nov. 1875. See the copy for 6 May 1875 for a good summary of the difficulties of federation.

imagination, but that they possessed a good understanding of the colonial relationship to be adopted in the 1870s and realised the limitations within which it was possible to work.

IV

The enthusiastic exponents of the plans for imperial federation lacked such an appreciation. They often displayed a remarkable ignorance of colonial aspirations, misunderstood colonial loyalty and ignored the feeling of a sense of 'nationhood', or rather of autochthonous development, which was gradually beginning to arise in many of the settlement colonies. The tendency to regard the proposals as of inestimable benefit and blessing to the out-lying portions of the empire was not always shared by the colonists. W. Jardine Smith protested against this patronising attitude in his article, 'The Imperial Question from an Australian Colonist's Point of View', in *Fraser's Magazine* of September 1871. Colonists were not inferior beings. On the contrary they had made great progress considering the limitations of time and the material available. He drew an illuminating comparison be-tween the methods used by the British government in suppressing a recent riot in Hyde Park and the expert handling, by a colonial government, of a similar breach of the peace by men of the North Eastern Railway Company in Victoria.

The colonists were proud of their achievements and their independence. And though many inhabitants of the mother country might still regard them as 'Englishmen over the seas', members of additional English counties, the colonists naturally concentrated on their own separate development. Those observers who expected the colonists to give up freely the independence gradually evolved under the system of responsible government were very much mistaken. Such plans would never be accepted. Yet it was precisely the idea of reasserting British authority in the colonies that lay behind many of the proposals for closer political union. Just as certain British newspapers had suggested that New Zealand's difficulties should be used to restore closer British control over that colony, so many of the imperial federalists looked for a resumption of British control over colonial legislation, commercial policy and waste lands. Jenkins and Westgarth, for example, obviously regarded the concession of responsible government as a mistake in need of rectification, and Earl Grey equally consistently called for a reassertion of British responsibility.

The control of waste lands was an old sore, and even in 1870 Macfie and Earl Grey hankered after re-establishing British authority. But commercial policy was the cause of most concern in the 1870s. Russell and Grey were staunch advocates of free trade and both sought means to control colonial economic policy. At the Westminster Palace Hotel conference in 1871 both Jenkins and Professor Sheldon Amos regretted the tendency of the colonists to erect tariff barriers; and the removal of protective duties on English goods was advocated as one of the benefits of union in a series of articles entitled 'The Federation of the English Empire' in the *Westminster Review* for April, July and October 1879.

Such benefits of federation as these would never be welcomed in the colonies. That such proposals could be put forward in the belief that the colonists would accept loss of control over their own revenue and commercial policy shows clearly how much the campaigners for closer empire unity had lost contact with representative colonial opinion. When they had posed as champions of the colonies during the agitation of 1869–70 they were disowned; they were now shown to be clearly out of touch with the views of the colonists. This paradox did not go unnoticed. Colonials in London who heard the papers on federation read before the Royal Colonial Institute continually pointed out how unacceptable these proposals were to those in the colonies.

H. B. T. Strangways, a former Premier of South Australia, probably laid his finger on the reason for this divergence of opinion when he pointed out that most of the group living in London seeking constitutional reform of the imperial structure were first-generation colonists, English-born settlers who had returned home, enriched or disillusioned, after living in the colonies for a number of years. Such men were naturally English in outlook, and in fact usually regarded themselves as 'Englishmen in exile'. Their outlook differed significantly from that of second-generation colonists, men actually born in the colonies who had fewer ties with the mother country. The Victorian-born Labilliere, for example, appreciated the colonial point of view when he suggested at the Westminster Palace Hotel conference, in opposition to the views of Jenkins and Amos, that union ought not to interfere with colonial commercial freedom. The 'busy-body absentees' in London, on the other hand, often regarded the problem of closer unity from the mother country's position and did not appreciate the strong views held locally by a younger generation of colonists. They often wished to replace harsh colonial realities, with which they had little sympathy, with the ideal of the affectionate mother country. Their sentimental vision was not to be clouded by everyday reality. And as they campaigned for closer political unity and tighter British control of colonial policy, the Australasian colonists were in fact demanding more administrative independence and negotiating with Kimberley the freedom to erect preferential duties. This emphasis on autochthonous development was bound to be a serious stumbling-block to any plan for imperial federation.

The energy and, occasionally, venom spent in pressing such plans were misdirected. The debates were academic and largely irrelevant. They were academic in so far as the schemes were impracticable, revolutionary and unacceptable to the colonists, the participants not even being recognised by the colonists. They were irrelevant in that they concerned theoretical issues and not questions of practical policy.

In the 1870s the most pressing problems concerned the periphery of empire – the government of indigenous populations and expansion in the tropics. The federalists were not in general interested in these problems. They were more concerned with the settlement colonies than with other parts of the empire.[45] Their activities undoubtedly contributed many characteristics to the British imperialism of later decades, but these men had little to do with the pioneers of the 'New Imperialism'. They wasted their energy on schemes that never materialised. Nothing constructive replaced the negative, separatist attitude. Where then did the impulses for imperial expansion come from in the 1870s? When it came to the test, the expansion of the empire in the 1870s was carried out by traditional agents – merchants, missionaries, the men on the spot – and the real debating theatres where pressure groups were formed were the traditional committees, such as the Anti-Slavery Society and Aborigines Protection Society, rather

[45] Even India was not usually included in the federation schemes; see S. Mehrota, 'Imperial Federation and India, 1868–1917', *J.C.P.S.*, I (1961) 29–40.

than a new body like the Royal Colonial Institute which for most of the decade was too aware of its non-political nature to play an official part in pressing various courses of action upon the government. Little wonder that the names of the early originators of a revived interest in empire devoted to the settlement colonies are hardly remembered today.

6

The Impulse for Expansion: The Philanthropists and the Tropics

THE doubts aroused by the policies of Gladstone's first government concerning Great Britain's relationship with her self-governing possessions fascinated and preoccupied colonial zealots throughout the 1870s. Yet some of the most difficult problems requiring urgent solution in this decade concerned not the colonies of English settlement but the periphery of empire, the area beyond the pale of British settlement into which British interests and influences had penetrated. The areas principally involved were Africa, south-east Asia and the Pacific. Here British politicians were reluctantly forced to consider the problem of governing indigenous populations and of expansion into the tropics.

Throughout the mid-Victorian era the British government had shown great reluctance in extending formal sovereignty to new areas of the earth. The problems and expense involved in establishing the necessary administrative machinery, and the attendant difficulties concerning relations with local rulers and inhabitants, were complex and costly. As Lord Derby later remarked, the British empire had black savages enough. Earlier attempts at maintaining friendly relations with aboriginal inhabitants had met with little success in Australia, New Zealand, Canada and South Africa. The report of the Aborigines Committee in 1837 had opposed British territorial expansion and favoured 'protecting' aborigines. Whether 'protection' meant 'assimilation', as it probably did, had never been ascertained.

A notable attempt at putting the committee's ideals into operation had been made in the 1840s by Sir George Grey during his governorships of South Australia (1841–5), New Zealand (1845–53) and the Cape (1854–61). But Grey's schemes, aimed at introducing 'mixed societies' in which Australian aborigines, Maoris and Bantus would become law-abiding citizens forming an integral part of a European economy and society, were so limited in scale that the results were negligible and the indigenous populations soon fell under the rule of the colonial governments.

In the face of repeated failure the British government reacted by leaving well alone and gave limited aid or advice only when absolutely necessary. This attitude was apparent in Lieutenant-Colonel W. J. Smythe's report of May 1861 on the proposed annexation of Fiji, in which he suggested that the island group should be left to develop gradually under western influence like Hawaii, for, he wrote,

> Judging from the present state of the Sandwich Islands, and the former condition of Tahiti, it would seem that the resources of the Pacific Islands can best be developed and the welfare of their inhabitants secured, by a native government aided by the counsels of respectable Europeans.[1]

A course of minimum intervention was advocated. Similarly, the report in 1865 of the Select Committee on West African Settlements suggested that British interests should be fostered through self-governing African states. The inhabitants of West Africa should be encouraged to exercise 'those qualities which may render it possible for us more and more to transfer to them the administration of all the Governments with a view to our ultimate withdrawal from all, except, probably Sierra Leone'.[2] But local attempts at establishing a Fante Confederacy, influenced no doubt by the writings of a government official, Dr J. A. Horton, an African graduate of Edinburgh University, who maintained

[1] Smythe to Newcastle, 1 May 1861, encl. no. 5, C.O. 83/1.
[2] Report of the Select Committee on West African Settlements, *Parl. P.*, Reports from Committees (1865) v 148.

that the Select Committee had laid down the great principle of establishing independent African nationalities, met only with objections, scorn and contempt from British officials. When in 1874 the British found it necessary to extend their influence in the Gold Coast 'protectorate', Fante protestations and dreams were swept aside.

In fact, as greater self-government was granted to the settlement colonies, Great Britain constantly found herself compelled to intervene in the tropical empire in the interests of good government. For example, during the years 1866–75 it was found necessary in the West Indies to abolish some of the old legislative assemblies, which had fallen under the power of the former slave-owning class, as they had become a bar to good government. By 1875 all the Caribbean colonies with the exception of Barbados, Bermuda and the Bahamas had been reduced to Crown colony status. While tightening her grip on certain parts of the empire, Great Britain also found it necessary to extend her hand in other areas, whether to assert her position in West Africa, to establish her influence in the Malay States or to combat lawlessness in the Pacific. These were the areas of imperial activity in the early 1870s, fields far removed from the agitation of 1869–71 and equally far removed from the thoughts of the federalists. A brief examination of the advances made at this time reveals the small part played in the revival of the imperial idea by the group of colonial agitators who emerged as champions of the empire in 1869. The expansion undertaken in the 1870s occurred at the behest of the merchants, the missionaries and the men on the spot. The Aborigines Protection Society, the Anti-Slavery Society, missionary societies and chambers of commerce were the real pressure groups. The agitators of 1869–71 contributed little more than the favourable atmosphere in which these committees worked.

I

Granville's conduct of colonial affairs had thoroughly aroused doubts in the minds of the government's critics about the future of the empire. Then, in June 1870, came the first formal acknowledgement that the government was considering actually abandoning a colony. It planned to cede the Gambia, a small insolvent colony, to France in return for small gains elsewhere on the West

African coast. The dismemberment of the empire seemed about to begin.

This was the third attempt at relinquishing troublesome colonies within a decade. In 1862 the Bay Islands Colony in the Caribbean had been ceded to the Republic of Honduras in spite of protests from the local inhabitants. In 1864 the Ionian Islands were given to Greece after a sarcastic speech by Disraeli in which he suggested that the government would next cede Malta and Gibraltar. Now it appeared that the Gambia headed the Gladstone government's list. Would this exchange be permitted in the electrified atmosphere of 1870? What would the small band of colonial agitators and the Royal Colonial Institute do to block this move? The answer was, very little indeed. Opposition came from an entirely different quarter.

The cession of the Gambia in return for three small settlements on the Ivory Coast had first been officially proposed by the French government in March 1866.[3] The proposal had been welcomed in the Colonial Office and Adderley, the Conservative Parliamentary Under-Secretary, had seen the suggestion as a convenient method for implementing the recommendations of the 1865 Select Committee. But some apprehension was felt about the reaction of the general public to such a move, and the Colonial Secretary, the Duke of Buckingham, had vetoed the plan as inopportune. In 1868, however, the Liberal government, prompted by Governor Sir Arthur Kennedy, revived the proposal and suggested a partition of the coast to the French government in February 1870.[4] The French were delighted by the prospect and all seemed set fair for an early agreement.

But the direction of the British government's policy had become known in the colony and several merchants who had trading interests in the Gambia set about rousing opposition to the proposed transfer. A group of merchants headed by the London firm of Forster & Smith and including several other traders of long standing in the Gambia – T. C. Chown, T. F.

[3] See R. Catala, 'La Question de l'Échange de la Gambie Britannique contre les Comptoirs français du Golfe de Guinée de 1866 à 1876', *Revue d'Histoire des Colonies Françaises*, xxxv (1948) 114–36; also J. D. Hargreaves, *Prelude to the Partition of West Africa* (London, 1963) pp. 126–65.

[4] For details of the various stages of the discussion, see memo. by A. Hemming, 8 Oct., on Grant to Carnarvon, 6 Oct. 1874, C.O. 87/107.

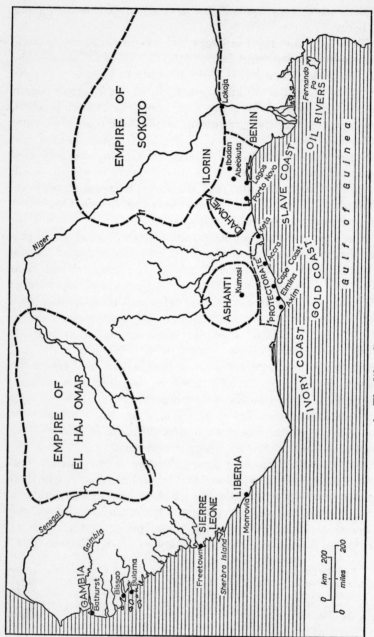

1 The West Coast of Africa, 1864-74

Quin and Thomas Brown – bombarded the Colonial Office with petitions and requests for information; Samuel John Forster secured the support of forty-one London firms; a petition from the inhabitants of Bathurst was presented to the Colonial Office; and Tomani Bojong, self-styled king of the Combo, sent in his own protest at being transferred to French protection.[5]

The merchants also began a campaign in the British press. Chown, Quin and Brown addressed themselves to *The Times* and visited the Colonial Office. Brown, a member of the Legislative Council of the colony, also roused the Wesleyan Missionary Society and interested the Manchester Chamber of Commerce who, after hearing a statement from him, sent in a memorial of objection in July 1870. The Bristol Chamber of Commerce followed suit three weeks later. Brown and Quin also circulated a printed memorandum on the Gambia to Members of Parliament.[6]

In June 1870 two Conservative M.P.s, Sir John Hay and R. N. Fowler, secured an undertaking from the Prime Minister that the Gambia would not be ceded without parliamentary assent. And on 15 July Sir John Hay, supported by E. B. Eastwick, Viscount Sandon and Baillie-Cochrane among the Conservatives and by the Liberals Thomas Bazley and R. A. Macfie, initiated a debate in the Commons protesting at the cession of British subjects against their will to a foreign power. The debate developed into a general attack on the government's colonial policy.[7]

Kimberley, the new Colonial Secretary, who had just taken up the seals of office, was clearly shaken by the clamour which faced him during the first few days of his secretaryship. After a long interview with the Gambia merchants on 14 July, the clash in the Commons on the 15th (the day France declared war on Prussia) and an attack by the Duke of Manchester in the Lords,

---

[5] C.O. 87/98 contains communications from Quin on 12 June; Forster & Smith, 18 June, 4 July, 3 Aug.; Brown, 12 July; Brown and Quin, 21 July; T. & T. C. Chown, 3 Aug. 1870. The Bathurst petition and that from the king of the Combo are to be found in Kennedy to Granville, 30 Apr., 15 June 1870, C.O. 87/96.

[6] Tregaskis to M.M.S., 11 May 1870, *M.M.S. Archives*, Gambia file, 1868–76; Manchester Chamber of Commerce to C.O., 4 July; Bristol Chamber of Commerce to C.O., 30 July; printed memo. from Brown and Quin for M.P.s, 26 July 1870, C.O. 87/98.

[7] 3 *Hansard*, 10 June 1870, cci 1842–3; 15 July 1870, cciii 339–67.

the new Colonial Secretary was only too relieved to shelve the plans for abandoning the Gambia when it became obvious that the necessary legislation could not be fitted into the session and that the Franco-Prussian war had brought the negotiations to a premature close. The project was never revived while Kimberley remained at the Colonial Office.

Thus the first concrete proposal by the Gladstone administration to cede a colony had been defeated in the critical summer of 1870 – not by the agitators who had caused such a storm of critical comment throughout the previous year, but by a small pressure group of local merchants who had enlisted the aid of London business interests, chambers of commerce and the small group of M.P.s who traditionally watched over British interests in West Africa. The 'imperialists' in the Cannon Street Hotel and the rooms of the Royal Colonial Institute had not raised a voice, let alone a finger, in effective protest.

II

Throughout the 1870s it was not colonies as such that attracted attention – there was no 'mass wave of imperialism'; instead it was issues such as the slave trade, humanitarianism and evangelicalism which received support from pressure groups in the lobbies of the House of Commons. This can clearly be shown in the agitation which culminated in the annexation of the Fiji Islands in 1874.

Ever since 1862, when the Palmerston government refused to accept the offer of cession of the islands made by Thakombau, self-styled Tui Viti or 'king of all Fiji', the British consul had often remained a helpless bystander as the lawlessness in the islands steadily mounted. The publicity accompanying the 1858 offer of cession and the growing importance attached to cotton cultivation, especially after the interruption to supplies caused by the American Civil War, had led to increased white settlement and investment in the islands culminating in the 'Great Fiji Rush' of 1870. The attendant lawlessness and the inability of the Fijian chiefs to combat this problem, despite a series of constitutional experiments in the 1860s, cried out for external intervention.[8]

Lord Kimberley, who took office just as the agitation against the negotiations for exchanging the Gambia was reaching its

[8] For details, see McIntyre, *Imperial Frontier*, pp. 221–66, 317–36.

climax, also found himself besieged with requests from the Australian colonies to annex Fiji. Kimberley was giving favourable consideration to a plan allowing New South Wales to annex the islands when the news of a *coup d'état* in Fiji, in which Thakombau had seized power and established yet another constitution, caused the Colonial Secretary to draw back and give *de facto* recognition to the new regime. However, this attempt to secure a breathing-space from action was not to last long. In December 1871 the murder of Bishop Patteson of Melanesia in the Santa Cruz islands caused a storm of protest at home.

The venerated missionary had been clubbed to death as an act of reprisal after a 'blackbirding' raid on the islands. The labour recruiters operated from Fiji, Queensland and New Zealand, raiding the New Hebrides, Solomon and Santa Cruz islands for labour to cultivate cotton in Fiji and Queensland, or went recruiting in eastern Polynesia for labour to collect guano, the valuable fertiliser, from Peru's off-shore islands. The British government had struggled with this rapidly growing problem for a number of years, but a bill making kidnapping a felony had met with objections from the Treasury, which had successfully vetoed a similar bill proposed by the Duke of Newcastle in 1862. The obvious difficulties concerning extra-territorial jurisdiction, Fiji being beyond British jurisdiction, were perplexing. The news of Bishop Patteson's murder led to a public outcry and further demands for the annexation of Fiji. More important, it brought to the forefront a significant pressure group of evangelicals and humanitarians which, combined with the commercial and colonial interests already pressing for government action, constituted a considerable lobby in favour of annexation.

The earlier proposal for annexation in 1858, which received favourable consideration from some government departments because of the strategic advantages to be gained from possessing the islands, had been urged by commercial interests, principally the Manchester Cotton Supply Association and Chamber of Commerce, and by humanitarian and missionary bodies, chiefly the Aborigines Protection Society and the Wesleyan Missionary Society. The missionaries had been particularly active. The Revd James Calvert had corresponded with Rear-Admiral J. E. Erskine, M.P., author of *Journal of a Cruise among the Islands of the Western Pacific*; the Revd William Arthur, general secretary to

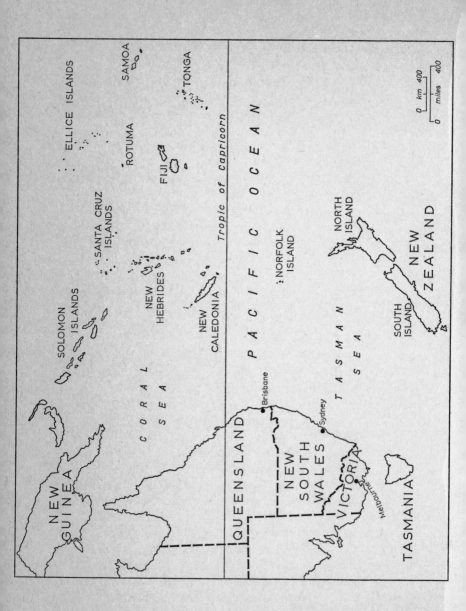

the society, had issued a pamphlet entitled *What is Fiji, the Sovereignty of which is offered to Her Majesty?*; and in the Australian colonies the missionaries joined hands with local commercial interests in advocating acceptance of the offer of cession. Alexander M'Arthur, son-in-law of the Revd W. B. Boyce, a former president of the Australian Methodist Conference and a general secretary of the Wesleyan Missionary Society in London, introduced a resolution in favour of annexation into the New South Wales legislature. An address advocating the same course was also received in the Colonial Office from the colony of Victoria.[9]

By 1871 this pressure group had regathered its forces and been considerably strengthened. The British Anti-Slavery Society now became more prominent. The secretary kept in close contact with the Aborigines Protection Society and the Wesleyan Missionary Society, even writing privately to the Revd James Calvert in Fiji. In October 1870 the society circularised the evangelical lobby – the Baptist Missionary Society, the Church Missionary Society, the London Missionary Society, the Reformed Presbyterian Church of Scotland Committee on Foreign Missions, the Society for the Propagation of the Gospel in Foreign Parts and the Wesleyan Missionary Society – in order to co-ordinate activity for publicising the evils of the Polynesian 'slave' trade.[10] In Parliament the supporters of the society, Arthur Kinnaird, R. N. Fowler, William M'Arthur, Admirals Wingfield and Erskine, and E. B. Eastwick, took up the cudgels. Arthur Kinnaird, a committee member of the Church Missionary Society and treasurer of the London Missionary Society, forwarded to Gladstone a letter, written by a Presbyterian missionary in the New Hebrides, concerning the activities of the *Latona* at Erromanga in the islands. The communication caused the Colonial Office to resurrect the Pacific Islanders' Protection Bill of 1862.[11] F. W. Chesson, secretary to the Aborigines Protection Society, tried to interest the Royal Colonial Institute with a paper on 'The Polynesian Labour Question', but that body refused to co-operate and the secretary, A. R. Roche, dissociated

[9] See Eldridge, *N.Z.J.H.*, I 171–84.

[10] A.S.S. circular, 30 Sept. 1870, *A.S.S. Papers*, Rhodes House, Oxford, Min. Book E.2/9.

[11] See O. W. Parnaby, 'Aspects of British Policy in the Pacific: The 1872 Pacific Islanders Protection Act', *H.S.A.N.Z.*, VIII (1957) 54–65.

the Institute from the views expressed in the paper.[12] But the real troublemaker from the government's point of view was Alderman William M'Arthur, M.P.

M'Arthur, the son of a Methodist minister, corresponded with Wesleyan missionaries in Fiji and spoke for the Wesleyan Missionary Society in Parliament. He became chairman of the London Wesleyan Conference in 1870. He was also on the committee of the Aborigines Protection Society and a member of the Anti-Slavery Society, the Evangelical Alliance and the British and Foreign Bible Society. His brother, Alexander, the New South Wales politician and trader who returned to London in the early 1860s, also belonged to the Aborigines Protection Society and the Anti-Slavery Society.[13] In June 1872 Alderman M'Arthur (supported by Admiral Erskine, a confidant of the Wesleyan missionaries and a spokesman for the Anti-Slavery Society), in calling for a 'protectorate' of Fiji, secured a declaration from Gladstone that on no account would Her Majesty's Government 'annex any territory, great or small, without the well-understood and expressed wish of the people to be annexed, freely and generously expressed, and authenticated by the best means the case would afford'.[14] Clearly, the next move would have to be made by the advocates for annexation.

In February 1873 M'Arthur enquired in the House of Commons whether the 1870 memorial from Fiji requesting British protection had been received. This document was duly forwarded to the Colonial Office by the Foreign Office in March 1873, after a report had arrived intimating that a letter in Thakombau's name had been despatched asking whether an offer of cession would be entertained by the British government. Kimberley, aware of the ever-increasing chaos in the islands and under pressure from his forthright Under-Secretary, Knatchbull-Hugessen, who was alarmed by American and German activity in the South Pacific, at last reluctantly agreed to endorse the proposed offer of cession. Gladstone, however, would have none of it. He could never give a promise 'to be party to any arrangement for adding Fiji and all that lies beyond it to the care of this

[12] Folsom, *Royal Empire Society*, pp. 136–7.
[13] For the activities of these two brothers, see T. McCullagh, *Sir William M'Arthur, K.C.M.G., a biography* (London, 1891).
[14] 3 *Hansard*, 25 June 1872, ccxii 217.

overdone and over-burdened Government and Empire'.[15] But Kimberley, stiffened by a deputation from the Aborigines Protection Society in May 1873,[16] remained adamant and Gladstone and the Cabinet finally agreed on 7 June to a Commission of Enquiry being sent to Fiji.

This decision was announced to the Commons a week later during a debate initiated by Alderman M'Arthur in which his call for annexation was endorsed by Admiral Erskine, Viscount Sandon and three supporters of the Aborigines Protection Society, vice-president Admiral Sir Charles Wingfield, committee member E. B. Eastwick and the banker Arthur Kinnaird. Gladstone's reply was not optimistic, although he privately admitted that 'the world without may be much more disposed to move in this matter than I am'.[17] Indeed, even the Royal Colonial Institute felt disposed at this stage to send a memorial to the Colonial Office urging annexation of the Fiji Islands, a move which they refused to repeat a year later.[18]

While awaiting the report of the two commissioners, E. Layard, H. M. Consul in Fiji, and Commodore J. Goodenough, senior naval officer of the Australian Station (who had obligingly visited the Wesleyan Missionary Society headquarters before leaving England), the advocates of annexation closed ranks. A 'Fiji Committee', formed under the auspices of the Aborigines Protection Society and the Royal Colonial Institute in August 1873, was re-formed shortly afterwards by the Aborigines Protection Society and the Wesleyan Missionary Society. This time the Royal Colonial Institute refused to associate itself with this body. F. W. Chesson, writing on behalf of the committee to C. W. Eddy, honorary secretary to the Institute, reminded him that the committee had been re-formed on the basis of two considerations :

1. That the Parliamentary leaders of the question are

---

[15] Gladstone to Kimberley, 26 Feb. 1873, *Kimberley Papers*, A/8c, quoted in McIntyre, *Imperial Frontier*, p. 255. See also the same author's 'New Light on Commodore Goodenough's Mission to Fiji, 1873–4', *H.S.A.N.Z.*, x (1962) 270–88.

[16] Deputation to Colonial Secretary, 14 May 1873, C.O. 83/4; see also *Australian and New Zealand Gazette*, 17 May 1873.

[17] Gladstone to Kimberley, 8 May 1873, *Kimberley Papers*, A/8c, quoted in McIntyre, *Imperial Frontier*, p. 255.

[18] Folsom, *Royal Empire Society*, p. 213.

responsible for the suggestion that a Deputation should
wait on the Prime Minister or the Colonial Secretary.

2. That also Mr Arthur has had an intimation conveyed to
   him from high quarters that if he wants Fiji annexed he
   must show that public opinion is in favour of annexation.[19]

But by the time this committee, which consisted of the M'Arthur
brothers, Arthur Kinnaird, the Revd W. Arthur and the Revd
W. B. Boyce, Admirals Wingfield and Erskine, and several M.P.s,
including Young, Jenkins and Corry, was fully constituted, a new
government had come into existence. The Gladstone administration had been replaced by that of Disraeli and the Earl of
Carnarvon now headed the Colonial Office. What would the new
Colonial Secretary do about Fiji?

Carnarvon was no more eager to annex the islands than his
predecessor. Nor did he like the way the two commissioners were
interpreting their instructions. One of his first acts was to telegraph the Governor of New South Wales requesting him to warn
the commissioners not to exceed their instructions by declaring
a British protectorate.[20] But the warning was of little avail.
Goodenough and Layard had become convinced soon after their
arrival that annexation was the only answer to Fiji's problems.
The settlers were clearly opposed to Thakombau's government;
peace was maintained only by the presence of the Royal Navy;
a virtual protectorate already existed; and Britain had an obvious
responsibility towards her settlers. They therefore worked to
engineer the offer of cession which they received on 20 March
1874.

The news of this development reached London in early April.
Queen Victoria was appalled at the thought of counting among
her subjects cannibals, stranglers of widows and perpetrators of
infanticide, but Disraeli privately advised her that these Fijians
were all Methodists and that it might be necessary to accept
the Sovereignty of this Southern Archipelago'.[21] The Colonial
Secretary was on tenterhooks. After Alderman M'Arthur had,
with great glee, drawn the attention of the Commons to the news
from Fiji, in the House of Lords Carnarvon could only plead

---

[19] Ibid., Chesson to Eddy, 28 May 1874.
[20] Carnarvon to Robinson, 23 Feb. 1874 (telegram), F.O. 58/142.
[21] Disraeli to Queen Victoria, 14 Apr. 1874, quoted in McIntyre, *Imperial
Frontier*, p. 328.

lack of official information. When the full report of the two commissioners arrived, however, he found, as feared, that he had been presented with a virtual *fait accompli*. He reported to Queen Victoria :

> looking to the opinion of New Zealand and Australia, and, as far as it can be gathered, of Parliament and this country, and looking also to the advantage which these islands possess as an intermediate station between America and Australia and the risks of great disorders arising unless some Government is constituted, it seems impossible to give a direct refusal to the cession.[22]

Accordingly, Carnarvon announced in the House of Lords on 17 July 1874 that if an unqualified offer of cession could be obtained by the Governor of New South Wales, the offer would not be denied. He concluded :

> I hardly like to say that England has a mission to extend her policy of colonisation in this part of the world, but at all events it does seem to me that there is an indirect duty which lies upon us, as far as we can, to take under our protection a place into which English capital has overflowed, in which English settlers are resident, in which it must be added, English lawlessness is going on, and in which the establishment of English institutions has been unsuccessfully attempted.[23]

M'Arthur and the members of the Aborigines Protection Society were jubilant. He sat 'spectacled and infinitely wise'[24] as Gladstone rose to denounce this 'sadly deluded philanthropy', warning the House of dark things to come :

> I see disagreeable and distorted phantoms stalking across the stage of this House. I see new Votes in the Estimates – new Votes for future wars in Fiji – new Votes for future engagements – a reproduction in an aggravated form of all we have had to lament in New Zealand.

Sir Wilfrid Lawson thought it better to leave the Methodists and cannibals to fight it out. Europeans had merely succeeded in

[22] Ibid. p. 332, Carnarvon to Queen Victoria, 13 July 1874.
[23] 3 *Hansard*, 17 July 1874, ccxxi 185.
[24] H. W. Lucy, *A Diary of Two Parliaments* (London, 1885), i 187–8.

introducing the principle of selectivity into Fijian eating habits : the cannibals only ate their enemies now.[25]

Carnarvon begged the Prime Minister for a Cabinet discussion of the question, but Disraeli, who was temporarily estranged from his Colonial Secretary because of the latter's conduct during a debate on the Public Worship Regulation Bill, refused to comply and left the matter entirely to Carnarvon's discretion.[26] Consequently Sir Hercules Robinson, the Governor of New South Wales, was despatched to Fiji and on 10 October 1874 Queen Victoria became the sovereign of another Crown colony and the proud possessor of Thakombau's favourite war club. As Sir Wilfrid Lawson, the genial champion of temperance, dryly observed : 'we have given them the measles and they have given us a war club'.[27]

Thus the Fiji Islands were reluctantly added to the empire at the discretion of the Colonial Secretary. The Liberal government had found itself virtually bound to intervene because of the political vacuum in the islands, and Kimberley later admitted : 'I think it would have been difficult to avoid taking Fiji.'[28] When the Conservative government came to power, Carnarvon found that the form such intervention was likely to take was almost decided on. Goodenough and Layard in exceeding their brief had virtually committed the British government to a policy of annexation – much to the joy of the small body of philanthropists in Britain and to the advantage of commercial interests in the Australian colonies. British rule had been extended through a curious mixture of moral obligation and political expedience. But Carnarvon was determined that this experiment in Polynesian government should remain a trial case. He refused to annex any more territory in the South Pacific and announced his intention to 'resist the cry for annexation' elsewhere.

III

The future of Fiji was not the only unresolved problem inherited by the Disraeli government. Carnarvon found himself in March

[25] 3 *Hansard*, 4 Aug. 1874, ccxxi 1287, 1295–9.
[26] Disraeli to Carnarvon, 8 Aug. 1874, quoted in Hardinge, *Life of Carnarvon*, II 74.
[27] 3 *Hansard*, 5 Aug. 1875, ccxxvi 570.
[28] Kimberley to Gladstone, 4 Nov. 1874, *Gladstone Papers*, Add. MSS. 44,225, p. 154.

1874 called upon to make equally far-reaching decisions concerning the future of the Gold Coast. The Conservative government came to power as the Ashanti war drew to its close and once again the British found themselves without a policy in West Africa.

The Cardwell policy of gradual withdrawal had perished in the heat of war and stood condemned in the words of Kimberley, the Liberal Colonial Secretary :

> for a long time to come our withdrawal would destroy all hope of improvement of the natives, who would speedily return to all their worst customs; and all prospect would be lost of opening the interior to commerce. Such a result would commend itself neither to philanthropists nor traders. For all present practical purposes therefore we may dismiss the question of retiring from the Coast.[29]

Carnarvon studied the problem afresh but was reluctantly forced to draw a similar conclusion. He refused, however, to accept that the choice was a simple question of withdrawal or annexation. Instead he hoped to find some way of meeting British obligations honourably without extending British sovereignty.

But what was to become of the 'protectorate' and the 'native custom' of domestic slavery? While the discussion continued in the Colonial Office with an intensive study of the situation by two of the younger clerks, a debate was initiated in Parliament on 27 April 1874 (and continued a week later on 4 May), in which it became clear that the body of opinion interested in Africa, the 'old Guard' headed by Sir John Hay and Arthur Mills and the 'sadly deluded philanthropists' led by Alderman William M'Arthur, would not tolerate any retreat from British responsibilities. A decision was impatiently awaited and Edward Jenkins, the new Radical M.P., whose speeches, it is said, struck terror into the hearts of many members, rapidly making him one of the least liked men in the House of Commons,[30] launched into an invective against the Disraeli government :

> It seems to me that H.M. Ministers suffer from a species of somnambulism, for they apparently walk about with their eyes

---

[29] Min. by Kimberley, 20 Feb., on M'Arthur's Question, 18 Feb. 1873, C.O. 96/104.

[30] Lucy, *Diary of Two Parliaments*, I 427–9.

open, but that their brains are shut. . . . The policy of the
Ministers is a policy of silence, for we do not hear a single
word as to the policy they intend to pursue.[31]

Eight days later Carnarvon announced his decision in the House
of Lords. There would be no withdrawal:

A great nation like ours must be sometimes prepared to discharge disagreeable duties; she must consent to bear burdens
which are inseparable from her greatness . . . it is certainly not
a desire of selfish interests or the ambition of larger empire
which bids us remain on the West Coast of Africa; it is simply
and solely a sense of obligations to be redeemed and of duties
to be performed.[32]

But neither was there to be any great advance. Instead the Gold
Coast forts were to be added to the island of Lagos and its out-
stations to form a new Crown colony on the model of the Straits
Settlements. Certain administrative improvements were to be
made and the problem of domestic slavery investigated.

This was hardly a new policy. Carnarvon had chosen to retain
the 'protectorate' and to meet British obligations by well-tried
means of informal empire. It is true that the new Crown colony
was soon empowered to legislate for the 'protectorate' (the 'protectorate' may be said to have been annexed administratively[33]),
but this hardly satisfied the government's critics who soon made
their views heard. The Hon. Evelyn Ashley (son of the factory
reformer), supported by W. E. Forster and G. J. Goschen,
introduced a motion into the Commons on 29 June 1874 calling
for the abolition of all slavery. The government was accused of
abolishing slavery only when it served their interests and of ignoring its existence when it proved inconvenient. Disraeli hurriedly
intervened to prevent a vote being taken by reassuring the House
that he personally hoped slavery could soon be abolished.[34]

Carnarvon had been quite content to pigeonhole the problem,
but Disraeli and the Cabinet now forced the Colonial Secretary
to reconsider his decision. Carnarvon reluctantly requested

---

[31] 3 *Hansard*, 4 May 1874, ccxviii 1649.
[32] 3 *Hansard*, 12 May 1874, ccxix 157–68.
[33] Order-in-Council, 6 Aug. 1874, *C.O. Confidential Prints* (Africa), C.O.
806/19, p. 6. See McIntyre, *Imperial Frontier*, p. 282.
[34] 3 *Hansard*, 29 June 1874, ccxx 607–41.

Governor George Strahan to enquire and report on the possibility of making an agreement with the 'protectorate' chiefs for the gradual abolition of domestic slavery.[35] Events then moved fast. Strahan, who had already discussed this problem with local chiefs on his own initiative, immediately recommended abolishing slavery as a legal status on the Gold Coast. Carnarvon was taken aback. But after having been convinced by Strahan that there was every chance of success, he endorsed the governor's plans for a series of local conferences. Having left the details and passed the responsibility to the man on the spot, the Colonial Secretary then sat back and watched as the governor formally took steps to make domestic slavery illegal. The proclamation was accepted quietly and Carnarvon, thanks to the initiative and courage of a local official, collected bouquets from his critics.

The Conservative policy announced in May 1874 had been mild enough. But the pressure exerted by a determined group of philanthropists had resulted in a major reform in Africa. This was one of those occasions when the colonial zealots succeeded in rousing the conscience of the House.

IV

Fear of a hostile reaction in Parliament was indeed an important factor in formulating policy and, on another occasion, forced the Disraeli government to give up its plans for reviving the Gambia exchange proposal with France. On this occasion the opposition was given a chance to crystallise and the Gambia Committee and the personnel involved resembled closely the pressure group who had urged the annexation of Fiji.

In April 1874 the French government revived the proposal to exchange the Gambia and in return offered the Ivory Coast and the Mellacourie.[36] Carnarvon welcomed the proposal. He recognised an easy mode of ridding the country of a sparsely populated and troublesome colony threatened by external aggression from the 'Marabouts' in the Combo and plagued internally by sanitary, economic and defence difficulties. The case for such an exchange seemed unanswerable. Furthermore, the British merchants were unlikely to revive the agitation of 1870 as only the Chown family

---

[35] For details, see McIntyre, *Imperial Frontier*, pp. 283–4.
[36] 'Correspondence respecting the Affairs of the Gambia and the Proposed Exchange with France', *Parl. P.* (1876) LII.

retained any substantial trading interests in the colony. In Britain the Foreign Secretary, Lord Derby, concluded: 'I see no harm in it; and after Fiji and the Gold Coast we are not likely to be reproached with a policy of colonial surrender'; but he warned the Colonial Secretary that 'the present Parliament is likely to be inspired with at least as much zeal for the integrity of the British possessions'.[37]

Carnarvon remained unperturbed and unhurried. He believed that once the obvious advantages of the exchange were explained, formal consultation with the Commons would suffice. Accordingly, no proposal was made to the French government until July 1875, when it was proposed to divide the coast into two spheres of influence leaving the British responsible in the Niger delta, the Gold Coast and Sierra Leone. At first French reaction was unfavourable, but so strong was the desire to achieve an understanding and maintain friendly relations with Great Britain that the French administration concurred.

Carnarvon now had to announce the terms to Parliament. But the Disraeli government had run into a storm. On 22 July 1875 the Prime Minister proposed dropping the controversial Merchant Shipping Bill after its inept handling by the responsible minister, the hapless Adderley. An embarrassing scene instigated by Samuel Plimsoll, who danced in rage on the floor of the House and shook his fist under the Prime Minister's nose, ensued in the Commons and a 'stopgap' bill was introduced instead. Disraeli, fearing opposition from the Gambia interest, was loath to introduce another controversial matter in the same parliamentary session. The matter would have to stand over. Accordingly, Carnarvon had to deny a report in *Le Moniteur* announcing that the arrangements for an exchange had been completed and stated in the Lords that negotiations were still pending, that the interests of the few British subjects would be safeguarded and that no decision would be taken until after parliamentary consideration in the new year. This delay was to wreck the project.[38]

The effect of this postponement was totally unexpected. The news that the project was still under discussion prompted those who opposed the exchange to organise their forces. In the Gambia, three Wesleyan missionaries, Babcock, Adcock and

[37] Derby to Carnarvon, 16 Dec. 1874, *Carnarvon Papers*, P.R.O. 30/6/8.
[38] See McIntyre, *Imperial Frontier*, pp. 287–9.

Fieldhouse, urged their parent society to oppose the plan and one of their number, Adcock, joined 150 Africans in signing a petition objecting to the transfer.[39] Letters from various Gambian merchants appeared in *The Times* during August 1875. Thomas Brown revived his earlier campaign, and in September Sir Thomas Bazley, the Liberal M.P. and merchant who was also a director and former chairman of the Manchester Chamber of Commerce, asked the Colonial Secretary to receive a deputation from that body. Another influential Manchester merchant with West African interests, J. F. Hutton, announced that the Chamber of Commerce had set up a committee to study the question. Carnarvon now requested from the French some concrete proposals for compensation to British trading interests before he approached Parliament.

In the opening weeks of 1876 the activities of the opposition intensified under the direction of the newly formed Gambia Committee. This *ad hoc* body, which operated like the Fiji Committee from rooms in the Canada Government Building, was under the chairmanship of Admiral Sir Charles Wingfield and had F. W. Chesson and C. Fitzgerald, a West Indian regiment officer, as honorary secretaries. The committee members included West African merchants T. F. Quin, David Brown, T. C. Chown and F. Swanzi, Sr, and the familiar representatives of the Aborigines Protection Society and the Wesleyan Missionary Society, Alderman William M'Arthur and his brother Alexander, Admiral Erskine, Samuel Gurney, the Revd W. B. Boyce and Dr Moffat of the London Missionary Society. This group, together with Edward Ashworth (president) and two members, T. Browning and J. F. Hutton, of the Manchester Chamber of Commerce, formed a deputation to Carnarvon expressing their concern about the proposed exchange.[40] Also in January 1876 the denizens of the Royal Colonial Institute surprisingly intervened and published a *Report on the Gambia Cession* drafted by Frederick Young. The Duke of Manchester subsequently addressed to the Colonial Office the objections of that august body to 'parting with any of the territories of the Empire'.[41]

[39] Babcock, Adcock and Fieldhouse to general secretary, 29 June 1875, *M.M.S. Archives*, Gambia file, 1868–76.
[40] *The Times*, 2 Feb. 1876.
[41] Reese, *History of the R.C.S.*, pp. 46–7; *P.R.C.I.* (1875–6).

About the same time two more pamphlets were published:
The Gambia and its Proposed Cession to France, by C. Fitzgerald,
secretary to the Gambia Committee; and *The Proposed Cession
of the British Colony of the Gambia to France*, by the Manchester
merchant J. F. Hutton, who was also trying to stir up French
antagonism to the exchange.[42] The Colonial Office received
additional memorials from the Liverpool Chamber of Commerce,
as well as representations from the firms of Spartali & Co.,
Swanzi & Co. and T. C. Chown. The redoubtable Thomas
Brown raised another petition from the local inhabitants which
further increased support from the British philanthropists.

Carnarvon was not unnaturally becoming apprehensive about
such widespread and well-organised opposition. But he was
pledged to bring the matter before Parliament and he trusted
that the terms would convince reasonable men of the advantages
of the exchange. But when, in the House of Lords on 17 February
1876, the Dukes of Manchester and Somerset, the Earls of
Lauderdale and Fortescue, and Lord Stanley of Alderley announced their implacable opposition to any cession of the
Gambia,[43] the Cabinet wavered and feared a complete rebuff of
their plans in the Commons. At this stage the negotiations with
France were suddenly broken off. A last-minute muddle had
arisen over the agreed terms and Carnarvon seized the opportunity to shelve the matter, blaming the Foreign Office for the
mess. Derby protested that the Colonial Office was 'in a hurry to
begin this negotiation, and in a hurry to break it off',[44] but the
Cabinet was relieved and Carnarvon insisted that the matter was
closed. Thus ended the second attempt to exchange the Gambia
with France.

Once again local missionaries and merchants had succeeded
in arousing not only the interest of the humanitarians and
evangelicals but the conscience of Parliament. The intervention
of this pressure group played an important role. Although there
was nothing like a coherently expressed body of 'public opinion',
the numbers of those interested in such problems were increasing
and they were beginning to organise themselves in a more
methodical fashion.

[42] Hargreaves, *Prelude to the Partition*, pp. 190, 193.
[43] 3 *Hansard*, 17 Feb. 1876, ccxxvii 374–94.
[44] Min. by Derby on memo. by C. B. Robertson, 21 Apr. 1876, quoted in
McIntyre, *Imperial Frontier*, p. 289.

Perhaps one of the most significant acts of the agitation concerning the Gambia, however, was the participation of the Royal Colonial Institute. In 1871 the Institute had been dubious about accepting a paper by F. W. Chesson on such a political topic as the Polynesian labour question.[45] The Institute had also refused to take part in petitioning the government about Fiji in 1874. But by 1875 that attitude was beginning to change, thanks, no doubt, to the influence of its president, the militant Duke of Manchester. In 1875, at the duke's suggestion, the Institute made an investigation into the Newfoundland Fisheries question despite the known disapproval of the Colonial Secretary. The Institute's interest in the proposed cession of the Gambia probably sprang from the belief that this move was to be made in return for the surrender of French claims to fishery rights in Newfoundland. After playing what its Council believed to be 'an important, if not determining, role in the subsequent decision of the Government to abandon the intended cession' of the Gambia,[46] the Institute was encouraged to take a more active interest in current topics. Their greatest opportunity came in the late 1870s with the movement pressing for the annexation of New Guinea.

v

The Australians had long cast covetous eyes on Papua, the part of New Guinea closest to their shores. After the publicity attached to the explorations of Captain Moresby, and when the London Missionary Society established itself on the south-east coast, the area became a subject of interest in Great Britain. One missionary, the Revd William Wyatt Gill, reported to the Governor of New South Wales that he hoped Great Britain would intervene and forestall the Germans, who were said to be interested in New Guinea.[47]

In March 1874 the new Colonial Secretary was forced to consider British policy when a letter from Labilliere urging British intervention in the area was received favourably in the Colonial Office. The Permanent Under-Secretary, Robert Herbert, a former Premier of Queensland, minuted:

[45] Folsom, *Royal Empire Society*, p. 136.
[46] Ibid. p. 215.
[47] See McIntyre, *Imperial Frontier*, pp. 342–50.

this is a much more important question to the Australian Colonies and to the Empire, than that of the annexation of Fiji. The great wealth and extent of New Guinea and its close proximity to Australia render the question of its ownership a somewhat pressing one. I do not think there is any hope of our being able to keep clear of interference with New Guinea. The brutalities of our traders must demand our frequent presence whenever they commence operations on its coast.[48]

Carnarvon requested the views of the Australasian governors. The result was only to be expected : the colonies were in general favourable to any action which would forestall intervention by foreign powers, but they were reluctant to assume the responsibility and expense of annexing New Guinea themselves.

Carnarvon was equally reluctant to contemplate any move by the British government. In April 1875 he received a deputation from the Royal Colonial Institute urging the annexation of the eastern half of New Guinea. Led by its forceful president, the Duke of Manchester, the deputation included many of the founder members of the original Colonial Society : Sir Charles Nicholson, James Youl, Leonard Wray, Sir Charles Clifford and Francis de Labilliere; two former colonial governors, R. G. MacDonnell and Sir James Fergusson, recently back from New Zealand; and a number of parliamentary watchdogs and representatives of the humanitarian and evangelical societies : W. T. McCullagh Torrens, Arthur Kinnaird, Lord Stanley of Alderley, R. N. Fowler, William M'Arthur and F. W. Chesson. Carnarvon thanked the deputation for their views but regretted that it was 'impossible to appropriate every territory and every island' and instead requested 'some breathing time before we are required to act on a large scale'.[49]

A policy decision soon became necessary, however, when the New Guinea Colonisation Association, a commercial venture sponsored by the Duke of Manchester and the eccentric Lord Stanley of Alderley, who had lived in the Straits Settlements for many years, requested official support for their scheme aimed at establishing settlements in Papua. Carnarvon decided that 'at present I am prepared to risk the cry for annexation' and

[48] Min., 3 Apr., on Labilliere to Carnarvon, 26 Mar. 1874, C.O. 234/34. See Reese, *History of the R.C.S.*, pp. 50–1.
[49] Ibid. pp. 52–3; also *The Times*, 3 May 1875.

announced that he could not admit that 'the responsibility of the measure rests exclusively with the Imperial Government' unless a foreign power intervened.[50] As there seemed no likely prospect of this, Carnarvon effectively shelved the question for a number of years. Nevertheless, the agitation continued.[51]

VI

In reality the part played by the Royal Colonial Institute in influencing the decisions of the government during the 1870s was little more than minor fringe activity. From this brief survey it may be seen that whenever any effective opposition to the government's policies in Africa and the Pacific occurred, apart from that stimulated by individual economic interests, it normally sprang from the activities of the various humanitarian and evangelical societies whose aid may or may not have been enlisted by local interests.

Undoubtedly the most active of these bodies was the Aborigines Protection Society. This fact was well known in the Colonial Office, where Herbert considered that 'this not very high-principled Society has been allowed undue latitude in bringing vague charges against Governments and dictating his duty to the Secretary of State'.[52] Nevertheless, the Aborigines Protection Society could organise support in varied circles, as the signatories to one memorial concerning the rights of civilised non-Europeans in South Africa clearly showed. These included Charles Darwin, T. F. Buxton, Lord Alfred Churchill, R. N. Fowler, Sir Charles Dilke, Joseph Chamberlain, A. J. Mundella, the M'Arthur brothers and Edward Jenkins.[53]

The British Anti-Slavery Society was another humanitarian group which took a close interest in government actions. Their main interests lay in the operation of slavery and the treatment of coolie labourers throughout the world. It was this society which caused the government hurriedly to retrace its steps in the

[50] Carnarvon to Robinson, 8 Dec. 1875, *C.O. Confidential Prints*, C.O. 808/15.

[51] Folsom, *Royal Empire Society*, p. 219; Reese, *History of the R.C.S.*, pp. 53–8.

[52] Min., 13 June, on A.P.S. to C.O., 12 June 1874, C.O. 96/113.

[53] A.P.S. to C.O., no date (July 1877), C.O. 48/484. See the *Transactions* and *Papers* of the society, Rhodes House, Oxford, for further details concerning the activities of this body.

issue of the Fugitive Slave Circular by the Admiralty. The Admiralty was prepared to surrender fugitive slaves under certain circumstances, but the Cabinet decided, at the last moment, that humanitarian opinion in the House was too strong for this to be sanctioned in 1875.[54] The evangelical societies also received a respectful hearing in the Colonial Office and were well represented by the Wesleyan Missionary Society, the London Missionary Society and the Church Missionary Society.

In general, the personnel of these various bodies are strikingly similar. For example, at one stage Samuel Gurney was president of both the Aborigines Protection Society and the Anti-Slavery Society, and Admiral Sir Charles Wingfield, T. F. Buxton, the M'Arthur brothers and R. N. Fowler were to be found as members, very often on the committees, of both societies. Most members were also active in the missionary movement: Admirals Wingfield and Erskine, and William and Alexander M'Arthur, were Methodists; T. F. Buxton, Sir Bartle Frere and Arthur Mills were members of the Church Missionary Society; R. N. Fowler, William M'Arthur and R. A. Macfie were also members of the Evangelical Alliance; Arthur Kinnaird was a Scottish Presbyterian and P. A. Taylor a Quaker. Thus the small group of philanthropists active in the societies and Parliament were a closely compact group. Doubtless the clue to the influence of these zealots lies in the varied connections and interests of such people as Alderman William M'Arthur, M.P., a woollen draper with Australasian connections and future Lord Mayor of London; R. N. Fowler, M.P., chairman of the Anti-Opium Society, treasurer of the Aborigines Protection Society, twice Lord Mayor of London, who belonged to an old Quaker banking family and in 1858 supported some forty religious societies;[55] F. W. Chesson, a journalist prominent in many philanthropic societies and involved with the Jamaica, Gambia and Afghan Committees, the Anti-Opium Society and the Eastern Question Association; R. A. Macfie, M.P., a sugar refiner, who was associated with the Royal Colonial Institute, the Evangelical Alliance, the National Association for the Promotion of Social Science and the Liverpool Chamber of Commerce; Edward Jenkins, barrister, journalist, Radical M.P., Canadian Agent-General 1874–6 and committee

[54] Buckle, v 296–8.
[55] J. S. Flynn, *Sir Robert Fowler* (London, 1893) p. 127.

member of the Anti-Slavery Society; and P. A. Taylor, Radical
M.P., Nonconformist freedom-fighter, proprietor of the *Examiner*
and partner in Samuel Courtauld's company of silk mercers. And
whereas it is noticeable that the economic interests which brought
pressure to bear on the Colonial Office in West Africa, Malaya,
the Pacific and elsewhere were many and varied, among the
philanthropists there was a marked continuity of personnel and
ideas.[56]

Nor were these philanthropic watchdogs a group peculiar to
the 1870s. Their existence can be traced throughout the mid-
Victorian period. In the mid-1860s, for example, J. S. Mill's
committee formed to prosecute ex-Governor Eyre for putting
down a rising in Jamaica with considerable force,[57] bore marked
similarity to many of the *ad hoc* committees formed in the 1870s.
The nerve-centre of Mill's committee was the Canada Government Building (the future headquarters of the Aborigines Protection Society and of many other pressure groups), and as usual
F. W. Chesson served as honorary secretary and P. A. Taylor as
the treasurer. Under the chairmanship of Charles Buxton the
committee included many familiar names : McCullagh Torrens,
T. F. Buxton, Alexander M'Arthur, Lord Alfred Churchill and
Chamerorzow, secretary to the Anti-Slavery Society until 1870.

In the late 1870s, during the Bulgarian atrocities campaign, a
'Parliamentary Committee on the Eastern Question' was formed
to watch developments in the east. Again the committee worked
from Canada Building, King Street, Westminster, and F. W.
Chesson served as honorary secretary with P. A. Taylor as his
associate. The moral conscience of the House of Commons was
represented by Evelyn Ashley, Sir Wilfrid Lawson (the temperance leader) and Henry Richard of the Peace Society.

[56] In Malaya, local interests were looked after by the London-based
Straits Settlements Association, founded in 1868 by a group of merchants
under the presidency of John Crawfurd, the veteran ex-governor. But this
pressure group received little attention until it secured parliamentary
representation. By 1872 the association had ten M.P.s among its members,
including Fowler. The eccentric Lord Stanley of Alderley, who had resided
in the Straits for some years, was another who kept a close watch on British
actions in the Malay States, and on one occasion his motion censuring the
government in May 1874 forced Carnarvon to make up his mind as to future
policy in this area. See McIntyre, *Imperial Frontier*, pp. 298–9.

[57] B. Semmel, *The Governor Eyre Controversy* (London, 1962); *A.S.S.
Papers*, Min. Book E.5/6.

Needless to say, the committee also included William and
Alexander M'Arthur, T. F. Buxton, A. J. Mundella and Edward
Jenkins, with the Revd William Arthur and Admiral Sir Charles
Wingfield in attendance.[58] From this committee sprang not only
the Eastern Question Conference but the Eastern Question
Association. Many of these men also served on the Afghan
Committee and the South Africa Committee in the 1880s. Thus
not only was the personnel of the various committees concerned
with philanthropic, religious and moral issues in the 1860s, 1870s
and 1880s remarkably similar, but they also operated over a
considerable period of time.

The solid work of the philanthropic group must, however, be
seen in perspective. There was a multitude of campaigns, but the
occasions when they exercised any real influence over government decisions, as in the abolition of domestic slavery on the
Gold Coast, the annexation of Fiji and in the amendment of the
Fugitive Slave Circular in 1875, were very rare indeed. Most of
the time pressure groups could exert influence only when external
factors favoured British action. Then they could amass arguments
and build up a case. But even then the role of such pressure
groups should not be over-emphasised. In South Africa, for
example, the largest field of British intervention and expansion
in the 1870s, the historian of that decade has noted a surprising
absence of commercial considerations and pressure groups at
work. Instead, C. F. Goodfellow painted a picture of imperial
policy as the product of personal hopes and visions, with non-
Europeans at the mercy of the irresponsible wills of individuals.[59]
Here, truly, was the mainspring of British policy. Rarely was
policy formulated in Whitehall. Occasionally circumstances were
ripe for the personal dreams of politicians, such as Carnarvon's
confederation scheme, to be put into effect, but more often than

[58] R. T. Shannon, *Gladstone and the Bulgarian Agitation, 1876* (London,
1963) p. 58. For the connection with the Jamaica Committee, see ibid.
pp. 206–9. F. W. Chesson, secretary to the A.P.S., seems to have been a key
figure in organising many of these *ad hoc* committees. For much of this
information on Chesson I am indebted to Mrs Susan Willmington.

[59] C. F. Goodfellow, *Great Britain and South African Confederation,
1868–81* (Cape Town, 1966) esp. pp. 217–19. However, Goodfellow is not
entirely reliable on this matter. Carnarvon's confederation scheme was at first
welcomed by the A.P.S. and South African mercantile interests. See the
report of the deputation of South African merchants, 26 Oct. 1876, C.O
879/10.

not it was the actions of the man on the spot, a Sir Bartle Frere in South Africa, a Jervois in Malaya, a Goodenough in Fiji, a Glover, Wolseley or Strahan in West Africa, a Lytton in India, who initiated the events which determined British 'policy'. Local conditions together with the aims and reactions of indigenous rulers and inhabitants dictated British intervention to a far greater extent than any pressure group in Great Britain.

VII

No British government wished to extend its sovereignty beyond the periphery of empire into the areas where British interests and settlers had penetrated. The traditional reluctance to intervene, influenced by former failures of 'acclimatisation' and administration, continued into the 1870s. When Britain found it necessary to deal with indigenous peoples, she generally drew on Indian experience and did so by indirect means. In Malaya the sultans were retained; in West Africa British influence but not territory was extended; in Fiji Sir Arthur Gordon ruled through the chiefs, as Sir William MacGregor attempted to do in Papua in the 1880s. In all these decisions the doctrine of trusteeship played an increasingly important role and the humanitarian element was due, to a large extent, to the watchdogs of the philanthropic societies. But if the more favourable attitude towards empire which came about in the 1870s gave them a louder voice, it did not guarantee them greater effect. Indeed, when they proposed the extension of British rule the societies sometimes found their greatest opponents within their own ranks, especially among the Quakers and Pacifists. What more determined custodian of the principles of the Manchester School could be found in the 1870s than P. A. Taylor, the Radical, Nonconformist M.P. for Leicester, who contested every item of government extravagance? Expansion was by no means popular in the 1870s.

It is noticeable, in fact, that in all the advances made in the 1870s the British government was carefully avoiding a deliberate policy of expansion, whether the government was Liberal or Conservative, that of Gladstone or Disraeli. The Conservative government's decision to annex Fiji and extend British influence in Malaya and the Gold Coast, all moves in perfect conformity with Kimberley's ideas, should not be regarded as 'forward movements' but rather as experiments in providing order and jurisdiction without assuming full sovereignty.[60] Even the annexation of Fiji was to be a limited experiment : Carnarvon refused to annex any more Pacific islands. The decision to appoint a High Commissioner for the Western Pacific was yet another experiment in securing law and order without assuming actual sovereignty.[61] Traditional Palmerstonian ideas of informal expansion and supremacy still held good.

Both Liberal and Conservative governments in the 1870s fought a rearguard action against expansion on the periphery of empire, in the tropical areas which were to become the prizes of the 1880s. The Conservative government's policy differed little from that of its predecessor. The expansionist pressure groups of humanitarians, missionaries and traders and specially constituted committees, the real pioneers of the 'New Imperialism', were equally unwelcome to both governments. The decisions to extend influence followed the lines of minimum intervention. In fact in the 1870s this was all that was normally desired : minimum intervention to achieve an immediate and limited objective.

And yet by 1880, as Koebner and Schmidt have shown,[62] 'imperialism' had become an anti-Disraeli slogan. Gladstone made much of this in his Midlothian campaign, and in the general election of 1880 the Liberals neatly dished the Conservatives over the question of imperial policy – the platform the Conservatives had used to mount unsuccessful attacks on the Liberals in 1870 and 1872. In 1880 Gladstone, who ten years before had been accused of wishing to dismember the empire, became Prime Minister again and Disraeli, defender of empire, was rejected by the electorate. What was the basis of that aspect of the Liberals' attack on Disraeli's 'imperialism'? Why did the charge become a useful political slogan in the armoury of the Liberals at a time when the British were reluctantly beginning to accept ideas of imperial mission and the 'white man's burden';

[60] McIntyre, *Imperial Frontier*, passim.

[61] W. D. McIntyre, 'Disraeli's Colonial Policy: The Creation of the Western Pacific High Commission, 1874–7', *H.S.A.N.Z.*, IX (1960) 279–94. See also D. Scarr, *Fragments of Empire: A History of the Western Pacific High Commission, 1877–1914* (Canberra, 1968).

[62] Koebner, *Imperialism*, pp. 135–65. According to *The Times*, 11 Mar. 1880, 'Imperialism was a word invented to stamp Lord Beaconsfield's supposed designs with reprobation'.

and when the country, on the verge of another phase of expansionism, was about to participate in the partition of large areas of the world? What, in short, was Disraeli's contribution to British ideas on 'imperialism'?

7

Disraeli's Imperial Ideas

AT the Crystal Palace banquet in June 1872 Disraeli posed as a defender of the empire which the Liberals had laboured to disband for forty years. In view of the agitation of 1869–70, and in the light of rapidly changing world conditions, it seemed a popular line of attack. But the empire bandwagon proved no asset to the Tory propaganda handcart. The so-called 'turn of the tide' was not followed by a wave of popular imperialism. Indeed, in 1880 the Liberals were able to utilise distrust of 'imperialism' and policies of intervention in their attack on the government; and Disraeli's manifesto was to be decisively rejected at the polls. Was there then a vast difference between the parties as Disraeli had tried to suggest? Professor Koebner has asserted that, on the contrary, 'a distinctive Conservative attitude to Empire questions was scarcely in evidence before the second Salisbury administration'.[1] We have already seen that in 1874 the policy of the Conservatives in the tropics differed little from that of their predecessors. What then did the years 1874–80 add to the British outlook on empire? What exactly was the significance of Disraeli's impact?

I

Disraeli remains one of several Victorian statesmen around whom controversy still rages. The passions aroused by his controversial career did not die with him. Indeed, the completion in 1920 by G. E. Buckle of the first detailed biography of this colourful political figure was the occasion of a violent attack on Disraeli's

[1] Koebner, *Imperialism*, p. 111.

political principles.[2] And the discussion has continued into the present decade, recently receiving perhaps its most majestic addition in the volume by Robert Blake.[3] The latest biographer, however, has devoted little attention to Disraeli's imperial ideas. Disraeli's contribution to British imperialism still awaits more detailed examination before the diametrically opposed views of his critics and admirers can either be cast aside or reconciled.

Disraeli's famous Crystal Palace address, delivered on 24 June 1872 at a banquet following a lively conference of the National Union of Conservative and Constitutional Associations, continues to be at the centre of the contending viewpoints. Most writers have awarded it a significant place either in Great Britain's imperial history or in the annals of the Conservative party. George Buckle called it 'the famous declaration from which the modern conception of the British Empire largely takes its rise', and C. A. Bodelsen heralded it as initiating 'the connexion between Imperialism and Conservatism'.[4] As recently as 1959 Sir James Butler referred to the address as a 'landmark in the history of the Conservative party, which had hitherto, with few exceptions, not noticeably differed from the Whigs in its views on colonial subjects'.[5] It is only in the last decade that the importance of the Crystal Palace speech has been challenged. According to one recent critic, 'friend and foe alike have accorded it a significance which it does not wholly deserve'.[6]

The contents of the speech, however, were subjected from the very first to the most varied of interpretations. Disraeli's words have been both praised and damned. Buckle's suggestion that the speech was a creative and prophetic act hardly survived the publication of his work. Professor J. L. Morison, in a spectacular

[2] J. L. Morison, 'The Imperial Ideas of Benjamin Disraeli', *C.H.R.*, I (1920) 267–80.

[3] R. Blake, *Disraeli* (London, 1966).

[4] Buckle, v 196; Bodelsen, pp. 120–3.

[5] Butler, 'Imperial Question in British Politics, 1868–80', *C.H.B.E.*, III 41. Similar interpretations have been put forward in Carrington, *The British Overseas*, pp. 666–7; Burt, *Evolution of the British Empire–Commonwealth*, pp. 449–50; J. A. Williamson, *The Modern Empire and Commonwealth* (London, 1958) pp. 183–5; Walker, *The British Empire*, pp. 80–1.

[6] S. R. Stembridge, 'Disraeli and the Millstones', *J.B.S.*, v (1965) 122. See also Koebner, *Imperialism*, p. 109. Blake noted that in the forty-five pages which Disraeli's Manchester Free Trade Hall and Crystal Palace speeches take up in Kebbel's edition of his speeches, the subject of empire occupies less than two pages.

tirade against anything appertaining to Disraeli, retorted in 1920 that Disraeli was completely ignorant of colonial questions and was panic-stricken by the most ordinary difficulties of colonial administration. Disraeli, in fact, had failed hopelessly at understanding 'the essence of the modern British Commonwealth'.[7] Four years later this point of view received additional impetus from the work of the distinguished Danish scholar whose *Studies in Mid-Victorian Imperialism* helped to formulate the orthodox historical interpretation of Disraeli's imperial ideas.

Professor Bodelsen suggested in 1924 that Disraeli's intervention in 1872 was due 'less to his own conviction of the greatness of the cause of Imperialism, than to the realisation that here was a new chance of "dishing the Whigs" and of monopolising for the Conservatives a cause which was sure to be popular with the constituencies'. Disraeli had shown little interest in colonial problems before 1872, except when he saw some advantage for the Conservative party, and was to play little part in colonial affairs after that date. Moreover, Bodelsen asserted, the ideas expressed in the speech which initiated 'the somewhat undeserved association of Imperialism with the Conservative party' were not only unoriginal but betrayed complete ignorance of colonial history and development. That Disraeli should have made such a speech at such a time merely indicated that the new ideas had gained the day.[8]

This interpretation still held good forty years later. Professor Koebner repeated and amplified the charges when he asserted that Disraeli's sudden concern for the integrity of the British empire was completely new and unexpected; previously he had shunned the subject. Disraeli was merely indulging in demagogic self-advertisement, and any 'attempt to antedate the "imperialism" of Disraeli and to understand his pertinent utterances made from 1872 onwards as the outgrowth of life-long convictions would be futile'. Moreover, the ideas he expressed were not only unoriginal and impracticable but lacked historical insight. The speech was basically 'a criticism in retrospect' aimed at the Liberal party. Its renown, however, was unjustified : 'It is quite mistaken to believe that the Crystal Palace speech inaugurated an ideological link between Empire championship and

[7] Morison, *C.H.R.*, I 271–3.
[8] Bodelsen, pp. 120–3.

Conservatism.' This was the conclusion of the foremost student of the semantics of imperialism.[9]

Students of Disraeli have reached different conclusions. The work of two recent writers and their detailed examinations of Disraeli's relevant utterances in the pages of Monypenny and Buckle has enabled an entirely different interpretation to be placed upon Disraeli's interest in the British empire.[10] Placed in a different perspective, it is not only possible to trace continuity in Disraeli's views on the importance to Great Britain of her empire, but it is also possible to show that most of the charges put forward by Disraeli's critics concerning his Crystal Palace speech were either unfounded, misplaced or irrelevant. But first, what did Disraeli have to say that sparked off so much controversy?

II

Disraeli rarely made speeches to mass audiences and the words he spoke at the Crystal Palace, of which so much has been made, were tantalisingly brief. He recurred to a familiar theme that the Liberals were the 'continental' or 'cosmopolitan' party while the Conservatives belonged to the truly 'national party'. The three great objects of Conservative ideology were to maintain the ancient institutions of the country, to uphold the empire and to carry out a programme of social reform. In all these aims, Disraeli asserted, the working classes were the Conservatives' natural allies: they 'are proud of belonging to a great country and wish to maintain its greatness . . . they believe on the whole that the greatness and the empire of England are to be attributed to the ancient institutions of the land'.

Disraeli then attempted to show that during the previous forty years there had been 'no effort so continuous, so subtle, supported by so much energy, and carried on with so much ability and acumen, as the attempts of Liberalism to effect the disintegration of the Empire of England'. The colonies had been constantly paraded as a drain on British resources, and when 'those subtle views were adopted by the country under the plausible plea of granting self-government to the Colonies, I confess that I myself

[9] Koebner, *Imperialism*, pp. 107–10.
[10] See Stembridge, *J.B.S.*, v 126–39; McIntyre, *Imperial Frontier*, pp. 20–6.

thought that the tie was broken'. It was not the grant of responsible government that Disraeli objected to, however, but the way
in which it was conceded :

> self-government, in my opinion, when it was conceded, ought
> to have been conceded as part of a great policy of Imperial
> consolidation. It ought to have been accompanied by an
> Imperial tariff, by securities for the people of England for the
> enjoyment of the unappropriated lands which belonged to the
> Sovereign as their trustee, and by a military code which should
> have precisely defined the means and responsibilities by which
> the Colonies should be defended, and by which, if necessary,
> this country should call for aid from the Colonies themselves. It
> ought, further, to have been accompanied by the institution of
> some representative council in the metropolis, which would
> have brought the Colonies into constant and continuous
> relations with the Home Government.

Fortunately the Liberal attempt at disbanding the empire had
failed because of the sympathy of the colonies with the mother
country :

> They have decided that the empire shall not be destroyed; and
> in my opinion no Minister in this country will do his duty who
> neglects any opportunity of reconstructing as much as possible
> our Colonial Empire, and of responding to those distant sym-
> pathies which may become the source of incalculable strength
> and happiness to this land. Therefore, gentlemen, with respect
> to the second great object of the Tory party also – the main-
> tenance of the Empire – public opinion appears to be in favour
> of our principles – that public opinion which, I am bound to
> say, thirty years ago, was not favourable to our principles, and
> which, during a long interval of controversy, in the interval
> had been doubtful.[11]

Thus spake Disraeli the words around which controversy has
raged ever since. Apart from the sparkle of Disraeli's oratory,
little interest was shown in the speech by contemporaries. *The
Times* saw no startling originality, calling it, in fact, a 'good
orthodox Conservative speech', and regarded it merely as 'an

[11] T. E. Kebbel (ed.), *Selected Speeches of the Late Earl of Beaconsfield*
(London, 1882) ɪɪ 523–34.

attempt to represent the Conservative party as exercising a constant healthy influence over the legislation of the last forty years'.[12]

The charges levelled against Disraeli by subsequent writers were to a large extent unfounded. It is untrue to suggest, for example, that these ideas were entirely new to the speaker, and indeed those historians who have made a detailed study of Disraeli's earlier writings, letters and speeches have been able to trace the ideas expressed – so unexpectedly we are told in 1872 – back to the 1830s and 1840s.[13] Disraeli had often reverted to the problem of colonial tariffs, the need for some sort of system for imperial defence and the idea of a representative council. And he had made similar remarks regarding the preservation of waste lands in 1849.[14] Even the attempt to equate the Liberals with the separatists was not new. Professor Koebner may have believed that Disraeli 'would have been at a loss, if he had been challenged to explain why he had failed to disclose the alleged Liberal conspiracy against the Empire at an earlier date'. But Disraeli would probably have retorted, quite truthfully, that he had done precisely this in 1863.[15] In fact the whole of the Crystal Palace speech had been more or less foreshadowed a decade earlier.

It is misleading to suggest, therefore, that the ideas Disraeli put forward in 1872 were new to the Conservative leader or that he had borrowed them from the Colonial Reformers or lifted them from the pages of *Blackwood's Magazine*.[16] It is true that Disraeli was not being original – the ideas had been well aired elsewhere – but the ideas were not suddenly adopted by Disraeli for political gain in 1872.

[12] *The Times*, 27 June 1872.

[13] The material for such a study can easily be found in W. Hutcheon (ed.), *Whigs and Whiggism: The Political Writings of Benjamin Disraeli* (New York, 1914) pp. 297–301, 408–30; Buckle, I 227, 283, 321; II 88–9; III 3-4, 23–4, 233–7, 333–5; IV 231, 434; 3 *Hansard*, CXII 1040–1; CXIX 143; CLXVIII 867–72; CLXIX 95–6; CLXXVII 1575–8; *The Times*, 7 June 1852, 29 June 1863.

[14] Buckle, III 233–7. Stembridge, *J.B.S.*, V 132, suggests that Disraeli's concern for waste lands was the 'only novelty at the Crystal Palace'.

[15] Koebner, *Imperialism*, p. 111. Cf. *The Times*, 29 June 1863: 'The Liberals are of the opinion that the relations between the metropolis and the people of the Colonies should be abrogated. We are not.'

[16] See Koebner, *Imperialism*, p. 107; Burt, *Evolution of the British Empire–Commonwealth*, p. 450; Thornton, *The Imperial Idea*, p. 10. Bodelsen (p. 123) suggests that Disraeli obtained his ideas from *Blackwood's Magazine*, CVI (1869) 772–6.

In fact many of the charges made against Disraeli are mis-placed. Disraeli was simply indulging in a piece of political propaganda at a well-publicised party conference and too much significance has been attached to his words by later writers. Disraeli could not have known that he was planting a 'great signpost at the start of the highway to the "New Imperialism"', or that he was anticipating the ideas of Joseph Chamberlain. And if certain historical commentators mistakenly attributed greater importance to Disraeli's words than was really justified, other writers committed a more grievous error in trying to show that he was tarred with the same brush with which he was trying to blacken his political opponents.

In his *Studies in Mid-Victorian Imperialism*, Professor Bodel-sen put forward the theory that Disraeli himself had held separatist views in the 1850s and 1860s, basing this opinion on two quotations from Disraeli's letters: 'These wretched colonies will all be independent, too, in a few years, and are a millstone round our necks',[17] written in 1852; and his equally famous statement to Lord Derby in 1866:

> what is the use of these colonial deadweights which *we do not govern*? . . . Leave the Canadians to defend themselves; recall the African Squadron; give up the Settlements on the west coast of Africa, and we shall make a saving which will, at the same time, enable us to build ships and have a good budget.[18]

Bodelsen maintained that these statements were representative of Disraeli's views on empire before 1872 and cited the opinions of Goldwin Smith, Grant Duff and Sir William Gregory in support of this interpretation.

It is this theory which has been most successfully demolished by recent students of Disraeli. S. R. Stembridge has shown that little credence can be given to the statements of Bodelsen's three witnesses and has suggested that the two most oft-quoted state-ments by Disraeli on empire were mere outbursts in moments of irritation. Professor McIntyre has suggested that these remarks should be read in a specific way and not constructed into an

[17] Disraeli to Malmesbury, 13 Aug. 1852, quoted in Earl of Malmesbury, *Memoirs of an Ex-Minister* (London, 1884) I 343–4.
[18] Disraeli to Derby, 30 Sept. 1866, quoted in Buckle, IV 476–7.

elaborate theory of aversion to empire.[19] In fact Disraeli's critics
never understood Disraeli's position. He was not a separatist in
the 1860s, nor was he an expansionist in the 1870s. Indeed,
whereas it has been asserted that Disraeli's limited interest in
colonial affairs after 1872 merely demonstrates the Conservative
leader's insincerity and opportunism, in reality this criticism
springs from a basic misunderstanding of Disraeli's imperial
ideas. Disraeli had never been, nor did he claim to be, interested
in individual colonial problems, but he was interested in the
potential value of the empire to British power and prestige. Had
his earlier critics appreciated this simple fact, they would not
have expected the Prime Minister to show any interest in colonial
problems after 1874 and would not have been surprised that
Disraeli's major concerns as Prime Minister were the Indian
empire and British foreign policy in the east.[20] In this respect
their criticisms were entirely misplaced.

In any case, as Professor Koebner has pointed out, the Crystal
Palace speech was nothing more than a 'criticism in retrospect,
not a programme or statement of policy':[21] Disraeli regretted
that the Liberals had not adopted a policy of 'imperial consolidation' in the 1850s. It is surely irrelevant, then, to criticise
Disraeli's ideas as being impracticable in the 1870s. In suggesting
that Great Britain should respond 'to those distant sympathies
which may become the source of incalculable strength and happiness to this land', Disraeli had not advocated turning the clock
back twenty years. No doubt, had the ideas mentioned by
Disraeli been implemented in 1872, the connection with the
colonies would have been severed, as Professors Morison, Bodelsen and Koebner asserted. But where is the evidence that Disraeli
had any intention of implementing such plans?[22] Equally
irrelevant is Professor Morison's lament that Disraeli failed 'to
understand the essence of the modern British Commonwealth'.[23]
It would have been extremely surprising if he had. It would be

---

[19] Stembridge, *J.B.S.*, v 124–6; McIntyre, *Imperial Frontier*, pp. 21–3.

[20] Disraeli's subsequent interest in purely colonial affairs can be traced in
Buckle, v 258–9, vi 515; *The Times*, 26 Jan., 2 Feb., 10 Nov. 1874, 10 Nov.
1875, 19 Sept. 1879; 3 *Hansard*, ccxxi 396, ccxxvii 1726, ccxli 1773.

[21] Koebner, *Imperialism*, pp. 109–10.

[22] Cf. Buckle, iii 233–7. Disraeli regretted in 1849 that it was *then* too
late to introduce colonial representatives into Parliament.

[23] Morison, *C.H.R.*, i 272.

equally inappropriate to castigate Joseph Chamberlain for not envisaging the development of the 'New Commonwealth'.

Finally, while it is true that, in trying to assume the mantle of empire for the Conservative party, Disraeli was stretching the truth in suggesting that the Liberals were a party of separatists and also ignoring the nature of the Conservatives' own contribution to colonial development, too much should not be made of this attempt to 'dish the Whigs' or to jump on a 'popular bandwagon'. Where was this vehicle, it may be asked? The empire references in Disraeli's speech fell flat. *The Times* asserted that the Liberals were the true saviours of empire; the Liberal *Daily News* contented itself with the remark that if this was Tory policy the empire would soon be in trouble; the *Daily Telegraph* and the *Morning Post* concentrated on non-colonial aspects of the speech, and even the *Spectator* found nothing to merit approbation.[24] And if Disraeli was slow in catching the bus Carnarvon had boarded in February 1870, he now found himself in strange company indeed: by 1872 Granville, Kimberley and Knatchbull-Hugessen had already joined the queue expressing belief in empire. Indeed, it has recently been suggested that Knatchbull-Hugessen may have indirectly prompted Disraeli's remarks. The Liberal Parliamentary Under-Secretary's challenge after Disraeli's Manchester Free Trade Hall speech – 'Hit us fairly in the face here; but don't stab us in the back at Conservative banquets'[25] – may have caused Disraeli to sharpen his knife and give the dagger a final twist, at another Conservative banquet in June 1872.

III

From the recent investigation into Disraeli's beliefs prior to his Crystal Palace speech in 1872, a new conception of Disraeli's ideas on empire has begun to emerge. Unlike the agitators of 1869–70 and the imperial federalists, Disraeli was not interested in the self-governing colonies, except in so far as the remaining responsibilities handicapped Great Britain's foreign policy. Unlike the small group of philanthropists, Disraeli was not interested in the government of indigenous populations or expansion in the

---

[24] *The Times, Daily News*, 25 June 1872; *Daily Telegraph, Morning Post*, 26 June 1872; *Spectator*, 29 June 1872.
[25] 3 *Hansard*, 31 May 1872, ccxi 933–4.

tropics, except in so far as these problems affected Great Britain's position and prestige as a world power. Disraeli was a master of ideas, not detail, and it was the part the possession of empire could play in assisting Great Britain's role in world affairs that interested him most. Disraeli was not interested in the petty problems of individual colonies, but he was intensely interested – solely interested – in ensuring that the obvious advantages the possession of empire gave to Great Britain should not be whittled away by misguided Liberals with their 'Little England' ideas.

Disraeli had always maintained that 'ships, colonies and commerce' were the foundations of England's greatness. He feared that the grant of responsible government would break the imperial tie and he begged the House of Commons in 1849 not to sacrifice 'the surest sources of your wealth and the most certain support of your power'.[26] And after having tried unsuccessfully for two years to interest Lord Stanley in a Conservative programme for imperial reconstruction,[27] Disraeli protested in the Commons at this 'deference to the dogmas of political economists and of abstract enquirers',[28] the prigs and pedants of an earlier decade.

The anomalies left by the grant of responsible government, especially the problem of military defence, worried Disraeli. Great Britain still had embarrassing responsibilities for Canadian defence, for example, though she possessed little control over Canadian policy. This was a political embarrassment, particularly aggravating when it upset his budgets. Moreover, the power of the United States was increasing daily. The mother country could not hope to defend Canada against an American attack, yet because no military code had been devised at the time Great Britain shed her political responsibilities, Great Britain still possessed potentially costly military obligations. The rise of the United States was a factor that Great Britain must take into account. Disraeli reminded his listeners in a speech at Aylesbury in 1859 :

The day is coming . . . when the question of the balance of power cannot be confined to Europe alone. . . . Remember always that England, though she is bound to Europe by

[26] 3 *Hansard*, 15 June 1849, cvi 365.
[27] Buckle, iii 3–4, 23–4, 233–7, 333–5.
[28] 3 *Hansard*, 3 Feb. 1852, cxix 143.

tradition, by affection, by great similarity of habits . . . is not
a mere Power of the Old World. Her geographical position,
her laws, her language and religion, connect her as much with
the New World as the Old.[29]

Disraeli was acutely conscious of extra-European developments, including the growth of China and the westernisation of
Japan. 'It is a privilege to live in this age of rapid and brilliant
events';[30] but the privilege was not without its dangers. Disraeli's
intervention in the debate concerning the sending of reinforcements to Canada during the *Trent* crisis (he warned the
Palmerston government against dampening the ardour of
the Canadians for their own defence) earned the praise of the
Colonial Reformers who were also campaigning against the evils
of the existing colonial system. And Disraeli was as shocked as
the Colonal Reformers when the Canadian government failed to
pass its Militia Bill in May 1862 ensuring adequate local defence
measures. In Parliament, Disraeli regretted the hasty grant of
responsible government without 'reasonable measures of self-
defence'. He remained 'anxious to maintain our colonial empire'
and he would not agree with the views of Sir George Cornewall
Lewis and J. A. Roebuck, who apparently favoured severing the
link with Canada : 'I think a great empire, founded on sound
principles of freedom and equality, is as conducive to the spirit
and power of a community as commercial prosperity or military
force.'[31] In fact Disraeli continued his attack on the views of the
so-called separatists with his famous jibe against 'prigs and
pedants' during the debate on the cession of the Ionian Islands
to Greece. He insisted that Britain ought to obtain and maintain
possession of the strong places of the world.[32]

In June 1863 Disraeli suggested that part of a popular and
truly irresistible Conservative programme should be a pledge to
maintain 'the majesty of the Empire'. He repeated this assertion
in March 1865 in a debate on Canada : it would be a grievous
political error to 'renounce, relinquish, or avoid the responsibility
of upholding and maintaining their interests'. The empire added

[29] Speech at Aylesbury, 1859, quoted in Buckle, iv 231.
[30] Ibid. p. 331, Disraeli to Mrs Brydges Williams, 9 Dec. 1862.
[31] 3 *Hansard*, 25 July 1862, clxviii 853–72.
[32] 3 *Hansard*, 5 Feb. 1863, clxix 96.

to Great Britain's strength in world affairs; surely it would be 'fatal and disastrous . . . to shrink from the duty which Providence has assigned us to fulfil'.[33] These assertions were in marked contrast to the much-quoted reference to 'colonial deadweights' in 1866 – when Disraeli, then Chancellor of the Exchequer, in a moment of understandable irritation, expressed his despair at seeing the eventualities which he had long warned against about to become costly realities. Nevertheless, Disraeli continued to advocate the important part the empire had to play in Great Britain's role as a world power: 'England is no longer a mere European Power; she is the metropolis of a great maritime Empire, extending to the boundaries of the farthest ocean.'[34]

Disraeli repeated these views in his celebrated attack on the 'exhausted range of volcanoes' at the Manchester Free Trade Hall in April 1872. He admonished his listeners for not taking a greater interest in foreign affairs. Great Britain's relations with Europe had undergone a momentous change. The Liberal government had played a feeble part in trying to prevent the Franco-Prussian war and in acquiescing in Russia's repudiation of the Black Sea clauses in the Treaty of Paris of 1856. Great Britain had suffered a further reverse in the *Alabama* arbitration. Disraeli pointed to the growing predominance of the United States, 'throwing lengthening shades over the Atlantic, which mix with European waters', but prophesied that the colonies would also 'in due time exercise their influence over the distribution of power'. He placed his hopes for Great Britain in 'that unbroken spirit of her people, which, I believe, was never prouder of the Imperial country to which they belong'. He concluded by commending to his listeners 'the cause of the Tory Party, the English Constitution, and of the Tory Empire'.[35] It is important to remember that this was the oration which directly preceded the famous Crystal Palace address.

In many respects Disraeli's remarks in the Manchester Free Trade Hall were much more in keeping with his personality than his subsequent remarks in June 1872. Foreign affairs clearly took pride of place. But it should also not be forgotten that the empire

---

[33] 3 *Hansard*, 13 Mar. 1865, CLXXVII 1575–8.
[34] Speech on Schleswig-Holstein, 1866, quoted in Buckle, IV 467.
[35] Kebbel, *Selected Speeches*, II 521.

section of the Crystal Palace speech was itself extremely brief and, apart from criticisms of former Liberal policy, was concerned with larger aspects of imperial policy. Disraeli ended this latter address by stating that the people of Great Britain would soon have to choose between 'national' and 'cosmopolitan' principles : the basic issue under discussion was

> whether you will be content to be a comfortable England, modelled and moulded upon continental principles and meeting in due course an inevitable fate, or whether you will be a great country, an imperial country, a country where your sons when they rise, rise to paramount positions, and obtain, not merely the esteem of your countrymen but command the respect of the world.[36]

Professor Koebner has justly remarked : 'It was that tirade, and not so much the retrospective Colonial programme that preceded it, which gave the speech an important place in the emergence of the concept of Imperialism.'[37]

Clearly, Disraeli comprehended the possibility of utilising British possessions to increase British influence and power. It was not 'colonial' policy that Disraeli was interested in but the effect of the possession of empire on British foreign policy; the empire was a 'visible expression of the power of England in the affairs of the world'.[38] It is misleading, therefore, to deduce from Disraeli's subsequent lack of interest in colonial problems that his remarks in 1872 were insincere and purely opportunistic. Such an interpretation springs from a complete misconception of Disraeli's ideas on empire. He made little use of the revived empire sentiment in the election of 1874. Virtually his sole effort at beating the patriotic drum, in trying to turn the Straits of Malacca question into an election issue, was a serious blunder, and he floundered amid details he did not understand.[39] Despite the assertion by R. L. Schuyler that 'the integrity of the Empire' was the most popular part of Disraeli's programme, it is probably more true to say that the electorate, having digested the

---

[36] Ibid. p. 534.
[37] Koebner, *Imperialism*, p. 111.
[38] Thornton, *The Imperial Idea*, pp. xii–xiii.
[39] W. D. McIntyre, 'Disraeli's Election Blunder: The Straits of Malacca Issue in the 1874 Election', *R.M.S.*, v (1961) 76–105.

Conservative programme for social reform, swallowed Disraeli's imperial ideas along with it.[40]

Thus the contemporary observers who expected, and those subsequent writers who have looked for, a new colonial policy in 1874 were misguided. In fact there were sound reasons for not expecting a sudden departure from former policy when the Conservatives came to power. The situation in 1874 certainly did not indicate that a new expansionist policy was likely to be adopted. Disraeli was 'very old and very worn when he got to the top of the tree';[41] he was an elderly widower of seventy whose health was far from robust. He was constantly ill throughout his second administration and died a year after leaving office. He complained: 'Power! It has come to me too late.'[42]

Nor was the Colonial Secretary, Lord Carnarvon, likely to inaugurate an expansionist policy. Though determined to support good government in the empire and maintain British honour and integrity, his main concern was for economy and security. Consequently he annexed territory with extreme reluctance. Lord Derby, the Foreign Secretary, was equally anti-expansionist in outlook and has been described as 'the most isolationist foreign secretary that Great Britain has ever known'.[43] He certainly wished to avoid all foreign entanglements and opposed both the occupation of Cyprus and the war against Afghanistan. Like Carnarvon, Derby left the Cabinet in 1878 at the prospect of war with Russia and was to leave the Conservative party in 1880. There seemed little reason to expect these men to inaugurate a new imperial policy in 1874.

In fact, though Disraeli's administration was rich in talent, there existed few strong bonds among its members. Disraeli's friendship with Derby became increasingly uneasy, his relationship with Carnarvon was often strained, and Lord Salisbury, the

[40] Schuyler, *Fall of the Old Colonial System*, p. 278. For an analysis of the Conservative victory in 1874, see Tyler, *Struggle for Imperial Unity*, pp. 21–3; H. J. Hanham, *Elections and Party Management: Politics in the Time of Disraeli and Gladstone* (London, 1959) pp. 221–6; Blake, *Disraeli*, pp. 535–8.

[41] Lord R. Churchill, in 'Elijah's Mantle', *Fortnightly Review*, XXXIX (1883) 615, quoted by Stembridge, *J.B.S.*, v 137.

[42] Sir J. A. Marriott, *Queen Victoria and her Ministers* (London, 1933) p. 120.

[43] A. J. P. Taylor, *The Struggle for Mastery in Europe, 1848–1918* (London, 1954) p. 233.

Secretary of State for India, the 'great master of flouts and jeers', was an equally difficult companion. Nor did there exist any great party planks on which these men could unite. After the first Cabinet meeting the Home Secretary, R. A. Cross, reflected, somewhat aghast :

> From all his speeches I had quite expected that his mind was full of legislative schemes, but such did not prove to be the case; on the contrary he had to entirely rely on the suggestions of his colleagues, and, as they themselves had only just come into office, and that suddenly, there was some difficulty in framing the Queen's speech.[44]

The Prime Minister almost seems to have expected individual policies from his ministers. He certainly had no wish to dictate colonial policy and left everything to Carnarvon and the Colonial Office. And in the Colonial Office the Permanent Under-Secretary, Robert Herbert, a former private secretary to Gladstone, and his Assistant Under-Secretary, Robert Meade, formerly private secretary to Granville, were unlikely to urge their chief into a policy of wholesale annexation.

The economic situation seemed to close the door against following an expansionist policy. Although Gladstone had succeeded not only in reducing taxation but in creating a £5 million budget surplus, the years of Disraeli's administration experienced a trade depression, poor harvests and a rise in industrial unemployment – hardly a situation in which to undertake costly new adventures.

Given Disraeli's ideas, then, and the environment in which he had to work, what could be expected of the new government? Firstly, little change in colonial policy and little intervention by Disraeli; secondly, a more active foreign policy, with Disraeli playing an important part in its formulation; thirdly, an inflated view of empire in general and a greater display of British power; and lastly, given Disraeli's personality, the occasional dramatic gesture and flash of brilliance. In other words, a quiescent colonial policy dominated by Carnarvon and an active foreign policy tempered by Derby's passivity. But no sudden 'forward movements' or costly undertakings unless Great Britain's security was gravely threatened. How far did these expectations work out in reality?

[44] Blake, *Disraeli*, p. 543.

IV

In the House of Commons it was taken for granted that the advent of a Conservative ministry would lead to a more favourable attitude towards empire. The Conservative Parliamentary Under-Secretary, James Lowther, wasted no time in asserting that 'the Government viewed the retention of our Colonial Empire as a subject of the greatest importance'.[45] But his Liberal predecessor, freed for once from the need not to embarrass his political superiors, was quick to remind the House that imperial sentiment was not the prerogative of one political party. It was rather a difference in outlook between two schools of thought :

The one school – represented by the hon. Member for Lambeth (Alderman M'Arthur) looked mainly to the advantages to be derived from such acquisition in the way of increased trade, extended commerce, the development of the resources of the annexed country and the consolidation of our Colonial Empire. The other school – represented by the hon. Baronet (Sir Charles Dilke) and the rt. hon. gentleman the Member for Greenwich (W. E. Gladstone) looked rather to the disadvantages and were disposed to magnify the difficulties which stood in the way of annexation.

For his part, Knatchbull-Hugessen – 'fussy, verbose, and patronising' as ever, 'ready on the shortest notice to give the benefit of his advice to Her Majesty's Government; or to any private members who may not have asked for it'[46] – maintained that 'a Country in the position of Great Britain could not avoid the responsibilities of that position, nor refuse addition to her territory from merely selfish considerations'.[47]

Knatchbull-Hugessen, it will be remembered, had often prodded his chief into action in the Colonial Office during the days of the Liberal administration. And in one sense both he and Kimberley were authors of the so-called 'forward movements' attributed to Disraeli, since the decisions Carnarvon implemented had often been discussed and approved in principle by his Liberal

[45] 3 *Hansard*, 4 Aug. 1874, ccxxi 1291–2.
[46] Lucy, *Diary of Two Parliaments*, I 317.
[47] 3 *Hansard*, 4 Aug. 1874, ccxxi 1293–5.

predecessors. The new policies were in reality 'the culmination of a period of tentative innovation' caused by a series of crises on the imperial frontier in the tropics,[48] and were not the result of a change in personnel in Downing Street.

The Conservative ministry did not desire any new commitments, except in areas of vital strategic significance. The existing network of commercial and naval bases was designed to secure the world's shipping routes for British trade and British concepts : missionaries and traders could carry the lamp while the government provided advisers who would bestow the benefits of civilisation without destroying the rights of indigenous peoples as free men. But during the 1870s the task of governing, protecting and advising 'native' peoples was not to admit of solution by traditional policies of *laissez-faire*. The various crises on the frontiers of empire cried out for British intervention.

The Conservative government was reluctant to move. Carnarvon decided on a series of strictly limited experiments in the administration of tropical dependencies. In every case he sought a course falling short of annexation which would still enable Great Britain to fulfil her obligations. In West Africa he was unwilling to extend British territory but was anxious to discharge British obligations in an honourable if economical way. His decision to construct a new Crown colony which would administer the 'protectorate' gave him a legal basis for exerting British control without assuming the sovereignty of the region. Similarly, in the Malay States Carnarvon adopted the resident system so as to achieve order without extending British rule,[49] and in the Pacific the creation of the Western Pacific High Commission was yet another experiment in providing order and jurisdiction without enlarging British territory. The annexation of Fiji, an experiment in Pacific island government, provided the Colonial Secretary, as the Permanent Under-Secretary suggested, with a formula for forestalling future demands for expansion :

the establishment of a separate Colonial Government in Fiji will afford H.M. Govt. increased facilities of considering the requirements of this country and of British subjects in the Pacific, and for the present you are not prepared to decide in

[48] McIntyre, *Imperial Frontier*, p. 6.
[49] Ibid. p. 316.

favour of or against any particular schemes for the development of British influence among the islands.[50]

There was to be no tidal wave of British expansion in the Pacific.

In all this activity Disraeli played little part. The amount of interest he took in the affairs of individual colonies can be gauged from a letter he wrote to Lady Bradford, shortly before the crucial debate on the issue of domestic slavery in the Gold Coast in June 1874 : 'I might be at Evelyn's [Lady Carnarvon's] tonight and see you! And I am detained by an infernal debate on the Gold Coast Policy of Evelyn's husband. Such is life! No wonder people go mad.'[51] Carnarvon firmly believed that Disraeli did not even bother to read the colonial papers he received. The Prime Minister certainly did not appreciate Carnarvon's long and persistent telegrams.[52] Rarely did his replies contain anything more than a few flattering remarks intended to retain the loyalty of a difficult subordinate.

In general, Disraeli's letters to his Colonial Secretary contained words of encouragement, not advice. After the establishment of a new Crown colony on the Gold Coast and the suppression (under pressure) of domestic slavery, he wrote : 'It is a masterly, indeed admirable performance, your conduct of your office cannot be too highly praised.'[53] With events in the Malay States the Prime Minister also showed little concern. Carnarvon was left to his own devices. Apparently the Cabinet was not even informed about the introduction of the resident system. Furthermore, Disraeli was preoccupied with purchasing the Suez Canal shares when the 'Perak crisis' blew up in 1875.[54] And when it came to taking a decision about Fiji, Disraeli was positively obstructive. Infuriated by the speeches of Carnarvon

---

[50] Min. by Herbert, 7 Nov., on Fergusson to Carnarvon, 24 June 1874, C.O. 209/232.

[51] Disraeli to Lady Bradford, 25 June 1874, quoted in Marquis of Zetland (ed.), *The Letters of Disraeli to Lady Bradford and Lady Chesterfield* (London, 1929) I 108.

[52] Carnarvon to Hardy, 19 July 1877, private and personal (copy), *Carnarvon Papers*, P.R.O. 30/6/12; Disraeli to Lady Bradford, 29 Dec. 1875, quoted in Zetland, *Letters of Disraeli*, I 312–13.

[53] Disraeli to Carnarvon, 26 Oct. 1874, quoted in Hardinge, *Life of Carnarvon*, II 79.

[54] McIntyre, *Imperial Frontier*, p. 311. Disraeli did, however, intervene a month later (ibid., pp. 312–13).

and Salisbury attacking the government's Public Worship Regulation Bill during its passage through the House of Lords, and disliking the expense involved in the annexation, he absolutely refused to arrange a Cabinet meeting at such a difficult moment, frigidly informing his Colonial Secretary : 'It was most unlucky that we were obliged to put off the Cabinet – but it was your vote, and perhaps speech, that occasioned that, for if I had not worked from the moment I rose till noon, the Commons would have rebelled. . . .' But he ended on a friendly note : 'However, I must leave the matter entirely to your discretion. There is none of my colleagues in whom I have more confidence than yourself, and I always say that your administration of your office is most able.'[55] After the annexation had been completed, however, he was delighted with his Colonial Secretary ('Carnarvon seems to be distinguishing himself') and boasted of the annexation at the Lord Mayor's luncheon as proof of the Tory faith in empire.[56] Even Carnarvon for the moment seemed carried away with his success and impetuously informed the Prime Minister : 'It is like a dream.'[57] The excitement soon passed.

For all his talk of the new morality of empire – of imperial mission, the discharge of disagreeable duties and of burdens inseparable from greatness – Carnarvon did not inaugurate a new phase in Great Britain's imperial history. The Conservative ministers merely reacted to events, their actions being guided to a large extent by the men on the spot. Although the decisions to extend British influence may serve as important landmarks in the regional history of the West African colonies, of Malaya and the South Pacific, the decisions did not proceed from any preconceived plans on the part of the Conservative ministers. Disraeli did not want 'forward movements'. Instead the Colonial Office hastily improvised solutions to a series of individual crises in the tropics. And Carnarvon's language merely served to conceal the fact that obligations reluctantly incurred had been met in the most minimal fashion.

Carnarvon, in fact, was intent on following an extremely

[55] Disraeli to Carnarvon, 8 Aug. 1874, quoted in Hardinge, *Life of Carnarvon*, II 73–4.

[56] Disraeli to Lady Chesterfield, 20 Oct. 1874, quoted in Zetland, *Letters of Disraeli*, I 161; *The Times*, 10 Nov. 1874.

[57] Carnarvon to Disraeli, 27 Oct. 1874, quoted in McIntyre, *Imperial Frontier*, p. 336.

conservative policy. Although deeply interested in the continuance and development of the fabric of empire, he did not look for new commitments. It was the strength and security of the existing empire that interested him most. Good government, economical government and, where possible, self-government were the bases of Carnarvon's policies – as they had been of all his liberal predecessors. In the long-neglected West Indies and in South Africa, Carnarvon followed a policy of consolidation in the interests of security, reliable government and economy. A policy of regional federation – the Canadian model – was adopted in order to strengthen individual colonies and to relieve Great Britain of some awkward responsibilities. But in neither of these regions did Carnarvon's ideas receive ready acceptance. As on the frontiers of empire, the set ideas of the Colonial Office were proving to be inadequate solutions for the problems of the late 1870s. But if Carnarvon successfully handled his initial difficulties, his reaction to later developments, as he became more and more involved in South African problems, had far less happy results. Events occurred which were not at all to Disraeli's liking.

v

Perhaps it was Carnarvon's earlier experience in the Colonial Office and the part he played in piloting the British North America Act through Parliament that convinced him of the benefits of regional federation for small struggling colonies. It certainly seemed a logical solution to the problems of the West Indies and had been advocated in the Colonial Office throughout the 1860s. Henry Taylor and Sir Frederic Rogers had first drawn up a plan for judicial and administrative consolidation in the interests of efficiency and economy during the secretaryship of Edward Cardwell (1864–6). The Earl of Kimberley had succeeded in federating most of the Leeward Islands (Antigua, St Kitts, Nevis, Montserrat and Anguilla) in 1871, but the work remained unfinished. Carnarvon decided to revive the plan to federate Barbados, Tobago and the Windward Islands (St Lucia, St Vincent and Grenada) so as eventually to form a British West Indian Confederacy.[58] The advantages of a strong federal legislature, the reduction in personnel, the diminished costs of joint public institutions and the benefits of a more efficient adminis-

[58] See Kimberley to Rawson, 1 May 1873, C.O. 28/218.

tration of justice, hospitals, asylums, prisons, poor-relief and education seemed obvious.

But Carnarvon showed neither tact nor understanding. He never grasped the strength of custom and conservatism among the upper classes in Barbados and mistakenly regarded opposition to reform from such quarters as a factious and vexatious agitation of not very important vested interests, which could, in the last resort, be cajoled or overawed into submission. He seemed to be completely unaware that conditions for spontaneous federation did not exist in the West Indies. And his promise that the proposed administrative reforms and unifications would not involve coercion of the Barbados legislature or important changes in the various island constitutions seems to have been the product of wishful thinking. Certainly, Carnarvon was not well served in this respect by one of his representatives in the West Indies, Sir John Pope-Hennessy, one of the most forthright and controversial colonial governors of the Victorian period, whose unrivalled talent for self-deception and ability to create opposition by his own impetuous acts, combined with excessive zeal on the part of certain local officials, brought public business to a standstill in Barbados. Carnarvon's visionary project floundered in 1876.[59] In many respects it was but a curtain-raiser to a more momentous failure in South Africa. Carnarvon's optimism was to lead to more disastrous events.

Here again, federation appeared to be the logical answer to the problems of the region, and it was a solution that had been canvassed for a number of years in the Colonial Office. Unfortunately, conditions for the spontaneous federation of the four British territories – Cape Colony, Basutoland, Griqualand West and Natal – and of the two Boer republics – the Orange Free State and Transvaal – again did not exist. Nevertheless, Carnarvon, seeing the growing seeds of disunion in this key area in the empire defence system, decided to press ahead with his policy of confederation.[60]

[59] See W. B. Hamilton, *Barbados and the Confederation Question 1871–85* (London, 1956).

[60] For the background to these events, see C. W. de Kiewiet, *The Imperial Factor in South Africa* (Cambridge, 1937); Goodfellow, *Great Britain and South African Confederation*; C. J. Uys, *In the Era of Shepstone: British Expansion in South Africa, 1842–77* (Lovedale, South Africa, 1933).

The British record in South Africa was one of vacillation. Every step forward had been followed by a pace backwards. An attempt at British disengagement in the 1850s failed to work. Great Britain had attempted to rid herself of territorial responsibilities in the hinterland of southern Africa by the Sand River and Bloemfontein Conventions, but the instability of the new Boer republics and the native strife they created only compromised the security and prosperity of the British possessions. At first the British government tried to stifle the potential threat from the Boer republics. But it soon came to see the danger of small, isolated states with divergent policies, attacking or being attacked by Bantu tribes, with the attendant risk of a general uprising of the African population, as well as the harmful effect upon trade and commerce of intercolonial separatism and mutual jealousies.

The need for a comprehensive African and frontier policy was vital. But the Cape Colony disliked the idea of shouldering the burdens of less affluent neighbours. Consequently in 1868, when the British government granted the Basuto ruler, Moshesh, protection against the Orange Free State, the Cape ministry refused to accept responsibility for the annexation of Basutoland. Similarly, in 1871, after the discovery of diamonds in Griqualand West, when the British government annexed the territory to prevent the republic enriching themselves, a new Crown colony had to be established separate from the Cape. After 1872 the Cape Colony used its new powers under responsible government to obstruct the making of a federation in which it would have to carry the finance and defence burdens of poorer states. For their part the Boers, thwarted in their attempts to reach a free port in St Lucia Bay in 1866 and at Delagoa Bay in 1868, and further embittered by the loss of Basutoland and Griqualand West, were in no mood to join a British-dominated federation. In any case, the frontier regions would have to be pacified and the differences between black and white settled before a successful union could be brought about. But the Basuto, Griquas, Zulus, Ba-Pedi and Gaika were in no mood to be pacified. None of the conditions for a successful federation seemed to exist.

Yet in 1875 Carnarvon decided that the time for action had come. Alarmed by the growing African unrest and the lack of unity in African policies, and worried by Boer attempts to assert

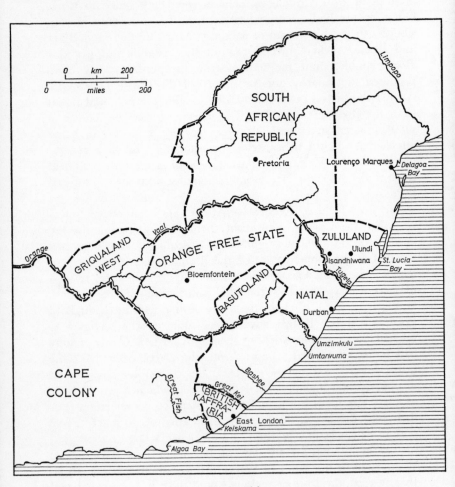

3 South Africa

their independence (President Burgers of the Transvaal had recently tried to enlist Dutch and German aid in building a railway from Pretoria to Delagoa Bay), Carnarvon suggested in May 1875 that a local conference of delegates from the republics and the colonies should meet to co-ordinate relations with the Bantu and also discuss the 'all important question of the possible union of South Africa in some form of confederation'.[61] Carnarvon, rather unwisely, went on to elaborate details of his scheme and even to suggest the names of delegates. This caused great offence in the Cape Colony, where further resentment was caused by the disallowance of an Act of the Cape Parliament and by the activities of Carnarvon's personal envoy, J. A. Froude, the historian. Then, in November 1875, Carnarvon sent a second ill-timed despatch suggesting a conference in London to discuss the position. By this stage the Colonial Secretary was well aware that neither the Cape nor the Boers would willingly accept any confederation scheme, but after President Burgers announced the conclusion of a commercial treaty with Portugal he decided that the two republics would have to be isolated and pressure brought to bear upon them. When the London conference failed, Carnarvon determined on the annexation of the South African Republic.

An opportunity soon presented itself. The Transvaal, on the verge of bankruptcy, was heavily defeated in a war with Chief Sekukini of the Ba-Pedi. The more formidable armies of Cetewayo were preparing to take advantage of Boer weakness, when Carnarvon seized the opportunity to secure acceptance of British rule. He informed Disraeli :

My hope is that by acting at once, we may prevent war and acquire at a stroke the whole of the Transvaal Republic, after which the Orange Free State will follow, and the whole policy for which we have been labouring will be fully and completely justified.

Disraeli, as usual, showed little interest : 'In all these affairs I must trust to you, and you are a person in whom I have much trust. Do what you think wisest.' Carnarvon reassured the Prime

---

[61] Carnarvon to Barkly, 4 May 1875, C.O. 48/477.

Minister that annexation would bring 'the *consequent* confederation . . . within sight', and Disraeli acquiesced.[62]

After the Transvaal had been annexed in April 1877,
Carnarvon introduced a permissive bill into the British Parliament to prepare the ground for South African federation.
Unfortunately, the annexation of the Transvaal had removed all
possibility of federal union. The British had finally alienated
those Transvaal Afrikaners, led by Paul Kruger, who cherished
Boer independence, and furthermore the British had inherited a
troublesome border dispute with the Zulus. Carnarvon's scheme
failed badly in 1877, and by the time Carnarvon resigned the
following year, Disraeli had become aware of the enormities of
'Twitters' blunders'.

Gladstone later included the annexation of the Transvaal in
his condemnation of Disraeli's costly interventionist policies. But
the Prime Minister and the Cabinet had played no part in the
South African venture. During the years 1878–80 there were
further scrapes – a Cape–Xhosa and Anglo–Zulu war in South
Africa, and a British invasion of Afghanistan. Were these the
results of British policy or did Disraeli merely drift into these
difficulties as well? In fact, how far is it true that the Disraeli
administration consciously adopted 'forward' policies in South
Africa and India at the end of the 1870s?

VI

The last thing Disraeli wanted was a series of imperial wars to
complicate his conduct of British foreign policy in the east. But
backpedal as fast as he tried, his administration soon became
involved in wars with Zulus and Afghans in which British
reverses were to contribute to the Conservative election downfall
in 1880. The turn of events in South Africa and India seriously
embarrassed the British Prime Minister.

After the resignations of Carnarvon and Derby in 1878,
Disraeli appointed Sir Michael Hicks Beach as Colonial Secretary,
and on the promotion of the Marquis of Salisbury to the Foreign
Office, Gathorne Hardy (now Viscount Cranbrook) became

[62] Carnarvon to Disraeli, 20 Sept.; Disraeli to Carnarvon, 20 Sept.;
Carnarvon to Disraeli, 15 Oct. 1876, quoted in Buckle, vi 414–15, and
Hardinge, *Life of Carnarvon*, ii 230, 234.

Secretary of State for India. Cranbrook's administration of his office was hardly competent (he was 'more interested in deer-stalking than in India'[63]), and during his first debate on India he promptly fell sound asleep. Similarly, Hicks Beach, although more attentive to administrative detail, had no previous experience of colonial affairs and knew nothing of Carnarvon's activities in South Africa. Both Secretaries of State therefore experienced difficulty in restraining their energetic local representatives, and Disraeli and the Cabinet were at last forced to show some interest in developments in South Africa and India.

In 1877 Carnarvon appointed Sir Bartle Frere, one of the most forceful proconsuls of his day, as Governor of the Cape Colony and High Commissioner for South Africa. Frere, who clearly expected to serve as the first Governor-General of a new South African federation, was the chosen instrument for Carnarvon's policies. But when it soon became obvious that federation was not immediately practicable, Frere, while biding his time, turned his attention to establishing British paramountcy over the African tribes south of the Zambesi. This led to the complications the British government feared most.

Frere believed that the power of the Zulus would have to be destroyed before the internal security of the South African colonies could be assured. The whole Zulu social structure was geared to warfare, and the British had not only assumed responsibility for protecting the Transvaal Boers but had inherited troublesome disputes over territory. A clash was clearly in the offing. Frere determined on a preventive war.[64] Carnarvon was aware of the dangers and warned him : 'We cannot now have a South African war on our hands and if the worst comes to the worst you must all temporise and wait for a better opportunity of settling these controversies'.[65] But Carnarvon's successor, Hicks Beach, who also agreed with Frere's objectives, seemed unaware that the High Commissioner's plan for subordinating the Zulus to a British protectorate could be achieved only by the use of force. It was not until September 1878 that the British Cabinet fully understood the direction of events in South Africa. Disraeli,

[65] Carnarvon to Frere, 2 Jan. 1878, *Carnarvon Papers*, P.R.O. 30/6/34.
[63] Blake, *Disraeli*, p. 661.
[64] See R. Coupland, *Zulu Battle Piece* (London, 1948); D. R. Morris, *The Washing of the Spears* (London, 1966).

who blamed the troubles on Carnarvon, was in despair at the thought of concurrent wars against the Zulus and Afghans. Writing to Lady Bradford, he declared:

> if anything annoys me more than another, it is our Cape affairs, where every day brings forward a new blunder of Twitters.
>
> The man he swore by was Sir Theophilus Shepstone, whom he looked upon as heaven born for the object in view. We sent him out entirely for Twitters' sake, and he has managed to quarrel with Eng., Dutch, and Zulus; and now he is obliged to be recalled, but not before he has brought on, I fear, a new war. Froude was bad enough, and has cost us a million; this will be worse. So much for Twitters.[66]

Hicks Beach immediately warned Frere to abandon all plans for a preventive war: 'the fact is that matters in Eastern Europe and India . . . wear so serious an aspect that we cannot have a Zulu war in addition to other greater and too possible troubles'.[67]

Nevertheless, despite all such warnings, the British High Commissioner deliberately disobeyed instructions and plunged recklessly ahead with an ultimatum to the Zulu king which he knew Cetewayo could never accept. The result was war. Unhappily, the campaign began with a major disaster. A Zulu army of 20,000 men, moving with extraordinary speed, slaughtered a small force of the 2nd Warwickshire Regiment (the South Wales Borderers) at Isandhlwana in January 1879. Reinforcements were hurriedly sent out. Disraeli was infuriated by this inopportune call on British reserves which jeopardised his whole foreign policy and seriously damaged the sadly dwindling British finances. Yet despite a private opinion that Frere 'ought to be impeached',[68] Disraeli resisted popular demands for the recall of the High Commissioner. Eventually British prestige was restored in July 1879 when the Zulu armies of Cetewayo were finally crushed

[66] Disraeli to Lady Bradford, 28 Sept. 1878, quoted in Zetland, *Letters of Disraeli*, II 189.

[67] Hicks Beach to Frere, 7 Nov. 1878, quoted in Goodfellow, *Great Britain and South African Confederation*, p. 161. For details of this period, see ibid. pp. 151–86; J. Martineau, *Life and Correspondence of Sir Bartle Frere* (London, 1895) II, chap. 19; Lady V. Hicks Beach, *Life of Sir Michael Hicks Beach* (London, 1932).

[68] Disraeli to Lady Chesterfield, 28 June 1879, quoted in Zetland, *Letters of Disraeli*, II 225.

A LESSON.

at Ulundi. But further fuel had been added to the Liberal charge of misguided ambition for territorial aggrandisement, and Gladstone included the Zulu war in his general indictment of the extravagant policies typical of 'Beaconsfieldism'.

In fact Disraeli's reputation for following an aggressive 'forward' policy was totally undeserved. The outcome was rather a product of the weakness of the Prime Minister than of any determined policy on his part. At first Disraeli ignored South African affairs, while he actively opposed the later developments. One observer concluded:

> Bartle Frere should have been recalled as soon as the news of his ultimatum reached England. We should then have escaped in appearance, as well as in reality, the responsibility of the Zulu war. So thought the majority of the Cabinet, so thought Dizzy himself. But the Queen was strongly opposed to it; and Hicks Beach was strongly opposed to it; and the Prime Minister was unable to resist his Sovereign and Colonial Secretary together.[69]

Disraeli accepted full responsibility for the disobedient acts of his proconsul. From the very first the Prime Minister and the Cabinet seem to have been unaware of the significance of Carnarvon's appointment of a man with Frere's expansionist views as High Commissioner in South Africa.

The same could not be said for the appointment of Lord Lytton as Viceroy of India. Disraeli noted: 'We wanted a man of ambition, imagination, some vanity and much will – and we have got him.'[70] Disraeli had in fact appointed another wilful proconsul who was to drag Great Britain into another unwanted war.

The problems of Afghanistan and relations with Russia haunted the Conservative administration throughout the years 1874–80. As Secretary of State for India, Salisbury believed that the Liberal policy of 'masterly inactivity' had been outdated by the Russian advance across central Asia. In the 1860s the Russians had gradually swallowed up the independent khanates of Turkestan – Chimkent, Tashkent, Samarkand, Bukhara – and

---

[69] A. Balfour, *Retrospect: An Unfinished Autobiography* (Boston, 1930) pp. 116–17.

[70] Disraeli to Salisbury, 1 Apr. 1877, quoted in Buckle, vi 379.

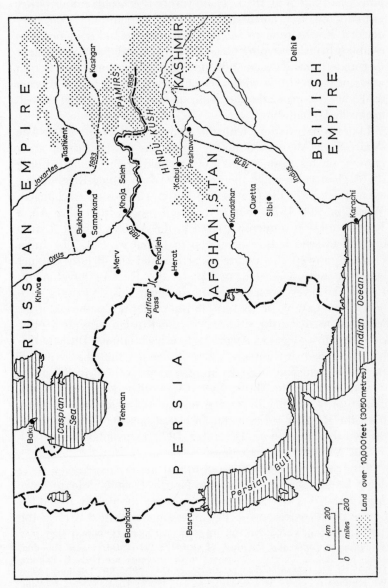

4 The Defence of India

Khiva had fallen in 1873. There was now a hostile major power virtually on the northern frontier of Afghanistan. Salisbury decided it was time to intervene across the Indus in order to establish British 'listening posts' at Herat, Kandahar and Kashgar to countermine Russian influence in Afghanistan. Lord Lytton was sent out to India with a secret despatch suggesting a mission to Kabul to persuade the Amir to accept permanent British agents in Afghanistan.[71]

Lytton's negotiations with the Amir made little progress. The Amir, Sher Ali, was naturally suspicious of the British army massing on his frontier and Lytton could not risk antagonising the Afghan ruler while the possibility of an Anglo-Russian war existed. But after the Congress of Berlin, circumstances changed. When, in July 1878, despite a formal protest from Sher Ali, a Russian mission suddenly arrived in the Afghan capital, Lytton decided to send a British mission to Kabul as well. The India Office approved this course of action and the British Cabinet belatedly sent a formal protest to the Russian government. Lytton, however, was not informed about this diplomatic protest.[72] And Lytton, in his turn, did not inform Cranbrook of his intention to make the dismissal of the Russian mission a prior condition to reopening Anglo-Afghan negotiations. Directly this became known in London, where it was felt that the arrival of the Russian mission might be in retaliation for the British transfer of Indian troops to Malta, Lytton was ordered to postpone the departure of the British mission until a reply had been received from the Russian government. In actual fact the Tsar withdrew the Russian mission in December 1878 to avoid violently upsetting Anglo-Russian relations.

But Lytton was not prepared to wait on events. After a short delay he authorised General Sir Neville Chamberlain to enter Afghanistan via the Khyber Pass, a route specifically forbidden by the British government. Chamberlain was turned back at the

---

[71] Salisbury to Lytton, 20 Feb. 1876, quoted in C. H. Philips (ed.), *The Evolution of India and Pakistan, 1858–1947: Select Documents* (London, 1962) pp. 446–8. For the background to these events, see Lady E. Balfour, *History of Lord Lytton's Indian Administration, 1876–80* (London, 1899); W. K. Fraser-Tytler, *Afghanistan* (Oxford, 1950); D. E. Ghose, *England and Afghanistan* (Calcutta, 1962); and D. P. Singhal, *India and Afghanistan: A Study in Diplomatic Relations, 1876–1907* (Brisbane, 1963).

[72] See M. Cowling, 'Lytton, the Cabinet and the Russians, August to November 1878', *E.H.R.*, LXXVI (1961) 60–79; Buckle, VI 380–1.

"SAVE ME FROM MY FRIENDS!"

"IF AT THIS MOMENT IT HAS BEEN DECIDED TO INVADE THE AMEER'S TERRITORY, WE ARE ACTING IN PURSUANCE OF A POLICY WHICH IN ITS
INTENTION HAS BEEN UNIFORMLY *FRIENDLY* TO AFGHANISTAN."—*Times*, Nov. 21.

frontier, an affront which led to war. Disraeli commented bitterly:
'When V-roys and Comms-in-Chief disobey orders, they ought
to be sure of success in their mutiny. Lytton, by disobeying
orders, has only secured insult and failure. . . . To force the
Khyber, and take Cabul is a perilous business.'[73] Nevertheless,
once again he decided to uphold the actions of a rebellious
Viceroy. He was even prepared to ignore the advice of his
Foreign Secretary. He wrote to Cranbrook:

> When you and the Viceroy agree I shall always wish to
> support you. No doubt Salisbury's views under ordinary
> circumstances would be more prudent but there are occasions
> when prudence is not wisdom, and this is one. There are times
> for action, we must control and even create events . . . what
> we want is to prove our ascendancy in Afghanistan and to
> accomplish that we must not stick at trifles.[74]

In his annual speech at the Lord Mayor's dinner, Disraeli
unhappily made pointed reference to the 'inconvenience' of
India's insecure north-western frontier – the foundation of the
charge that he planned the Afghan war in order to achieve a
'scientific frontier'.[75] Fortunately all went well and after a
brilliant campaign by General Roberts peace was made and a
British mission installed in Kabul. But just as the Viceroy's
actions seemed to have been vindicated, another bombshell hit
the Disraeli government. In September 1879 the British mission
was massacred in Kabul by mutinous Afghan soldiers. A second
punitive war had to be fought. Another outcry occurred in Great
Britain and Gladstone added another item to his list of Disraeli's
misguided and extravagant adventures abroad – an adventure in
which Disraeli had originally expressed no desire to take part.

Certainly, however unsuccessful the government's 'imperial'
policies had been, there was clearly little ground for the Liberal
accusation of the deliberate adoption of a costly and unnecessary
policy of blatant imperialism. But then it was not so much
colonial or even Indian policy that the Liberals were thinking of
(although Gladstone included the Royal Titles Bill, the annexation of the Transvaal, and the Zulu and Afghan wars in his

---

[73] Disraeli to Cranbrook, 26 Sept. 1878, quoted in Buckle, VI 382.
[74] Cowling, *E.H.R.*, LXXVI 74.
[75] A charge apparently accepted by Stembridge, *J.B.S.*, V 137.

indictment against the Disraeli administration), but Disraeli's 'empire', the sphere of foreign policy. It was in Disraeli's handling of the Eastern Question that the Liberals claimed to have discovered the most threatening aspects of Disraeli's imperial dreams.

8

The Empire of Disraeli's Dreams

DISRAELI's contribution to British imperial history needs to be reassessed. With the so-called 'forward movements' of the early years of his administration he had almost nothing to do. The decisions extending British influence in various parts of the world were not even part of a consistent Conservative philosophy, but merely the outcome of earlier events. For the 'forward movements' of the later years of his administration Disraeli also had little responsibility. He deplored the direction of events in South Africa and India and censured in private the activities of the men he supported in public. The actions of the men on the spot, very often in flagrant disregard of the instructions of Her Majesty's Government, were more responsible for the Zulu and Afghan wars than the vacillation of Disraeli and his Cabinet.

'Beaconsfieldism' was substantially a product of Disraeli's weakness as Prime Minister rather than his strength. He failed to oversee adequately the work of individual ministers and he failed to ensure the necessary departmental co-ordination and consensus of opinions. On one occasion Disraeli actually confessed : 'In a Cabinet of twelve members there are seven parties.'[1] The Prime Minister and the Cabinet often found themselves forced into corners from which it proved difficult to escape. Sometimes the difficulty was of Disraeli's own making. From being largely uninterested in imperial affairs, by the mid-1870s the Queen had become intensely interested in the overseas empire, partly, no doubt, as a reaction to Gladstone's failure to 'keep up

[1] Buckle, VI 194.

the empire', but largely as a result of Disraeli's own tuition. The Queen now began to give whole-hearted support to the men of her empire, including Sir Bartle Frere and Lord Lytton, who opposed her enemies the Zulus, the Afghans and the Russians. To the Prime Minister these men of the periphery were enthusiasts who disobeyed orders and whose interventionist policies were likely to result in higher estimates and unpopular wars. Disraeli had tried to reduce the imperial question to one of empire or no empire: the men on the spot differentiated between a static, disintegrating empire and a dynamic, well-organised and expanding empire. These were the men who now received the Queen's support. 'Balmoral is becoming a serious nuisance', noted Lord Salisbury,[2] and royal pressure can certainly be traced in the progress of the Public Worship Regulation Bill of 1874 and in the Royal Titles Bill of 1876. Disraeli was often pushed a little further than he really wished to go.

He was not a warmonger. He denounced the Ashanti war from the very beginning;[3] resisted pressure to exert a greater control over Egypt after his purchase of the Suez Canal Company's shares; and his handling of the Eastern Question, the Cyprus Convention apart, was thoroughly Palmerstonian in character.

Disraeli's foreign policy must be kept in perspective. He entered office determined that Great Britain should once again have a voice in European affairs. But apart from a determination to do something (and it is not precisely clear what that 'something' was), he possessed no ideas other than the traditional Palmerstonian conception of British interests and approach to defence strategy. As Robert Blake concluded: 'Having at last obtained power he had curiously little idea what to do with it.'[4] Disraeli never bothered to master details. 'He detests details', fumed Carnarvon, 'he does no work . . . Mr Corry is in fact Prime Minister.'[5] And for the first three years of his administration Disraeli had no consistent foreign policy. For most of the time the Prime Minister was at odds with his Foreign Secretary, who with the assistance of his wife apparently revealed Cabinet secrets to the Russian ambassador in an attempt to foil Disraeli's

[2] Salisbury to Carnarvon, 27 May 1877, quoted in Blake, *Disraeli*, p. 547.
[3] Disraeli to Northcote, 11 Sept. 1873, confidential, quoted in Buckle, v 258–9; *The Times*, 26 Jan., 2 Feb. 1874.
[4] Blake, *Disraeli*, p. 549.
[5] Hardinge, *Life of Carnarvon*, ii 78.

schemes.[6] Even the incisive Salisbury found himself floundering, with his authority undermined during the Constantinople Conference of 1876–7. It seemed impossible to reconcile Disraeli's desire to uphold Turkish territorial integrity, as a barrier to the Russian advance on British routes to India, with the British public's insistence that Turkish rule over Christian populations in south-eastern Europe should be abolished. As a result, British foreign policy was entirely paralysed during the years 1876–7. Salisbury concluded: 'English policy is to float lazily downstream, occasionally putting out a diplomatic boat-hook to avoid collision.'[7] While Derby remained in the Cabinet, Disraeli's desire for Great Britain to play a leading role on the world's stage was successfully countered – by the inactivity and antipathy of his own Foreign Secretary.

After Lord Salisbury had been installed in the Foreign Office, however, there was both greater harmony of purpose in the Cabinet and a more decisive control of British foreign policy. By 1878 circumstances had changed and the British government had more freedom to manoeuvre. The decision to support the Turks against Russian encroachments on the Ottoman empire in Asia, in return for the promise of reforms in government, was endorsed in Great Britain, British public opinion being less concerned with the plight of misruled Moslem peoples in Asia than it had been with that of the Christian populations in south-eastern Europe.

The Congress of Berlin and the claim to have achieved 'peace with honour' saw the high point of Disraeli's career. Disraeli dominated the summit meeting and his presence was necessary to enforce British demands. But even so, Disraeli could have achieved little without his second-in-command: the details of policy and negotiation were left entirely in the capable hands of Salisbury. Disraeli's frail constitution was seriously overtaxed during the Congress and Salisbury carried a greater burden than his chief. The Cyprus Convention, for example, owed much more to the Foreign Secretary than it did to the Prime Minister. As Salisbury commented: 'What with deafness, ignorance of French and Bismarck's extraordinary mode of speech, Beaconsfield has

---

[6] Blake, *Disraeli*, pp. 623, 627–8, 634–7.

[7] Salisbury to Lytton, 9 Mar. 1877, quoted in Lady G. Cecil, *Life of Robert, Marquis of Salisbury*, 4 vols. (London, 1921–32) II 130. For a recent analysis of foreign policy during these years, see C. J. Lowe, *The Reluctant Imperialists* (London, 1967) I 1–93.

the dimmest idea of what is going on, understands everything crossways and imagines a perpetual conspiracy.'[8] Nevertheless, as the most recent biographer of Disraeli states, 'there is no doubt that foreign policy from the Suez Canal purchase to the Berlin Congress and beyond, was essentially Disraeli's'.[9] During these years Disraeli provided the framework and set the tone for the conduct of British foreign policy; and it was in his approach to the Eastern Question that his vision of the purpose of empire became most apparent.

Disraeli's concept of the British empire in the world, increasing the power and influence of Great Britain, caused observers to link Conservatism and empire. For the first time the close involvement of imperial affairs with foreign policy became obvious to the general public. During Disraeli's premiership Indian and imperial interests became synonymous with the British national interest. The purchase of the Suez Canal Company shares, the Royal Titles Act, the sending of Indian troops to Malta and the occupation of Cyprus were all part of a design to defend British naval lifelines and the approaches to India. Disraeli's foreign policy, like his view of empire, became increasingly dominated by that brightest of jewels in the imperial diadem.[10] The emergence of India as the focal point of British foreign policy can easily be traced. Specific reference was made to 'the Provinces of my Eastern Empire' in the Queen's Speech of February 1875, and the 'Eastern Empire' received greater publicity later in the year when the British government purchased the Khedive's Suez Canal shares. The following year the Queen was made Empress of India. All these actions were intended to reaffirm British power in the east.

I

In November 1875 Disraeli discovered that the bankrupt Egyptian Khedive was negotiating for the sale of his last remain-

[8] Salisbury to Lady Salisbury, 23 June 1878, quoted in Cecil, *Salisbury*, II 287.

[9] Blake, *Disraeli*, p. 653.

[10] See A. W. Preston, 'British Military Policy and the Defence of India: A Study of British Military Policy, Plans and Preparations during the Russian Crisis, 1876–80', unpublished Ph.D. thesis (London, 1966); also R. L. Kirkpatrick, 'British Imperial Policy, 1874–80', unpublished D.Phil. thesis (Oxford, 1953).

THE LION'S SHARE.

"GARE À QUI LA TOUCHE!"

ing asset, 176,602 ordinary shares in the Suez Canal Company, with two rival French syndicates, one of which had an option on the shares due to expire on 19 November. Disraeli persuaded the Cabinet that the control of this important seaway, which considerably shortened the routes to India, China and Australia, should not be allowed to fall completely into French hands. Accordingly, the Khedive was informed on 17 November that the British government wished to purchase his shares. Nine days later the Khedive was £4 million richer and the shares were safely deposited in the British consulate in Cairo. It was a dramatic coup, a personal victory for Disraeli. Great Britain now held 44 per cent of the Suez Canal Company shares, admittedly not a controlling interest as Disraeli would have liked to believe, but, as later events were to prove, an extremely profitable investment in a seaway dominated by British commerce and in turn dominating British sea routes to India, the Pacific and the Far East. To Disraeli it was an action upholding British power :

> Some may take an economical view of the subject, some may take a commercial view, some may take a peaceful view, some may take a warlike view of it; but of this I feel persuaded – and I speak with confidence – that when I appeal to the House of Commons for their vote they will agree with the country, that this was a purchase which was necessary to maintain the Empire, and which favours in every degree the policy which this country ought to sustain.[11]

Another opportunity to further the policy of imperial greatness which the country 'ought to sustain' soon arose. A personal wish of the Queen to be Empress of India was turned into 'the semblance of deep and organised policy'.[12]

The Queen's Speech of February 1876 referred briefly to the acquisition of the Suez Canal Company shares and then dwelt on the recent tour of the Prince of Wales in India. In a speech seconding the address, Mr Mulholland (M.P. for Downpatrick) remarked on the success of the tour which had given the Indian princes 'a common pride in the greatness of the Empire – a greatness of which, as dignitaries, they themselves to some extent partake. We, too, when we have read of the assembly of those

[11] 3 *Hansard*, 8 Feb. 1876, ccxxvii 102.
[12] Disraeli to Salisbury, 11 Jan. 1876, quoted in Buckle, v 458.

"NEW CROWNS FOR OLD ONES!"

(ALADDIN *adapted.*)

feudatory Princes, have, perhaps, realised the greatness of that Eastern Empire, as we never realised it before.' He therefore welcomed the announcement that the Queen was to adopt a new royal style and title in her capacity as ruler of India, as crowning 'this great Empire that we have built up in the East, by assuming a title long foreshadowed by events'.[13]

The assumption of the imperial title had been in the air since the proclamation of British rule in 1858. The question no doubt appealed to Disraeli's sense of imperial splendour and dignity. When the Empress-Queen began to demand her imperial crown, Disraeli doubtless saw an opportunity to signify to the world at large, and to Russia in particular, that 'it was the unanimous determination of the people of this country to retain our connection with the Indian empire'.[14] Thus, on 17 February 1876, he introduced a bill into the Commons providing for an unspecified addition to the Queen's royal titles.

In his speeches during the passage of the bill, however, Disraeli revealed an ignorance of the Indian empire as complete as his ignorance of colonial affairs. His picture of the Indian masses clamouring to pay homage, not to a distant suzerain but to the crowned head of India, was as ill-informed as his references to the British colonist who 'finds a nugget' or 'fleeces a thousand flocks' before returning to Great Britain to live in rich retirement. Compelling rhetoric, a romantic idea no doubt, but hardly an accurate description of Indian and colonial realities.[15] In fact Disraeli's attempt at linking the growing empire sentiment with India was a failure. Opposition to the adoption of the alien title of Empress, with its continental associations, was unexpectedly strong and the bill had a tough passage through Parliament. Much was written and spoken about the dangers of Disraeli's actions to English constitutional usage before the bill was passed, mainly out of respect for the known wishes of the Queen.[16] In future Disraeli was to be much more cautious in the use of imperial language. He was careful to stress imperial interests as part of the British national interest. But even this term was to

[13] 3 *Hansard*, 8 Feb. 1876, ccxxvii 65–7.
[14] 3 *Hansard*, 17 Feb. 1876, ccxxvii 408–10.
[15] Disraeli's speeches detailing his romantic concept of empire can be found in 3 *Hansard*, ccxxvii 407–10, 424–8, 1719–27; ccxxviii 278–81, 293–4, 319–24, 492–501.
[16] Koebner, *Imperialism*, pp. 117–24.

become suspect after it had been used to shield the 'unspeakable Turk'.

II

On 23 June 1876 the Liberal *Daily News* published a horrifyingly detailed account of atrocities committed by Turkish irregular troops against the peasantry in Bulgaria, where a revolt had been raging for most of the year. There followed a loud humanitarian outcry in England. The misgovernment of the Porte was notorious. Yet Disraeli obstinately refused to endorse the demands of the European powers for immediate governmental reforms, acting coolly towards the Andrassy Note and rejecting outright the Berlin Memorandum. Indeed, the Turks were encouraged in their obstinacy by the presence of British warships in Besika Bay, just outside the Dardanelles. Disraeli appeared to be supporting the Turkish policy of repression. It was not surprising, then, that the Liberal opposition should charge the Conservative government with being morally implicated in the massacre of 12,000 Bulgarians.

Disraeli, who had previously tried, mistakenly, to brush off the question of 'atrocities', was forced to admit in the last debate of the session in August 1876 that a massacre had indeed occurred. It was, he agreed, a deplorable event. But he rejected Sir William Harcourt's charge that the government upheld Turkey through 'blind superstition, and from a want of sympathy with the highest aspirations of humanity'. He informed the House : 'what our duty is at this critical moment is to maintain the empire of England'. The massacre of 12,000 peasants, he obstinately declared, did not justify a change in existing British foreign policy, securely based as it was on the Treaty of Paris of 1856 and the less well-known Tripartite Treaty of Guarantee concluded shortly after.[17] These were Disraeli's last words in the House of Commons.

It would be a mistake to conclude that Disraeli had, at this stage, determined on preserving Turkish territorial integrity. Far from it : 'All the Turks may be in the Propontis as far as I am concerned', he declared.[18] His interests lay elsewhere. He was more concerned with making an emphatic assertion of British

[17] 3 *Hansard*, 11 Aug. 1876, ccxxxi 1146.
[18] See Buckle, vi 53; also the conclusions of Blake, *Disraeli*, pp. 595–6.

NEUTRALITY UNDER DIFFICULTIES.

Dizzy. "BULGARIAN ATROCITIES! I CAN'T FIND THEM IN THE 'OFFICIAL REPORTS'!!!"

independence and with striking a blow at the *Dreikaiserbund*. It was not until the Russians declared war on Turkey in 1877 that Disraeli decided on the need to bolster the crumbling regime. As the Russians advanced towards Constantinople, it looked as if the Russian empire would soon face the British empire in the Mediterranean as well as on the Indian border. And however aware of the changing pattern of great-power relationships Disraeli may have been, he certainly possessed no ideas on the defence of British interests other than the 'old Crimean policy' and the traditional Palmerstonian approach to defence strategy.

Palmerston had twice risked war over the Eastern Question (and once actually waged it in the Crimea) in order to preserve the *status quo*. By upholding Turkish territorial integrity Palmerston had sought, in Europe, to prevent the emergence of Russia as a Mediterranean power, and in Asia to prevent the possibility, however remote, of an overland march through Syria on Egypt and the Red Sea, or through the Tigris–Euphrates valley on the Persian Gulf. The integrity of the Ottoman empire had been the crux of his policy. In short, the Eastern Question in Europe and policy towards Persia and Afghanistan in Asia all involved the general problem of Russian expansionism and the security of India. Thus the outbreak of the Russo-Turkish war in the spring of 1877 marked the failure of the attempt to control the Russian advance by diplomacy. Disraeli immediately reverted to the traditional British policy of supporting the Turk, a course which Gladstonian Liberals and conscientious Christians found repugnant. And as Gladstone, excited by popular passion, tried to whip up a moral crusade (his pamphlet *The Bulgarian Horrors and the Question of the East* published in September 1876 was a bestseller), Disraeli denounced Gladstone's activities as 'worse than any of those Bulgarian atrocities which now occupy attention' and asserted that the 'permanent and imperial interests of England would prevail'. The more Turcophobe Gladstone became, the more Russophobe was Disraeli.[19]

Disraeli seems to have held a fairly consistent (if rather ridiculous and ill-founded) belief in a Russian menace over the whole area between Europe and India, which posed a threat to

---

[19] *The Times*, 21 Sept. 1876; Blake, *Disraeli*, p. 607.

the British empire.[20] But while it was generally agreed by the majority of British politicians that it was in the national interest to safeguard the routes to India and the *status quo* in the Persian Gulf and the Dardanelles, the extent to which the integrity of the Ottoman empire remained a British interest was disputed. There was disagreement even within the Cabinet. Was Constantinople the 'key to India'? Sir Stafford Northcote and Lord Salisbury did not think so. Salisbury wrote to Lord Lytton in March 1877:

> I feel convinced that the old policy – wise enough in its time – of defending English interests by sustaining the Ottoman dynasty has become impracticable, and I think that the time has come for defending English interests in a more direct way by some territorial rearrangement.

And again, in May 1877, he grumbled:

> The commonest error in politics is sticking to the carcases of dead policies. When a mast falls overboard you do not try to save a rope here and a spar there in memory of their former utility; you cut away the hamper altogether. And it should be the same with a policy. But it is not so. We cling to the shred of an old policy after it has been torn to pieces; and to the shadow of the shred after the rag itself has been torn away.[21]

Much of the trouble, he remarked, came from using maps on too small a scale. Surprisingly, Disraeli, who had visited the places in his early manhood, was an offender in this respect. He had no time for those of his colleagues who suggested that British defensive strategy should be based on Cairo:

> Many in England say, Why not? England might take Egypt and so secure our highway to India. But the answer is obvious. . . . If the Russians had Constantinople, they could at any time march their Army through Syria to the mouth of the Nile, and then what would be the use of our holding Egypt? Not even the command of the sea could help us under such circumstances. People who talk in this manner must be utterly ignorant of geography. Our strength is on the sea.

[20] See B. H. Sumner, *Russia and the Balkans, 1870–80* (Oxford, 1937) for a discussion of Russian policy at this time.

[21] Cecil, *Salisbury*, II 130, 145.

THE AWKWARD SQUAD.

(See Blue Book.)

Sergeant. "ON YOUR EASTERN QUESTION—RIGHT-ABOUT-TURN!" Company Officer (aside). "AH, THEY ALWAYS WERE SLOW AT THEIR 'FACINGS!'"
Sergeant (to himself). "MUST GET 'EM ROUND SOMEHOW!"

Constantinople is the Key to India, and not Egypt and the Suez Canal.[22]

Like Palmerston before him, Disraeli seems to have genuinely believed that whoever held Constantinople could threaten the Suez Canal area. This was a remote possibility at best : an obsession, notes Robert Blake, that 'stemmed from ancient habit rather than clear thought'.[23] Nevertheless, for Disraeli the defence of Constantinople remained an overriding British interest in his concern for the safety of India and its approaches.

When hostilities between the Russians and Turks began, Disraeli was convinced that these British interests could be maintained only by the threat of war backed up by military preparedness. The Cabinet was divided and Gladstone, emerging from retirement, attacked the government's position during the 'Five Nights' Debate' on the Eastern Question in May 1877 : 'English interests', he charged, were being used to cloak a calculated policy of imperial aggression which could lead only to weakness and warfare. India had first been conquered and now it was being maintained that, in order to secure the safety of British rule, Great Britain must interfere in every political development which occurred along the routes to India. In Gladstone's view, the empire which had symbolised freedom and voluntaryism was being turned into a military machine for the use of the Prime Minister of England.[24] He feared that a new concept of 'empire' was being born : the term, he noted, was being associated increasingly with military and political power over vast alien populations.

This attack on the nature and purpose of the British empire spread to the pages of *The Nineteenth Century* during the summer of 1877 when Gladstone became involved in an acrimonious debate with Edward Dicey, the editor of *The Observer*.

III

In June and August 1877 Dicey contributed two articles to the periodical advocating a British occupation of Egypt in the

[22] Barrington memo., 23 Oct. 1876, quoted in Buckle, vi 84. This is a record of Disraeli's words on the subject in an interview with Lord Barrington in October 1876.

[23] Blake, *Disraeli*, p. 578.

[24] 3 *Hansard*, 7 May 1877, ccxxxiv 408–14.

interests of empire security. Such an action, he maintained, would forestall a Russian move into the Mediterranean and secure the Suez Canal and our routes to India. Great Britain had acquired her empire because she was strong, and in protecting her possessions she should not shrink from extending her dominions. The power and greatness of Great Britain, Dicey asserted, depended upon this imperial position. The burden of empire was part of Great Britain's 'manifest destiny'.[25]

Such an interpretation was anathema to Gladstone. He let forth a broadside in reply entitled 'Aggression on Egypt and Freedom in the East' (August 1877). The empire was a burden, he admitted, but it was a burden of honour, a trust that should one day be shed. It was also a national weakness. 'The root and pith and substance of the material greatness of our nation lies within the compass of these islands, and is, except in trifling particulars, independent of all and every sort of political dominion beyond them', Gladstone countered. India, he informed Dicey, 'does not add to but takes from our military strength'. Great Britain, he concluded, had 'no interest in India except the well-being of India itself'.[26]

To Dicey this highflown philanthropy was so much moral humbug. In reply, he entirely rejected the thesis that the possession of empire could be justified only by the benefits it conferred, directly or indirectly, on subject peoples. The British empire, he emphasised, had been established for the sole benefit of Great Britain. We ruled India 'because we deem the possession of India conducive to our interests and our reputation, because we have got it and intend to keep it'. The empire, in fact, added not only to British power but to British greatness:

We have followed our star, fulfilled our destiny, worked out the will implanted in us; and to say that we have been influenced in the main by any higher motive seems to me self-deception. Still, though to assert that we have gone forth to foreign lands for the sake of doing good would be sheer hypocrisy, we may fairly say that we have done good by going

[25] E. Dicey, 'Our Route to India' and 'The Future of Egypt', in *The Nineteenth Century*, I (June 1877) 665–85; II (Aug. 1877) 3–14.
[26] W. E. Gladstone, 'Aggression on Egypt and Freedom in the East', *The Nineteenth Century*, II (Aug. 1877) 149–66.

and are doing good by stopping. . . . Whatever else we may have failed to do, the mere existence of our Empire has brought new life into lands stagnant for ages, has stirred up dormant energies, has instilled the rudimental ideas of individual liberty, equality before the law and public duty.[27]

This was the justification of empire Dicey put forward in opposition to the views of Gladstone, the leader of that 'anti-imperialist Theory of English Statecraft'. Obviously, Gladstone's conception of a voluntary association of self-governing colonies, each constantly asserting its own independence, had vastly less appeal than the notion of a compact, centralised and armed empire ready to defend British interests at a time when Great Britain feared Russian expansionism and faced the growing might of the military machines of Europe. Dicey had become, in Professor Koebner's words, 'the literary spokesman of an Empire spirit which was illiberal and militant, a spirit which the political crisis in the Near East had helped to hatch'.[28] And as this crisis deepened in the early months of 1878, the new outlook on empire was emphasised when Disraeli once again resorted to imperial rhetoric.

IV

In January 1878 the Russians finally occupied Adrianople and the Turks sued for peace. In Great Britain, as fears concerning Russian designs on the Straits grew larger, Disraeli asked for a £6 million vote of credit. At the prospect of war with Russia the Colonial Secretary, Lord Carnarvon, promptly resigned. Disraeli then took the further precaution of sending a British fleet to Constantinople when an armistice was signed on 31 January. A British expeditionary force under Lord Napier of Magdala was also planned as war-fever mounted.

British fears were confirmed when, on 3 March 1878, the Porte finally signed the Treaty of San Stefano. Russian gains in the Balkans and Armenia were acknowledged and Russia became for the first time, through her influence over Albania and an enlarged Bulgaria, a Mediterranean power. Disraeli informed the Cabinet that the crisis point had been reached. The whole

[27] E. Dicey, 'Mr Gladstone and Our Empire', *The Nineteenth Century*, II (Sept. 1877), 292–308.
[28] Koebner, *Imperialism*, p. 133.

ON THE DIZZY BRINK.

Lord B. "JUST A LEETLE NEARER THE EDGE?"
Britannia. "NOT AN INCH FURTHER. I'M A GOOD DEAL NEARER THAN IS PLEASANT ALREADY!"

balance of power in the Mediterranean had been destroyed. The empire was in peril. He proposed, therefore, to send an expeditionary force secretly from India to seize a *place d'armes* – either Cyprus or Alexandretta – in order to counter the Russian conquests in Armenia and to watch over British interests in the Persian Gulf. A second member of the Cabinet, the Foreign Secretary, Lord Derby, now resigned. It was also decided to call up the reserves 'for the maintenance of peace and for the protection of the interests of the empire'. These were the twin pillars of Disraeli's platform, and Disraeli returned to the ornate language of his speeches on the Royal Titles Bill when he conveyed this decision to the House of Lords on 8 April 1878. He concluded by declaring:

> I have ever considered that Her Majesty's Government of whatever party formed, are the trustees of that Empire. That Empire was formed by the energy and enterprise of our ancestors, my lords; and it is one of a very peculiar character. I know no example of it, either in ancient or modern history. No Caesar or Charlemagne ever presided over a dominion so peculiar. Its flag floats on many waters; it has provinces in every zone, they are inhabited by persons of different races, different religion, different laws, manners, customs. Some of these are bound to us by the ties of liberty, fully conscious that without their connection with the metropolis they have no security for public freedom and self-government; others are bound to us by flesh and blood and by material as well as moral considerations. There are millions who are bound to us by our military sway because they know that they are indebted to it for order and justice. All these communities agree in recognising the commanding spirit of these islands that has formed and fashioned in such a manner so great a proportion of the globe.[29]

The foreign policy of Great Britain, the centre of the empire, could not but be an imperial one.

The speech foreshadowed the announcement, a week later, of the despatch of 7,000 Indian troops to Malta, a result of that 'military sway' exercised by the British Prime Minister (without the aid of Parliament) on behalf of the British people. Such an

[29] 3 *Hansard*, 8 Apr. 1878, ccxxxix 761–77.

action did not go uncontested. An opposition motion declaring the despatch of Indian troops a violation of the Bill of Rights was debated on three successive nights in May. The new Colonial Secretary, Sir Michael Hicks Beach, defended the government's action as necessary 'to show quickly and decisively to the world that we were able, if need be, to wield the Forces of a united Empire'.[30] The motion was lost, but the outcry against the military concept of empire continued in the press and the suspicion remained that the government was prepared to by-pass Parliament, a suspicion that was not diminished when the main provisions of the Treaty of Berlin were ratified without the knowledge of that body.

Disraeli and Salisbury returned from the Congress of Berlin triumphantly proclaiming 'peace with honour'. The San Stefano Treaty had been disposed of, the 'big Bulgaria' divided and British interests secured in Asia. A new military alliance had been concluded with Turkey, and Cyprus occupied in the interests of peace and the maintenance of the empire. The Liberal opposition was aghast, not simply at the prospect of further foreign commitments engaged in without the authority of Parliament, but at the way in which the new military concept of empire, which had emerged during the crisis with Disraeli's blessing, was flaunted before an almost hysterical British public. In the House of Lords, Disraeli indulged in a typical piece of imperial rhetoric :

Her Majesty has fleets and armies that are second to none. England must have seen with pride the Mediterranean covered with her ships; she must have seen with pride the discipline and devotion which have been shown to her and her Government by all her troops, drawn from every part of her Empire. I leave it to the illustrious duke [the Duke of Cambridge] in whose presence I speak, to bear witness to the spirit of imperial patriotism which has been exhibited by the troops from India, which he recently reviewed at Malta. But it is not on our fleets and armies, however necessary they may be for the maintenance of imperial strength, that I alone or mainly depend in that enterprise on which this country is about to enter. It is on what I most highly value – the consciousness that in the Eastern Nations there is a confidence in this country, and that,

[30] 3 *Hansard*, 20 May 1878, ccxl 264.

5 The Balkans after the Congress of Berlin, 1878

while we know we can enforce our policy, at the same time they know that our Empire is an Empire of liberty, of truth, and of justice.[31]

Disraeli's empire was India-oriented ('In taking Cyprus the movement is not Mediterranean, it is Indian', the Prime Minister gleefully announced), a centralised, military unit controlled increasingly, it seemed to opponents, by the British Prime Minister to further purely British ends. A new imperial age was being born. The government was 'striving to pick up the thread – the broken thread – of England's old Imperial traditions', Lord Salisbury proudly proclaimed at a Conservative banquet, and, referring to those who did not possess the same grandeur of imperial vision, he sneered :

For a short time there have been men, eminent in public affairs, who have tried to persuade you that all the past history of England was a mistake – that the duty of England, the interests of England, was to confine herself solely to her own insular forces, to cultivate commerce, to accumulate riches, and not, as it was said, to entangle herself in foreign policies. They were men who disdained empire, who objected to colonies, and who grumbled even at the possession of India. Even for their own low purpose the policy of these men was a mistake. The commerce of a great commercial country like this will only flourish – history attests it again and again – under the shadow of empire, and those who give up empire in order to make commerce prosper will end by losing both.[32]

The present government, Salisbury concluded, did not suffer from this delusion.

V

Such a declaration was anathema to Gladstone, who penned yet another rebuke to the Disraeli government in the September issue of *The Nineteenth Century*, entitled 'England's Mission'. Gladstone began by criticising Disraeli's claim to have brought back peace with honour. Where was the honour, he enquired, in making an alliance with the oppressors of Christians and in

[31] 3 *Hansard*, 18 July 1878, CCXLI 1753–74.
[32] Speech at Knightsbridge, 27 July 1878, quoted in Cecil, *Salisbury*, II 302–3; *Daily News*, 29 July 1878.

violating European law by occupying Cyprus? What was the use
of this small island in any case? It was merely a symbol of that
expanding imperial appetite that had first swallowed up the Fiji
Islands and then the Transvaal. The government's policy was
simply one of 'territorial aggrandisement, backed by military
display'. Increased commitments usually meant strained resources,
but the great British nation was being seduced into believing that
extent of territory constituted greatness and that security depended on the amount of fear generated in foreign breasts.

Gladstone then explained the real difference between the two
parties in their attitude towards colonies:

> It is the administrative connection, and the shadow of political
> subordination, which chiefly give them value in the sight of
> the party, who at home as well as abroad are striving to cajole
> or drive us into Imperialism. With their opponents, it is the
> welfare of these communities which forms the great object of
> interest and desire.

The Liberal view of empire was one of growing communities,
freely associated, bound to the mother country by ties of kindred
and affection, of friendship and trust:

> We do not want Bosnian submissions. Especially is it in-
> expedient to acquire possessions which, like Cyprus, never can
> become truly British, because they have acquired indelibly an
> ethnical character of their own. In them we remain as masters
> and as foreigners, and the connection at its best has not the
> ennobling features which, in cases like America and Australasia,
> give a high moral purpose to the subsisting relation, and
> compensate for the serious responsibilities which in given
> contingencies it may entail.[33]

This, Gladstone insisted, was a far nobler view of empire than
the alien concept, currently being preached, of an empire based
on the use of force, enveloped by this ostentatious display of
splendour, and used in an unscrupulous manner by a scheming
party leader to undermine the authority of Parliament and the
British constitution. It was a very sharp attack indeed. In the
Commons, Sir William Harcourt continued the attack and

[33] W. E. Gladstone, 'England's Mission', *The Nineteenth Century*, IV
(Sept. 1878) 560–84.

declared that the government 'had roused a spirit which they could not repress; they had summoned this war spirit as their slave, and it had become their master. . . . The policy of the Government was an Imperial policy. Yes, it was an Imperial policy – it was a servile copy of the Imperialism of the Second Empire.'[34]

An ideological battle over the two opposed views of empire now began.[35] When Disraeli spoke of 'Empire and Liberty' in his speech at the Guildhall in November 1879, Gladstone retorted that it meant 'Liberty for ourselves, Empire over the rest of mankind'.[36] The climax of Gladstone's assault on the principles behind Disraeli's foreign and imperial policies came, however, before massed audiences during the Liberal leader's Midlothian campaign of 1879–80.

On his Scottish tour during November and December 1879 Gladstone restated the basic tenets of Liberalism and of the party's foreign policy. Time and again the Liberal leader insisted that the strength of Great Britain lay within the shores of the United Kingdom, not in ever-increasing dominion overseas. The Disraeli government had not increased Great Britain's international standing by annexing the Fiji Islands and the Transvaal, by occupying Cyprus, by interfering in the affairs of the Malay States, or by becoming involved in the financial affairs of Egypt, which could yet prove to be the embryo of an African empire. Foreign ventures led only to disaster, as the Zulu and Afghan wars had witnessed. Great Britain, Gladstone asserted, had overreached the limits of prudence and incurred obligations she could not meet. It was a fundamental tenet of Liberal foreign policy not to profess any claim not allowed to another. Yet the British people were being urged to act as instructors to the other nations of the world. It was true the Indian empire ought to be upheld – it was a pledge to be redeemed and not an object for exploitation as Disraeli seemed to think[37] – but this did not mean that Great Britain had the right to interfere in all developments

[34] 3 *Hansard*, 13 Dec. 1878, CCXLIII 768.
[35] Koebner, *Imperialism*, pp. 147–65.
[36] Speech at West Calder, 27 Nov. 1879, quoted in W. E. Gladstone, *Midlothian Speeches 1879*, Victorian Library ed. (Leicester U.P., 1971) p. 128.
[37] For a survey of Conservative policy towards India, see R. J. Moore, *Liberalism and Indian Politics, 1872–1922* (London, 1966) pp. 15–27.

affecting every avenue of approach to our eastern possessions :
'That, gentlemen, is a monstrous claim.'[38]

In his speeches during this 'festival of freedom' Gladstone was
careful to disavow the charge that he was a separatist. He had
always believed in empire, he said. Great Britain could be justly
proud of the free communities she was rearing for nationhood,
but this was a far cry from revelling in military dominion over
alien peoples. He accepted rule over backward nations where it
had already been established as 'moral trusteeship', but asserted
that every nation had the right to conduct its own affairs : 'if
one thing more than another has been detestable to Europe, it
has been the appearance upon the stage from time to time of
men who, even in the times of the Christian civilisation, have
been thought to aim at universal dominion'.[39] Disraeli's foreign
policy was stifling national independence and that spirit of liberty
it should be seeking to preserve, both at home and abroad. He
denounced specifically the doctrine that the British government
could wage wars and raise troops anywhere in the British empire
without the consent of Parliament, provided Parliament did not
have to foot the bill. Nothing could be more certain to rouse
Gladstone's righteous wrath than the use of Indian troops during
the parliamentary recess in a campaign against Afghanistan :
nothing could be more immoral. The war was a flagrant abuse of
Afghanistan's freedom. 'We have', he roared,

> gone up into the mountains; we have broken Afghanistan to
> pieces; we have driven mothers and children forth from their
> homes to perish in the snow; we have spent treasure, of which
> a real account has never yet been rendered; we have under-
> gone an expenditure of which as yet I believe we are aware of
> but a fraction.

All for the sake of a vainglorious imperialism that had shaken
the foundations of the Indian empire. 'Remember that the
sanctity of life in the hill villages of Afghanistan among the
winter snows', he urged his audience, 'is as inviolable in the eye
of Almighty God as can be your own.'[40]

Such impassioned denunciations doubtless thrilled the ears of

[38] Glasgow, 5 Dec. 1879, quoted in *Midlothian Speeches*, p. 196.
[39] Ibid. p. 128, 27 Nov. 1879.
[40] Ibid. p. 204, 5 Dec. 1879; p. 94, speech at Dalkeith, 26 Nov. 1879.

THE COLOSSUS OF WORDS.

Gladstone's listeners and the minds of his reading public. But the absence of any effective reply (Disraeli boasted that he had not 'read a single line' of Gladstone's 'pilgrimage of passion'[41]) gave the impression that no effective reply was possible. By the election of 1880 'imperialism' had become a damaging political smear-word and Gladstone's accusations remained unanswered. If the existing agricultural and industrial depression had not already sealed the fate of the Conservative government, Gladstone certainly scored an outstanding personal success at the hustings. The crowds who had roared in support of Disraeli on his return from the Congress of Berlin, and had subsequently been carried away by enthusiasm for military display, warmed, in 1880, to Gladstone's denunciation of imperialist ventures, costly foreign policy and unpopular wars. When the Conservative government disappeared from the scene, the Disraelian concept of empire temporarily went with it.

VI

What then was Disraeli's contribution to British imperialism? He paid scant attention to the Gladstonian empire of settlement. He was *not* concerned with colonial policy : as we have seen, in the annexation of Fiji and the Transvaal, the occupation of Cyprus, and the extension of British influence in West Africa, the Malay States and the South Pacific, he had scarcely participated. Even the 'imperial' policies associated with 'Beaconsfieldism' – the Zulu and Afghan wars – were not part of an imperial vision. Disraeli's contribution to these events was purely negative, a failure to oversee policies, restrain Cabinet ministers and control the men on the spot. Disraeli's apparent endorsement of the idea of expansion belonged to the realm of histrionics.

But in Disraeli's handling of British foreign policy in the east, a new vision of empire did emerge – a centralised, military empire backing up the strength of Great Britain in her role as a world power and providing both resources and armies beyond the control of Parliament. Here was the empire of Disraeli's dreams, which has been obscured by the myths of 'forward movements' and 'Beaconsfieldism'. Gladstone recognised the challenge and fought a running battle with the Prime Minister, over the future character of the British empire, during the years 1877–80. The

[41] Blake, *Disraeli*, p. 700.

views of the two schools of thought which dominated policy for
the next fifty years were spelt out in public debate as never
before; and the British public for the first time became aware of
the close connection between foreign policy, the empire and the
routes to the east.

In 1863 Disraeli had written of the need for Great Britain to
'get possession of the strong places of the world if it wishes to
contribute to its power'.[42] What contribution did Disraeli's policies
make? It is doubtful if his acquisitions added to the strategic
strength of the empire at all. The occupation of Cyprus, for
example, has been heavily criticised by historians as hasty,
inopportune and ill-advised, especially when French agreement
was secured only by assenting to the proposed annexation of
Tunisia, including the port of Bizerta, from which the British
routes to India could be effectively challenged.[43] And similarly,
the 'forward movement' Salisbury initiated in India, where one-
third of the British army was already stationed, only succeeded
in stretching the strained resources of trained manpower even
further. Professor D. C. Gordon was probably right in concluding
in his study of imperial defence policy : 'Disraeli's imperialism
was essentially rhetorical : it added little to the Empire's power.'[44]

Nevertheless, Disraeli's imperial vision did make an indelible
impression on British public opinion and added a new dimension
to the British imperialism of later decades. Professor Koebner has
recorded that when Gladstone proved himself equally incom-
petent in the conduct of imperial affairs, 'empire' was soon
purged of that 'evil smell that had clung to it in the mudslinging'
of 1876–80. Then, 'Disraeli's name acquired a new glitter; a
legend of his imperial vision began to grow and his name was
often associated with the awakening of the imperial spirit'.[45]
Disraeli did indeed contribute to the imperial idea. He contributed a new vision of an expanding, militant empire which
was often linked with an undemocratic and illiberal imperial
spirit glorifying British achievements and rule overseas. This was
an imperial vision far removed from that of twenty years before,

[42] 3 *Hansard*, 5 Feb. 1863, CLXIX 96.
[43] See H. Temperley, 'Disraeli and Cyprus', *E.H.R.*, XLVI (1931) 274–9;
Thornton, *The Imperial Idea*, p. 34; Blake, *Disraeli*, p. 651.
[44] D. C. Gordon, *The Dominion Partnership in Imperial Defence, 1870–
1914* (Baltimore, 1965) p. 40.
[45] Koebner, *Imperialism*, pp. 166–7.

a vision of empire which not only influenced the development of British imperialism in the late-Victorian period, but retained a lasting grip on certain sections of British public opinion until well into the twentieth century.

9

England's Mission

DISRAELI ceased to be Prime Minister in April 1880. Parliament was dissolved on 24 March and voting began a week later. The results of the first day's polling came as an unwelcome surprise : the Liberals made a net gain of fifteen seats in sixty-nine constituencies. By the following day Conservative hopes for victory were negligible. Gladstone, who had just undertaken a second whirlwind tour of Midlothian, announced in West Calder that the nation 'had found its interests mismanaged, its honour tarnished, and its strength burdened and weakened by needless, mischievous, unauthorised, unprofitable engagements, and it has resolved that this state of things shall cease, and that right and justice shall be done'.[1] Gladstone's triumph in Midlothian was now complete : 'I am stunned but God will provide.'

In the House of Commons the Liberals received a handsome majority of over one hundred seats. Disraeli's policy, stigmatised by Lord Derby as one of 'occupy, fortify, grab and brag', had been decisively defeated at the polls. And so the Liberals returned to office with their mid-Victorian ideas of limited, economical government, of informal rule and free trade, and their policies of limited intervention and minimum responsibility. Gladstone, perceiving in all this the hand of the Almighty ('the Almighty has employed me for His purposes, in a manner larger, or more especial than before, and has strengthened me, and led me on accordingly'), marvelled at the downfall of Beaconsfieldism which was 'like the vanishing of some vast magnificent castle in an Italian romance. It is too big, however, to be taken in all at

[1] Morley, *Life of Gladstone*, II 611.

SUNSET.

(After B. R. Haydon.)

once.'[2] The clock seemed to be put back ten, even twenty, years. Nevertheless, the atmosphere of the 1880s was radically different from that of two decades earlier. The 1870s had witnessed some very significant changes in political opinions as well as in the direction of colonial policy.

I

Following the debates of the years 1868–70, when Earl Granville was thought by some critics to be contemplating the dismember-ment of the empire, separatist ideas had been trounced. To this extent Professor Bodelsen was right in suggesting that 'the decisive defeat of Separatism took place, not as commonly believed, in the eighties, but already in the early seventies'.[3] But though the anti-empire outlook had been overcome, nothing positive replaced it. Federalists, philanthropists and the various business interests concerned, failed to achieve general acceptance for their ideas. Thus Bodelsen went too far in asserting that the years 1869–74 saw 'the turning point in the history of English public opinion on the colonial question'.[4] Admittedly, these years saw the demise of certain political ideas, but there is little evidence to suggest that separatism had ever established a strong hold over mid-Victorian 'public opinion', or that there was any significant change in the general attitude of the electorate towards the British empire before the 1890s. Although many existing prejudices had been removed, there was no popular movement in favour of imperialism. There was certainly little demand for a general expansionist policy. The critics of Lord Granville's alleged policy, the defenders who declared that the empire was in danger and then pressed the need for consolidation, aimed at the maintenance of the empire, not its extension. Once the nega-tive separatist attitude had been removed, this allowed the small expansionist pressure groups a louder say, but did not guarantee them greater effect. In fact the so-called 'forward movements' of the 1870s, Fiji apart, had little to do with the colonial lobby and even less to do with Lord Granville's critics. As Professor J. E.

[2] Ibid. II 615; III 1.
[3] Bodelsen, pp. 8–9. Dr I. M. Cumpston notes the complete absence of separatism in her article 'The Discussion of Imperial Problems in the British Parliament, 1880–85', *T.R.H.S.*, XIII (1962) 29–47.
[4] Bodelsen, p. 8.

Tyler concluded, as long ago as 1938, the imperialist revival of the last two decades of the nineteenth century

> lay in the logic of the immense changes which were now coming over world politics, changes which precipitated a general reaction against *laissez-faire* in which imperialism was to play its signal part. It was due neither to the particular sins of Granville nor the protests of his critics. Nor was it but a passing phase. Born of a new age, it could only die, as it was born, along with it.[5]

In reality, Bodelsen's protest movement was in the long run little more than the agitation of a rather insignificant group of men who, ignoring changing world circumstances and the non-white areas of the empire, later lost themselves amid plans for federation of the settlement colonies.

A more sympathetic approach to colonial needs was, however, in evidence after the disappearance of Granville and Rogers from the Colonial Office. Typically, Rogers, for ever suspicious of new projects, sourly minuted in April 1868 :

> Settlers and merchants are always ready to call for operations of which they are to reap the benefit in the shape of security of commerce, etc., and Government to bear the cost in the way of military proceedings, embassies etc. And Governors are only too apt to fall in with a policy which gives interest and importance to their proceedings.[6]

But Kimberley and Carnarvon and the new Permanent Under-Secretary, Herbert, appreciated colonial susceptibilities more fully and were not so afraid to face expansion. Herbert noted, for example, after the annexation of the Fiji Islands and the proposed establishment of the Western Pacific High Commission : 'Further annexation will come at the proper time, but to tell the world (Germany, United States, France etc.) that we *now* contemplate it would be to defeat the object and prevent us from quietly acquiring paramount influence among the islands.'[7] But these men can hardly be described as determined expansionists.

---

[5] Tyler, *Struggle for Imperial Unity*, p. 20.
[6] H. Hall, *The Colonial Office: A History* (London, 1937) p. 240.
[7] Min. by Herbert, 5 May, on Vogel to Carnarvon, 4 May 1875, *Carnarvon Papers*, P.R.O. 30/6/47, p. 225.

The new Conservative administration was equally reluctant to
annex new areas, especially when it involved areas on the
periphery of empire. The political changeover in 1874 hardly
affected colonial policy.

Disraeli's flamboyant and romantic 'imperialism', however,
with its concentration on the east, the empire of trade and power
as opposed to the empire of settlement, shifted the field of activity
to the arena of foreign policy. This transference of emphasis
paralleled the temporary shift of focus in the colonial policy of
the mid-1870s, away from discussions concerning the proper
relationship between self-governing colonies and the mother
country, to the problem of governing, advising and protecting
indigenous populations in South Africa, Fiji, the Gold Coast and
the Malay States, where pressing problems required urgent
solution. The problem of the government of non-European populations and the controversy Gladstone stirred up in 1877–80
revived anew the sense of moral obligation and of an imperial
'mission'.

II

Imperial trusteeship was by no means a novel idea; it had been
part of the intellectual climate of British opinion since the trial
of Warren Hastings. The tradition of a paternalistic, civilising,
evangelising mission had a long and influential pedigree. In 1850
a writer in the *Edinburgh Review* declared :

> It is a noble work to plant the foot of England and extend her
> sceptre by the banks of streams unnamed, and over regions yet
> unknown – and to conquer, not by the tyrannous subjugation
> of inferior races, but by the victories of mind over brute matter
> and blind mechanical obstacles. A yet nobler work it is to
> diffuse over a new created world the laws of Alfred, the
> language of Shakespeare, and that Christian religion, the last
> great heritage of man.[8]

The imperial idea retained its place in Victorian minds even at
the time when the teachings of the Manchester School are said to
have carried the day. Those who advocated separation may have
been at their most vociferous in the so-called 'Little England era',
but the majority view expressed in Parliament and the press was

[8] *Edinburgh Review*, xci (1850) 61.

still in favour of the maintenance of empire. In November 1860 the *North British Review* stated :

> to those who regard a vast empire as founded for some higher purpose than the creation and development of wealth, the wilful dismemberment of such an empire seems nothing less than the breaking up of some vast and complex machinery for the progressive civilisation of the human race, and an impious rejection of an instrument put into our hands by Providence for working out some great purpose of His government. . . . Colonial self-government is only another term for an extension . . . of freedom and . . . liberty. . . . This we believe to be the noble 'mission' of Great Britain.[9]

To this belief, as Professor A. P. Thornton has argued,

> the Victorian conscience still adhered, and neither Trollope nor anyone else who commanded and wished to retain the public ear, disputed the point that mission was a duty laid upon us. . . . Mission was an imperial idea before the politicians adapted it, and it was to have a longer history than political imperialism itself.[10]

We have already noted the almost universal acceptance by Victorians of imperial obligations once they had been incurred. Gladstone insisted that the government of India was 'the most arduous and perhaps the noblest trust, that ever was undertaken by a nation',[11] and even Goldwin Smith and John Bright conceded that Great Britain had a mission to stay in India in order to prevent the return of disunity. To these dour observers the imperial mission was a charge and a responsibility, a trust regrettably handed down to them by their predecessors. While Victorian philanthropists optimistically regarded Great Britain as the moral guardian of civilisation everywhere, these men possessed none of that 'arrogance of power' so common in the mid-Victorian heyday of wealth and political domination which caused so many observers to believe that the *Pax Britannica* brought nothing but benefit to those under its sway.

[9] *North British Review* (Nov. 1860) 86–7.
[10] Thornton, *The Imperial Idea*, p. 38.
[11] Speech at Glasgow, 5 Dec. 1879, quoted in *Midlothian Speeches,* p. 199.

Responsible politicians were more cautious than the humanitarians. Nevertheless, the politicians themselves paid lip-service to the sense of mission. While announcing his Fijian policy in the House of Lords in July 1874, Carnarvon said :

> I am loath to use words which seem too strong for the occasion and therefore I hardly like to say that England has a mission to extend her policy of colonisation in this part of the world, but at all events it does seem to me that there is an indirect duty which lies upon us, as far as we can, to take under our protection a place into which English capital has overflowed, in which English settlers are resident, in which it must be added, English lawlessness is going on, and in which the establishment of English institutions has been unsuccessfully attempted.[12]

Similarly, when detailing his administrative reorganisation of the West African settlements, Carnarvon had spoken of Great Britain's moral obligations :

> A great nation like ours must be sometimes prepared to discharge disagreeable duties; she must consent to bear burdens which are inseparable from her greatness . . . it is certainly not a desire of selfish interests or the ambition of larger empire which bids us remain on the West Coast of Africa; it is simply and solely a sense of obligations to be redeemed and of duties to be performed.[13]

These were fine words. But when relieved of the burdens of office Carnarvon spoke in even loftier tones. After his resignation from Disraeli's Cabinet in 1878, Carnarvon discussed that 'newly coined word "imperialism"' and alluded, in his grand manner, to England's mission :

> if we turn to that far larger empire over our native fellow-subjects of which I have spoken, the limits expand and the proportions rise till there forms itself a picture so vast and noble that the mind loses itself in the contemplation of what might be under the benificent rule of Great Britain. . . . There we have races struggling to emerge into civilisation, to whom

[12] 3 *Hansard*, 17 July 1874, ccxxi 185.
[13] 3 *Hansard*, 12 May 1874, ccxix 157–68.

emancipation from servitude is but the foretaste of the far higher law of liberty and progress to which they may yet attain; and vast populations like those of India sitting like children in the shadow of doubt and poverty and sorrow, yet looking up to us for guidance and for help. To them it is our part to give wise laws, good government, and a well ordered finance, which is the foundation of good things in human communities; it is ours to supply them with a system where the humblest may enjoy freedom from oppression and wrong equally with the greatest; where the light of religion and morality can penetrate into the darkest dwelling places. This is the real fulfilment of our duties; this, again, I say, is the true strength and meaning of imperialism.[14]

For Carnarvon at least the imperial idea had assumed a high sense of mission by the end of the 1870s.

Yet Carnarvon's brand of true 'imperialism' was in fact not so far removed from Gladstone's pride in the virtues of the British constitution and the benefits of civilisation it could bestow on less fortunate peoples. Even Lord Salisbury, who had observed colonial life at first hand as a young man and had written cynically in the 1850s and 1860s about the alleged 'progress of colonisation', by the late 1870s had come to subscribe to a similar doctrine. In a celebrated speech at a Conservative banquet in Knightsbridge, on his return from the Congress of Berlin in July 1878, he declared that it was the purpose of the Disraeli government to pick up 'the broken thread of England's old Imperial traditions . . . the one object we have in view is that peace and order shall be maintained, and that races and creeds which for centuries back have lived in feud should henceforth live in amity and goodwill'. Other powers, he hoped, would 'heartily co-operate with us in our civilising mission'.[15] Clearly, this was another aspect of the imperial idea freely subscribed to by both political parties at the end of the mid-Victorian age.

In the 1860s the relationship between Great Britain and the colonies in Canada, Australia, New Zealand and South Africa

---

[14] From an address to the Edinburgh Philosophical Institution on 5 Nov. 1878 entitled 'Imperial Administration', reprinted in the *Fortnightly Review*, xxiv (Dec. 1878) 751–63.

[15] Speech, 27 July 1878, quoted in Cecil, *Salisbury*, ii 302–3.

had dominated discussions on the British empire. The imperial idea most spoken about then consisted of a belief in preparing these colonies of British settlement for eventual self-government. In the 1870s, however, politicians once again became aware of the problems of the imperial frontier in the tropics. The doctrines of imperial trusteeship which had for so long poured forth from Exeter Hall once again came to the fore. And for the last generation of the Victorian era the imperial idea assumed a new trait. England's mission came to signify, as Professor Thornton has written,

> to lead the world in the arts of civilisation, to bring light to the dark places, to teach the true political method, to nourish and to protect the liberal tradition. It was to act as trustees for the weak, and to bring arrogance low. It was to represent in itself the highest aims of human society.[16]

In short, late-Victorian imperialism, that 'greater pride in empire which', as Lord Rosebery defined it, 'is a larger patriotism', became a faith, a faith (admittedly degraded in many minds) to support the idea that the white race was destined to conquer and rule the inferior races of the world.

However, before the 1880s there had been some abstract justification of conquest and dominion over subject populations and professions of a belief in a divine mission to rule. Theories concerning the identity of might and right and of the right of superior races to dominate inferior ones certainly existed. They formed not only a part of Froude's philosophy but were accepted by most British travellers and traders and were undoubtedly reflected in the reactions of many missionaries and explorers (David Livingstone is a celebrated exception) to indigenous societies.[17] These ideas played an increasingly important role in future decades as popular ideas of Darwinian theories filtered through to the reading public first in newspapers and then in novels. Pseudo-scientific publicists and popularisers planted racism

[16] Thornton, *The Imperial Idea*, pp. ix–x.
[17] See R. Maunier, *The Sociology of Colonies: An Introduction to the Study of Race Contact* (London, 1949); H. A. C. Cairns, *The Prelude to Imperialism: British Reactions to Central African Society, 1840–90* (London, 1965); and A. Holmberg, *African Tribes and European Agencies* (London, 1966).

in the minds of the multitude,[18] and yet another facet was added to the imperialism of the late-Victorian decades. As Professor Tyler has noted, 'it is possible to discern as early as 1868 the beginning of a whole philosophy of imperialism in the Teutonic racialism and the idea of trusteeship for backward peoples which Dilke elaborated in *Greater Britain*'.[19]

Nevertheless, the most respectable brand of 'imperialism' in the early 1880s concerned the possibility of closer union with the self-governing colonies. No doubt in reaction to the events of Disraeli's premiership, Professor J. R. Seeley observed in his popular lectures on *The Expansion of England*: 'When we inquire . . . into the Greater Britain of the future we ought to think much more of our Colonial than our Indian Empire.'[20] The further acquisition of territory, especially in aid of British trading and philanthropic enterprise beyond the existing imperial frontiers, was still frowned upon. True to the mid-Victorian outlook, as one contemporary textbook on the colonies stated in 1883, 'the policy of England discourages any increase of territory in tropical countries already occupied by native races'.[21] Even Disraeli, the leader of Seeley's 'bombastic school' of imperialism, it must be noted, had not preached imperial expansion. Clearly, by the end of the 1870s no mass wave of imperialist fanaticism existed. There were no expansionists in the great offices of state, there was no expansionist colonial policy and no desire to acquire undeveloped parts of the world. Gladstone's election victory in 1880 was intended to restore the economical approach to government at home and the tradition of non-intervention and minimum responsibility abroad. As the new Prime Minister remarked: 'We believe that the responsibilities of this great empire . . . are sufficient to exhaust the ambition or strength of any minister or

[18] See A. Ellegård, *Darwin and the General Reader: The Reception of Darwin's Theory of Evolution in the British Periodical Press, 1859–72*, Göteborgs Universitets Arsskrift, vol. LXIV (Gothenburg, 1958); L. J. Henkin, *Darwinism and the English Novel, 1860–1910* (New York, 1940); also H. Arendt, *Origins of Totalitarianism* (London, 1958).

[19] For an analysis of racial theories in contemporary writings, see L. L. Snyder, *Race: A History of Modern Ethnic Theories* (New York, 1939); and C. Bolt, *Victorian Attitudes to Race* (London, 1970).

[20] J. R. Seeley, *The Expansion of England: Two Courses of Lectures* (London, 1883) p. 11.

[21] J. S. Cotton and E. J. Payne, *Colonies and Dependencies* (London, 1883) part ii, p. 114, quoted in Robinson, 'Imperial Problems in British Politics, 1880–95', *C.H.B.E.*, III 127.

of any parliament, and we do not wish to overload them or break them down.'[22] Why then did Great Britain become entangled in the scramble for territory in Africa, south-east Asia and the Pacific?

III

In the early 1880s the 'imperialists' were still chiefly federalists interested in the future of the settlement colonies. A few of their number, along with the philanthropists, missionary societies and vested business interests, did, however, support certain colonial demands for extensions of British rule designed to forestall foreign annexation or prevent foreign intervention in what were regarded as British spheres of influence. This group, who believed that only formal extensions of empire could protect British interests threatened by insecurity or foreign expansion beyond the existing imperial frontiers, became the advocates of a new expansionist policy. Alderman M'Arthur, for example, woollen draper, banker and humanitarian, 'hoped that Her Majesty's Government would not look coldly upon projects for the extension of our trade, but would rather regard the trader as an ally in the great work of civilising Africa'. If only the government would protect and extend British commerce, he argued, it would 'assist Great Britain to maintain her individual supremacy, and at the same time further the great cause of peace, civilisation and Christianity'.[23] But the traders, philanthropists and 'imperialists' made little headway in politics. Public inertia and indifference, as well as fear of increased financial burdens, favoured the non-interventionists or 'consolidators', who believed that international diplomacy and informal influence were sufficient to maintain the existing situation. Imperial aggrandisement was still an unpopular idea. There was no spontaneous or irresistible outburst of mass emotion. As Dr R. E. Robinson has written, the imperialism of the 1880s was still a matter of chance and the opportunism of a few powerful personalities. The impetus to expansion, when it arose, came from outside British politics or from behind locked doors. The general public adopted the expansionist philosophy only after the event.[24]

---

[22] 3 *Hansard*, 17 Mar. 1882, ccLxvii 1190.
[23] 3 *Hansard*, 2 May 1876, ccxxviii 2002–4.
[24] Robinson, *C.H.B.E.*, iii 129–30, 179–80.

What then did the years 1868–80 contribute to the history of British imperialism? The answer may be found in two significant dislocations which occurred in British policy during the 1870s. These consisted of breakdowns in established lines of both colonial and foreign policy.

In the colonial field, traditional policies of informal supremacy, moral suasion, confederation panaceas and gentlemanly agreements between the leading European powers to avoid elbowing each other on the periphery of empire had begun to fail and were gradually being replaced by limited territorial annexations, extensions of administration and the establishment of spheres of paramountcy. Rogers, Kimberley, Carnarvon and Herbert all prophesied that Great Britain would soon be drawn deeper into Africa, south-east Asia, the Far East and the Pacific. Gladstone heartily deplored 'the disposition of John Bull to put his head . . . into a noose'.[25] According to W. D. McIntyre's analysis, the mid-Victorians became 'caught up in a current of colonial expansion which they did not fully understand, which they sought to avoid, but which they were unable completely to check'.[26] Certainly, before the 1870s were out, explicit claims to British paramountcy had been made in the Malay States and the South Pacific, and such claims were implicit in the government's extension of administration in West Africa. Professor McIntyre concludes: 'The concept of "paramountcy" was the highest common factor in Britain's response to her troubles on the frontier in the tropics' during the 1870s.[27] Mid-Victorian politicians were determined to follow limited objectives. McIntyre has suggested elsewhere, however, that Herbert would have liked to see a 'sort of Monroe Doctrine in the South Pacific'.[28] Such a concept was freely talked about for South Africa too. As early as 1876 Carnarvon informed Sir Bartle Frere:

> I should not like anyone to come too near us either on the South towards the Transvaal, which *must* be ours; or on the north too near to Egypt and the country which belongs to Egypt.

[25] Gladstone to Kimberley, 21 Aug. 1873, *Kimberley Papers*, A/52, quoted in McIntyre, *Imperial Frontier*, p. 384.
[26] Ibid. p. 374.
[27] Ibid. p. 370.
[28] McIntyre, *H.S.A.N.Z.*, IX 291.

In fact when I speak of geographical limits I am not expressing my real opinion. We cannot admit rivals in the East or even the central parts of Africa: and I do not see why, looking to the experience that we have now of English life within the tropics – the Zambesi should be considered to be without the range of our colonisation. To a considerable extent, if not entirely, we must be prepared to apply a sort of Munro (*sic*) doctrine to much of Africa.[29]

Clearly, the whole fabric of empire was becoming more brittle – dangerously brittle in the light of the second dislocation in the field of foreign affairs.

At the same time the balance of power in Europe had begun to shift after 1870 and Russian expansionism in Asia increasingly threatened British interests. Great Britain had to secure India as well as safeguard her routes of communication. Disraeli realised all these dangers but possessed no alternative strategy to the old 'Crimean policy'. He continued to support Turkish territorial integrity and tried to use the military power of the British empire. As a result, the issues involved, the pacifist and interventionist attitudes towards foreign policy, were thrashed out in public as never before during the years 1877–80. Derby and Carnarvon resigned when Disraeli departed from mid-Victorian ideals, as Lord Salisbury at the Foreign Office began the long series of reappraisals of Great Britain's position in the world which laid the basis of British policy towards Europe for the rest of the century. On his return to power in 1880 Gladstone was shocked to discover that Disraeli's world, 'one of jealous nations, competing for favourable positions in the sun',[30] was now the real world of international relations.

These unforeseen changes in the direction of colonial and foreign policy were the chief legacy of the 1870s. They led to greater British involvement in regional problems as territory was extended, control of administration tightened and local officials took sides in indigenous disputes. It also involved a reassessment of European rivals in the colonial sphere. Where Germany had previously been welcomed in New Guinea, Fiji, Samoa and the

[29] Carnarvon to Frere, 12 Dec. 1876, *Carnarvon Papers*, P.R.O. 30/6/4, no. 67.
[30] Thornton, *The Imperial Idea*, p. 50.

Malay States, she was now feared, and French activity in south-east Asia was regarded with suspicion. Foreign competitors were now watched much more closely. Salisbury noted in 1879, for example, that 'the attention of all other countries is at the present time so much towards the acceptance of important strategic positions in the Pacific that if this opportunity is allowed to pass by it seems very probable that some other nation would interpose claims which would prevent it from being renewed'.[31] In the unsettled and changing situation of the early 1880s, any action either by a European power or an indigenous ruler calculated to disrupt the *status quo* could lead to possible conflict. But why did the European scrambles for territory and attempts to partition large areas of the world occur at this time?

A tentative answer may be offered. Gradually, the European powers came to feel that their interests and prestige were involved, whether it was the prestige of the humiliated who, like Gambetta, asserted that in Africa France would take the first faltering steps of the convalescent, or the prestige of the newcomer, like Bismarck, whose map of Africa lay in Europe. Whenever any power feels its prestige and security threatened, an upsurge of nationalism is usually the result. In the closing years of the nineteenth century this took the form of attempts by most European powers to achieve increasing imperial dominion: 'Empire, if correctly organised, was power, wealth, fame, influence.'[32] Since 1870 the stage had gradually been set for a new phase of overseas expansion; all that was lacking was the spark to set the activity in motion.

By the late 1880s European diplomacy had become intertwined with prestige on the periphery of empire where any unilateral action was likely to disturb the *status quo*. No power could expect to act in a vacuum any longer. Many countries felt impelled to interfere in distant areas when power vacuums occurred, expressly to forestall the intervention of a rival. Such interference in its turn often provoked further imperial crises or resulted in the growth of black nationalism. In such circumstances the metropolitan powers became more inclined to back the actions of their men on the spot, who were always ready to intervene in matters beyond their jurisdiction and who were in

[31] Salisbury memo., 11 Oct. 1879, F.O. 12/54.
[32] Thornton, *The Imperial Idea*, p. 49.

fact often used by local rulers in their own manoeuvring for power.

Thus three important trends in the 1870s pointed towards an upsurge of 'imperialism' in later decades: European trends; relations between certain regions and the metropolitan powers; and entirely local internal developments in these regions. First, the change in the international atmosphere after 1870 was all-important: France humiliated, Germany with her new-found unity and power, Great Britain struggling to maintain her position, Russia on the look-out for further extension of her frontiers, Turkish territorial integrity in danger of collapse in Europe, and the United States emerging as a new force to be reckoned with on the world's stage. As each country sought to maintain, regain or acquire commercial or political supremacy, this rivalry was translated into conflicts on the periphery of empire. Once it had been deemed necessary, as in the 1870s, to establish spheres of paramountcy, it also became necessary to oppose outside intervention in these areas. And as more countries turned away from *laissez-faire* and began to erect tariff barriers, the 'open door' also began to disappear. Strategic and commercial reasons were brought into play. Precautionary claims had to be made to preserve each country's interests and forestall rivals. It then became impossible not to join in the partition for fear of being left out altogether. The inevitable reaction was a tendency to divide up the remaining areas, unoccupied by Europeans, in Africa and the Pacific. China and Persia narrowly escaped a similar fate. These were the European bases of the 'scramble', springing from a new international rivalry, great technological advances, and the need to secure existing interests, routes of communication, markets and sources of raw materials, backed up by the demands of the humanitarians and missionary societies and by the hope, however mistaken, of further economic gains – an outlook so neatly summed up by Cecil Rhodes as 'philanthropy plus 5 per cent'.

But the new burst of imperial activity in evidence after 1880 was not of European stimulus alone. The new rivalry must also be seen as the logical development of a long period of European trade and rule in Africa and the Pacific. C. W. Newbury has shown, for example, how concession hunting in West Africa and commercial rivalry led to local expansion. The French had no need to search for 'pin-pricks' in the British side (supposedly in retaliation for the British occupation of Egypt in 1882); the causes of conflict were already there, a logical development of local rivalry.[33] Such causes had long existed but they were now beginning to multiply rapidly, though open clashes were usually avoided. The new European rivalry and change in the international atmosphere explains why such local friction could spark off a scramble for territory.

There were also some purely local reasons, as Gallagher and Robinson have shown, why metropolitan powers felt compelled to intervene. Internal crises, the breakdown in local government, an upsurge of black nationalism, could lead to European intervention, admittedly sometimes with extreme reluctance. The response to local nationalism hardened and protectorates were declared in areas threatening existing spheres of informal supremacy. All this increased the danger of European rivalry and conflict.

The gradual convergence of these three separate threads – European diplomatic and commercial rivalry, local friction between individual powers on the periphery of empire, and internal crises in existing colonies and spheres of influence – pointed to a new phase of imperial expansion. There was no going back. The British reaction to these developments was normally a defensive one. Events often took statesmen by surprise. Lord Salisbury, commenting on developments in Africa, noted : 'I do not know exactly the cause of this sudden revolution. But there it is!'[34] Statesmen often did not know what they were doing as they drew arbitrary lines on maps and sought to preserve their prestige or their commercial and strategic interests. The occupation of Egypt by Great Britain in August 1882, the French ratification of the Brazza–Makoko treaty in the autumn of that year, Leopold II's activities in the Congo and the German irruption into Africa and the Pacific in 1884–5 set in motion a scramble for territory in Africa, the Pacific, the Middle East and south-east Asia.

The causes of this phenomenon are complex. The varying motives of different powers in separate areas illustrate the

---

[33] C. W. Newbury, 'Victorians, Republicans and the Partition of West Africa', *J.A.H.*, III (1962) 493–501.

[34] Speech at Glasgow, May 1891, quoted in Cecil, *Salisbury*, IV 310.

multiple aspects of what, for good or ill, has come to be called
'imperialism'. What then was the British role in all this? The
British occupation of Egypt in 1882 has been held responsible by
some historians for inaugurating the 'scrambles'. But this seems
to be an over-simplification. It may help to explain why a
partition in Africa occurred at all, but it does not explain why
this phenomenon spread to south-east Asia and the Pacific. This
has much more to do with international necessities, local colonial
pressures and, above all, the drive which led Europe to impose a
power solution. The British action in 1882 was not the obviously
fateful step it has been made out to be. It was carried out only
after all attempts at joint action had failed, and Gladstone and
his Cabinet sincerely regarded it as a purely temporary measure.
Henri Brunschwig has shown that French public opinion was not
over-excited : the reversal of 1882 was insignificant compared
with the humiliation of 1870. And Jean Stengers has insisted that
the British occupation affected French relations with Belgium
more than any other power, leading to the ratification of the
Brazza–Makoko treaty.[35]

But even so, these clashes between Great Britain, France and
Belgium could have been sorted out peacefully among the existing colonial powers; each was seeking to avoid friction. The
emergence of Germany as a colonial power, however, provided a
new ingredient and a real turning-point. If the British occupation
of Egypt and the activities of Brazza and Leopold II help explain
why a partition occurred in Africa, the irruption of Germany
(and later Italy and the United States) explains why the
'scramble' came about and why it spread to other parts of the
world. The 1884 Berlin Conference on West Africa led the
partition to take its particular form, with the emphasis on the
provision of effective signs of occupation and administration.
Chartered companies were used as a cheap method of fulfilling
such obligation. These in their turn provided a further stimulus
to expansion.

It is obvious that the initial causes of European intervention
were often based in a particular locality – mounting commercial
rivalry, internal crises and power vacuums. Here, more studies
of nationalism and the policies of indigenous rulers and, above

[35] H. Brunschwig, *French Colonialism: Myths and Realities, 1871–1914*
(London, 1966); Stengers, *J.A.H.*, III 469–91.

all, a closer examination of the activities of the men on the spot would prove well worth while. These men were at the heart of the new upsurge of imperial expansion and supplied the metropolitan powers with their information. Nevertheless, the causes of the 'scrambles' were primarily European; European rivalry and diplomacy electrified the atmosphere and led to large-scale partition. The main reasons for the British participation were economic and strategic – the protection of existing assets and the hope of further economic gains. European prestige was also involved and it would be interesting to know exactly what part racialist doctrines played in this new outbreak of European chauvinism and imperialism. British politicians, at least, did not act under any such popular pressures. Although by the end of the 1880s the new expansionist school may have been clamouring for a new tropical empire for future commercial and philanthropic development, imperialism was still not a popular appetite or mass emotion. Not until the 1890s did empire become, in Dr Robinson's words, 'a popular nostrum for curing depression and unemployment, for easing national insecurity and ensuring future greatness'.[36] How then did the imperial idea come to assume the character A. P. Thornton attaches to it in this period?

IV

By 1890 British policy and attitudes had undergone an important change. Faced with nationalist intransigence, oriental fanaticism, new rivals in Africa and new enemies in the Mediterranean, Salisbury had accepted that supremacy in Egypt was becoming crucial as the balance of power in Europe and the Mediterranean altered. The pivot of British policy moved from Constantinople to Cairo and the defensive strategy of the northern frontiers of India was then applied to the Sudan, Uganda and the hinterlands of Zanzibar. Great Britain now had an interest in tropical Africa. It was a new policy adopted to defend old needs : the 'frontiers of fear' were on the move. Traditional concepts of informal supremacy, moral suasion and free partnership had proved impracticable or had been rudely rejected by Orientals and Africans, by Boers and Irishmen. With this decline of mid-Victorian aspirations and ideals, mid-Victorian optimism and superiority faltered as well. The emphasis shifted to control and

[36] Robinson, *C.H.B.E.*, III 180.

administration, and British policy became even more concerned with prestige and with hypothetical dangers.

The factors underlying the new international situation, which necessitated a great deal of rethinking concerning Great Britain's position in the world, can be traced back to the 1870s and most clearly manifested themselves in 1878, when circumstances led Disraeli to adopt a more aggressive foreign policy and to disregard mid-Victorian canons of conduct, a course which brought about the resignations of Derby and Carnarvon. Even the return of Gladstone and his attempts to achieve disengagement, which received partial success in South Africa and Afghanistan, failed to alter the growing involvement of Great Britain in regional problems. By the 1880s a policy of informal supremacy was insufficient in the face of foreign expansion, existing British commitments, increasing local difficulties and the need to defend British interests and lines of communication in a world where tariff barriers were rising and British manufactures were facing increasing competition. The stage was set for the 'struggle between the Gladstonian upholders of the mid-Victorian anti-expansionist tradition and leaders of the Forward and expansionist movement'[37] in Great Britain, and for the scramble for colonies in Africa, south-east Asia and the Pacific which characterised the last two decades of the nineteenth century.

Thus the continued prominence of the empire as an important factor in British politics towards the end of the last century was largely dictated by external considerations, both European and regional. It was a defensive reaction in the face of new forces which were disturbing the *status quo*. The revived interest in imperial overseas activity did not spring from the actions of the small group of agitators who later became the advocates of federation. Nor was the so-called 'imperialism' of Disraeli responsible. Stripped of its frills, this amounted to nothing more than a mixture of hot air and power politics. But it was an indication of things to come. Gladstone, despite his own wishes and personal beliefs, found himself painting much of the map red. After 1880 the imperial idea was revitalised. The birth of the 'New Imperialism' was long drawn out and complicated, and in 1880 the infant was still very weak indeed. It needed a change of environment, different European and regional conditions, to

[37] Ibid. p. 130.

allow the child to flourish and turn into the *enfant terrible*, the popular imperialism of the 1890s and the early twentieth century.

These conditions were provided in the 1880s during a period of new international rivalry, of economic depression, and of rising foreign competition and tariff discrimination which only increased the need to protect and expand existing markets and sources of raw materials. To the demands of philanthropists, anti-slavers and the missionary societies who since the 1870s had constantly urged, for humanitarian reasons, the extension of imperial dominion, and to the more self-interested aspirations of colonial governments, were now added the pleas of private enterprise, of the City, chambers of commerce and manufacturers' associations. The continuation of British commercial prosperity became linked with the campaign for the betterment of subject races and the education of black 'savages'. The extension of the *Pax Britannica* would, it was suggested, bring safety, personal freedom and new economic and intellectual opportunity to all. As awareness of the empire and its problems increased, so did the government's vulnerability to expansionist pressures.

And so, in the last decades of the nineteenth century, as imperialism acquired a new moral purpose, the urge towards greater imperial expansion received widespread support, from the Queen, the Imperial Services, the children of the old landed aristocracy, from the new financial aristocracy, the new educated middle class (children of the successful manufacturers of the early-Victorian age), products of the new public schools, and the new clerical class of the late-Victorian age, educated, well paid, but in no position to gain a position of influence within the confines of Little England. The new imperialism of tropical responsibility mean 'employment for the worker, markets for the manufacturer, and civilisation and freedom for the African tribes'.[38] Imperial expansion had taken on a high moral purpose. Commerce, Christianity and civilisation were to advance hand in hand. The moral conception of an imperial civilising mission became as popular as it had ever been in the early-Victorian age, and the great Lord Salisbury bowed before what he called a 'great civilising, Christianising force'.[39]

[38] Ibid. p. 159.
[39] Cecil, *Salisbury*, IV 336.

Thus by the 1890s, when imperial expansion was thought to be in the British interest, 'imperialism' had conveniently been purged of that tinge of oriental despotism which Disraeli had associated with it, although his spirit glorifying British achievements and rule overseas remained. The imperial spirit animating an imperial code continued to influence the thoughts of the British governing classes until well after the Second World War. The moral duty of trusteeship in the tropics had been recognised afresh in the 1870s and had restored a dimension to the imperial idea which had not been particularly prominent, at least in the public mind, in the mid-Victorian age. Imperial trusteeship was now stronger than ever, reinforced by Darwinian ideas and theories concerning racial superiority. 'Today there is no cause so hopeless as the Little England cause', declared the *Graphic* on 12 June 1897. 'The Imperial idea is now triumphant because it is founded in the economic necessities of the component parts of the Empire and fertilised by Liberal ideas of government.'

In the late-Victorian era the imperial idea was dominated by a sense of 'mission' and 'obligation'. England's mission remained, according to the intellectual climate of the day, twofold : to guide the colonies of British settlement along the final stages of the road to colonial nationhood (albeit within the bounds of an imperial federation), and to bring the benefits of 'civilisation' to the more underdeveloped parts of the empire. As Joseph Chamberlain explained in a speech before the Royal Colonial Institute in March 1897 :

> We feel now that our rule over these territories can only be justified if we can show that it adds to the happiness and prosperity of the people, and I maintain that our rule does, and has, brought security and peace and comparative prosperity to countries that never knew their blessings before. In carrying out this work of civilisation we are fulfilling what I believe to be our national mission.[40]

This was an exposition of the 'virtues' of imperialism at a time when most authorities agree that the imperial idea had reached its zenith. Soon afterwards, with the Boer war, a revulsion set in against imperialism. Then the imperial idea was formulated afresh. But the British policy-makers clung tenaciously to their

[40] Speech, 31 Mar. 1897, quoted in Koebner, *Imperialism*, p. 210.

doctrine of trusteeship in Asia, Africa and the Caribbean countries as they blindly groped their way towards the realisation of the ultimate goal of self-government. It was a goal which Gladstone, the greatest prophet of 'England's mission' in the 1870s, would freely have applauded, had he been alive to witness both the replacement of Disraeli's concept of a militant, centralised empire by a voluntary association of free states in the form of a Commonwealth, and the return once again, after the passing of a century, to dear little England.

Appendix
Biographical Notes

THESE notes, compiled from the *Dictionary of National Biography*, are intended to identify some of the more important but less well-known participants in the narrative. They do not contain full biographical details. Faulty entries in the *D.N.B.* have been corrected wherever possible.

ADDERLEY, Charles Bowyer (1814–1905), 1st Baron Norton; helped found settlement of Canterbury in New Zealand; Cons. M.P., 1841–78; Under-Sec. for Cols., 1866–8; Pres. of Board of Trade, 1874–8.

ARTHUR, Revd William (1819–1901), Wesleyan divine; missionary in India, 1839–41; sec., W.M.S., 1851–68; pres., Methodist College, Belfast, 1868–71; hon. sec., W.M.S., 1888–91.

ASHLEY, Anthony Evelyn Melbourne (1836–1907), son of 7th Earl of Shaftesbury; Lib. M.P., 1874–85; Under-Sec. for Board of Trade, 1880–2, and C.O., 1882–5.

ATKINSON, Major Sir Harry Albert (1831–92), Minister for Colonial Defence, N.Z., 1864–5; best known as a company commander in the Taranaki Volunteer Rifles when he invented the 'search and destroy' tactics against guerrillas; N.Z. Premier, 1876–7, 1883–4, 1887–91.

BAILLIE-COCHRANE, Alexander Dundas Ross Wishart (1816–90), 1st Baron Lamington; Cons. M.P., 1841–52, 1858, 1859–68, 1870–80.

BAZLEY, Sir Thomas (1797–1885), cotton spinner and merchant; Lib. M.P., 1858–80; pres., Manchester Chamber of Commerce, 1845–59.

BIRCH, Arthur N. (1837–1914), C.O. official, Colonial Sec., British Columbia, and administered colony, 1865–6; Acting Lieut.-Gov. of Penang, 1871.

BLAINE, Henry, former member of Cape Parliament.

BOWEN, Sir George Ferguson (1821–99), colonial governor; Gov. of Queensland, 1859–68; New Zealand, 1868–73; Victoria, 1873–9; Mauritius, 1879–83; Hong Kong, 1883–6.

BOYCE, Revd William Binnington (1803–89), former pres., Australian Methodist Conference; sec., W.M.S., 1858–76.

BUCKINGHAM AND CHANDOS, Richard Plantagenet Campbell Temple Nugent Brydges Chandos Grenville, 3rd Duke of (1823–89), Cons. M.P., 1846–57; Sec. of State for Cols., 1867–8; Gov. of Madras, 1875–8.

BURY, William Coutts Keppel, Viscount (1832–94), 7th Earl of Albemarle; Civil Sec. and Superintendent of Indian Affairs in Canada, 1854–7; Lib. M.P., 1857–9, 1860–5, 1868–74; 1st pres., R.C.I., 1868–71; became Cons. and Roman Catholic; Under-Sec. at W.O., 1878–80, 1885–6.

BUXTON, Sir Thomas Fowell (1837–1915), Lib. M.P., 1865–8; Gov. of South Australia, 1895–8.

NEWCASTLE, Henry Pelham Fiennes Pelham Clinton, 5th Duke of (1811–64), Peelite M.P., 1832–51; Sec. of State for War and Cols., 1852–4; Sec. of State for War, 1854–5; Sec. of State for Cols., 1859–64.

NICHOLSON, Sir Charles (1808–1903), medical practitioner; spent years 1834–62 in New South Wales and Queensland; member of Legislative Council, N.S.W., 1843–59; Speaker, 1847–56; Pres. of Legislative Council, Queensland, 1860; principal founder, Vice-Chancellor and then Chancellor of University of Sydney, 1854–62.

NORMANBY, George Augustus Constantine Phipps, 2nd Marquis of (1819–90), ex-army officer; Lib. M.P., 1847–58; Lieut.-Gov. of Nova Scotia, 1858–67; Gov. of Queensland, 1871–4; New Zealand, 1874–9; Victoria, 1879–84.

NORTHBROOK, Thomas George Baring, 1st Earl of (1826–1904), Under-Sec. at India Office, 1859–61, 1861–4, at War Office, 1861, 1868, and at Home Office, 1864; Sec. to Admiralty, 1866; Gov.-General of India, 1872–6; 1st Lord of the Admiralty, 1880–5; special commissioner to Egypt, 1884.

NORTHCOTE, Sir Stafford Henry (1818–87), 1st Earl of Iddesleigh; Cons. M.P., 1855–85; Sec. of State for India, 1867; Gov. of Hudson's Bay Co., 1869–74; Chancellor of the Exchequer, 1874–80; Foreign Sec., 1886.

PAKINGTON, Sir John Somerset (1799–1880), 1st Baron Hampton; Cons. M.P., 1837–74; Sec. of State for War and Cols., 1852; 1st Lord of the Admiralty, 1858, 1866; Sec. of State for War, 1867–8.

POPE-HENNESSY, Sir John (1834–91), Cons. M.P., 1859–65, 1890–1; Gov. of Labuan, 1867–71; West African Settlements, 1872–3; Bahamas, 1873–4; Windward Islands, 1875–6; Hong Kong, 1877–82; Mauritius, 1883–9.

RICHARD, Henry (1812–88), Congregational pastor, Old Kent Road, London, 1835–50; sec., Peace Society, 1848; Lib. M.P., 1868–88; advocate of international arbitration.

ROBINSON, Sir Hercules George Robert (1824–97), 1st Baron Rosmead; Lieut.-Gov. of St Kitts, 1854–9; Gov. of Hong Kong, 1859–65; Ceylon, 1865–72; New South Wales, 1872–9; New Zealand, 1879–80; Cape of Good Hope and High Commissioner for South Africa, 1880–9, 1895–7.

ROCHE, Alfred R. (1819–76), father editor of Morning Post; civil servant in Canada; campaigned for development of North Western Territories of Hudson's Bay Co. under pseudonym 'Assiniboia' in Montreal Gazette; hon. sec., R.C.I., 1868–71.

ROGERS, Sir Frederic (1811–89), 1st Baron Blachford; one of founders of the Guardian; leader writer for The Times; Registrar to Joint Stock Cos., 1844; Colonial Land and Emigration Commissioner, 1846; Permanent Under-Sec. at C.O., 1860–71.

ROGERS, James Edwin Thorold (1823–90), political economist; 1st Tooke Prof. of Statistics and Economic Science, King's College, London, 1859–90; Drummond Prof. of Political Economy, Oxford, 1862–7, 1888; M.P., 1880–6.

SEWELL, Henry (1807–79), sec. and deputy chairman of Canterbury Assoc. for Colonisation of New Zealand, 1850; member of House of Representatives, N.Z., 1853–6, 1860, 1865–6; of Legislative Council, 1861–5, 1870–3; 1st Premier of N.Z., 1856; Colonial Treasurer and Commissioner of Customs, 1856–9; Attorney-General, 1861–2; Minister of Justice, 1864–5, 1869–72.

SHEPSTONE, Sir Theophilus (1817–93), British resident among Fingo, 1839; Agent for Natives in Natal, 1845; Sec. for Native Affairs, 1856; annexed and administered Transvaal, 1877–9; Administrator in Zululand, 1884.

CARNARVON, Henry Howard Molyneux Herbert, 4th Earl of (1831–90), Under-Sec. for Cols., 1858–9; Sec. of State for Cols., 1866–7, 1874–8; Chairman of Commission on Imperial Defence, 1879–82.

CAVE, Stephen (1820–86), Cons. M.P., 1859–80; Paymaster-General, 1866–8; chairman, West India Committee, and director of Bank of England.

CHESSON, Frederick William (1833–88), journalist prominent in many philanthropic societies; wrote for Morning Star, Daily News, Adelaide Observer, South Australia Register and Evening Journal; edited for short while The Dial; assistant sec., A.P.S., 1854–66; sec., 1866–88; organised Manchester Peace Conference, 1853; founded London Emancipation Society, 1859; member of N.A.P.S.S.; Law Society; Jamaica, Gambia, Fiji, Afghan and Greek Committees; Anti-Opium Society; helped organise Eastern Question Conference and Association.

CHILDERS, Hugh Culling Eardley (1827–96), emigrated to Melbourne, 1850; prominent politician in Victoria to 1856; 1st Vice-Chancellor of University of Melbourne; Agent for Victoria in London, 1857; Lib. M.P., 1860–92; 1st Lord of the Admiralty, 1868–71; Chancellor of Duchy of Lancaster, 1872–3; Sec. of State for War, 1880–2; Chancellor of the Exchequer, 1882–5; Home Sec., 1886.

CHURCHILL, Lord Alfred (1824–93), Cons. M.P., 1845–7; supporter of Palmerston, 1857–65; chairman, African Aid Society.

CLIFFORD, Sir Charles, member of House of Representatives, N.Z., 1853–60; Speaker, House of Representatives, 1854–60.

CORRY, Montagu William Lowry (1838–1903), 1st Baron Rowton; private sec. to Disraeli, 1866–81; founder of poor man's hotel, 'Rowton Houses'.

DENISON, Sir William (1804–71), colonial governor; Tasmania, 1847–55; New South Wales, 1855–61; Madras, 1861–6.

DICEY, Edward James Stephen (1823–1911), author and journalist; leader writer for The Times, 1861; editor Daily News, 1870; editor The Observer, 1870–89.

DILKE, Sir Charles Wentworth (1843–1911), Lib. M.P., 1868–86, 1892–1911; Under-Sec. at F.O., 1880–2; Pres. of Local Government Board, 1882–5; ruined by divorce case, 1886.

EASTWICK, Edward Backhouse (1814–83), Prof. of Hindustani at Haileybury College, 1845; Assistant Political Sec., India Office, 1859; private sec. to Lord Cranbourne at India Office, 1866–7; Cons. M.P., 1868–74.

EDDY, Dr Charles W. (1821–74), Oxford M.B., 1849; held Ratcliffe Travelling Fellowship for 10 years during which time he lived in Europe, Australia and Canada; sec. to Danube & Black Sea Railway Co., 1862–74; hon. sec., R.C.I., 1871–4.

ERSKINE, Admrl John E. (1806–87), Lib. M.P., 1865–74; author of Journal of a Cruise among the Islands of the Western Pacific; associated with W.M.S.

FORSTER, William Edward (1818–86), Yorkshire woollen manufacturer; left Quakers in 1850; Lib. M.P., 1861–86; Under-Sec. for Cols., 1865–6; Vice-Pres. of Privy Council, 1870–4; Chief Sec. for Ireland, 1880–2; 1st chairman, Imperial Federation League, 1884.

FORTESCUE, Chichester Samuel (1823–98), Lord Carlingford; Lib. M.P., 1847–74; Under-Sec. for Cols., 1857–8, 1859–65; Chief. Sec. for Ireland, 1865–6, 1868–71; Pres. of Board of Trade, 1871–4; Lord Privy Seal, 1881–3; Lord Pres. of the Council, 1883–5.

FOWLER, Sir Robert Nicholas (1828–91), from Quaker banking family (became Anglican, 1858); Cons. M.P., 1868–74, 1880–91; chairman, Anti-Opium Society; twice Lord Mayor of London.

FRERE, Sir Henry Bartle Edward (1815–84), served in Indian Civil Service, 1834–61; Gov. of Bombay, 1862–7; member of Council of India, 1867; commissioner to Zanzibar to negotiate slave-trade treaty, 1872; Gov. of Cape Colony and High Commissioner for South Africa, 1877–80.

FROUDE, James Anthony (1818–94), historian; editor *Fraser's Magazine*, 1860–74; travelled in South Africa, 1874–5; Regius Prof. of Modern History at Oxford, 1892–4.

GORST, Sir John Eldon (1835–1916), emigrated to New Zealand, 1859; served as civil commissioner in Waikato, 1862, wrote classic account of the Maori king; Cons. M.P., 1866–8, 1875–1906; reorganised Conservative party machinery, 1868–74; helped found Fourth Party, 1880; Solicitor-General, 1885; Under-Sec. at India Office, 1886.

GOSCHEN, George Joachim (1831–1907), 1st Viscount Goschen; Lib. M.P., 1863–85; Lib. Unionist M.P., 1886–1900; Pres. of Poor Law Board, 1868–71; 1st Lord of the Admiralty, 1871–4, 1895–1900; investigated financial position of Egypt, 1876; Chancellor of the Exchequer, 1886–92.

GRANVILLE, Granville George Leveson-Gower, 2nd Earl (1815–91), Colonial Sec., 1868–70, 1886; Foreign Sec., 1851–2, 1870–4, 1880–5.

GREY, Sir George (1812–98), colonial governor; explored north-western Australia, 1837; Resident Magistrate, Albany, Western Australia; Gov. of South Australia, 1841–5; New Zealand, 1845–53, 1861–8; Cape of Good Hope, 1854–61; Superintendent of Auckland, 1875; Member of House of Representatives, N.Z., 1875–9, 1880–95; Premier, 1877–9.

GREY, Sir Henry George, Viscount Howick, 3rd Earl (1802–94), Under-Sec. for Cols., 1830–3; Under-Sec. at Home Office, 1834–5; Sec.-at-War, 1835–9; Sec. of State for War and Cols. 1846–52.

HARCOURT, Sir William George Granville Venables Vernon (1827–1904), Whewell Prof. of International Law, 1869–87; Lib. M.P., 1868–1904; Solicitor-General, 1873–4; Home Sec., 1880–5; Chancellor of the Exchequer, 1886, 1892–5.

HAY, Rear-Admiral Sir John (1821–1908), Cons. M.P., 1862–5, 1866–85; a Lord of the Admiralty, 1866–8.

HERBERT, Sir Robert George Wyndham (1831–1905), Colonial Office official; private sec. to Gladstone, 1855; Colonial Sec., Queensland, 1859; member of Legislative Council and 1st Premier of Queensland, 1860–5; Assistant Under-Sec. at C.O., 1870; Permanent Under-Sec., 1871–92; Agent-General for Tasmania, 1893–6.

HICKS BEACH, Sir Michael Edward (1837–1916), 1st Earl of St Aldwyn; Cons. M.P., 1864–1906; Chief. Sec. for Ireland, 1874, 1886–7; Col. Sec., 1878–80; Chancellor of the Exchequer, 1885, 1895–1902.

HUTTON, James F., Manchester merchant; pres., Manchester Chamber of Commerce, 1884–5; Cons. M.P., 1885–6; director of United Africa Co. and British East Africa Co.

JENKINS, John Edward (1838–1910), lived in Canada many years, father a prominent Presbyterian minister in Montreal; barrister; General Resident Agent and Superintendent of Colonisation for Dominion of Canada in London, 1874–6; Radical M.P., 1874–80.

KIMBERLEY, John Wodehouse, 1st Earl of (1826–1902), Under-Sec. at Foreign Office, 1852–6, 1859–61; British Minister at St Petersburg, 1856–8; Lord Privy Seal, 1868–70; Sec. of State for Cols., 1870–4, 1880–2; Sec. of State for India, 1882–5, 1886, 1892–4; Foreign Sec., 1894–5.

KINNAIRD, Arthur Fitzgerald (1814–87), 10th Baron Kinnaird; private sec. to Earl of Durham, 1837; Lib. M.P., 1837–9, 1852–78; head of banking firm of Ransome, Bouverie & Co.

KNATCHBULL-HUGESSEN, Edward Hugessen (1829–93), 1st Lord Brabourne; Lib. M.P., 1857–80; Under-Sec. at Home Office, 1860, 1866; Under-Sec. for Cols., 1871–4; became a Cons. in 1880.

LABILLIERE, Francis P. de, Victorian colonist; author; instrumental in founding the Imperial Federation League.

LAWSON, Sir Wilfrid (1829–1906), Lib. M.P., 1859–65, 1868–1900, 1903–; temperance leader.

LOWE, Robert (1811–92), 1st Viscount Sherbrooke; emigrated to Sydney, 1842; member of Legislative Council of New South Wales, 1843–; leader writer for *The Times*, 1850; Lib. M.P., 1852–80; Chancellor of Exchequer, 1868–73; Home Sec., 1873–4.

LYTTON, Edward Robert Bulwer, 1st Earl of (1831–91), poet and diplomat, son of Sir Edward Bulwer-Lytton; occupied several posts in British legation at Washington, Florence, The Hague, Vienna, Belgrade, Copenhagen, Athens, Lisbon and Paris; Gov.-General of India, 1876–80; Ambassador at Paris, 1887–91.

M'ARTHUR, Alexander (1814–1909), brother of William M'Arthur; emigrated to Australia, 1841, and began a firm in Sydney; prominent politician in New South Wales legislature; m. daughter of Revd W. B. Boyce, pres. Australian Methodist Conference; returned to England, 1862–3; Lib. M.P., 1874–80.

M'ARTHUR, Sir William (1809–87), Irish woollen draper in Enniskillen, Londonderry and London; established houses with his brother at Sydney, Melbourne and Auckland; Lib. M.P., 1868–85; chairman, London Wesleyan Conference, 1870; Lord Mayor of London, 1880–1; one of founders of London Chamber of Commerce, 1881.

MACDONALD, Sir John Alexander (1815–91), Canadian politician; 1st Prime of Dominion of Canada, 1867–73; one of commissioners of Treaty of Washington, 1871; Premier and Minister of the Interior, 1878–91.

MACFIE, Robert Andrew (1811–93), sugar refiner, established Macfie & Sons, Liverpool, 1838; original director of Liverpool Chamber of Commerce; trustee of Liverpool Exchange; Lib. M.P., 1868–74.

MACLEAY, Sir George (1809–91), son of former Colonial Sec. of New South Wales, 1825–37, who founded Linnaean Society and gave Botany Bay its name; played important role in promoting foundation of South Australia when, in company with Charles Sturt, he discovered the Murray; Speaker of Legislative Council of N.S.W., 1843–6.

MANCHESTER, William Drogo Montagu, 7th Duke of (1823–90), cavalry officer; Cons. M.P., 1848–55; pres., R.C.I., 1871–8.

MEADE, Sir Robert Henry (1835–98), entered F.O., 1859; private sec. to Granville, 1864–6, 1868–70; Assistant Under-Sec. at C.O., 1871; Permanent Under-Sec., 1892–6.

MERIVALE, Herman (1806–74), Prof. of Political Economy at Oxford; Assistant Under-Sec. at C.O., 1847; Permanent Under-Sec. 1848–59, and at India Office, 1859–74.

MONSELL, William (1812–94), 1st Baron Emly; Lib. M.P., 1847–74; Under-Sec. for Cols., 1868–70; Postmaster-General, 1871–3.

MUNDELLA, Anthony John (1825–97), hosier manufacturer and director of Bank of New Zealand; Radical M.P., 1868–97; Pres. of Board of Trade, 1886, 1892–4.

SMITH, Goldwin (1823–1910), Stowell Law Prof. at University College, Oxford, 1846; Regius Prof. of Modern History, Oxford, 1858–66; Prof. of English and Constitutional History, Cornell University, 1868–72 (non-resident prof. to 1881); settled in Toronto, 1871; lecturer in English History at Cornell, 1875–94; pres., American Historical Association, 1904.

STANLEY OF ALDERLEY, Henry Edward John Stanley, 3rd Baron (1827–1903), orientalist; travelled extensively in the east, said to have lived in Singapore as an Arab; became a Moslem convert; supported Indian National Congress.

TAYLOR, Peter Alfred (1819–91), partner in Samuel Courtauld & Co., silk mercers, 1850–66; chairman of committee of Society of Friends, 1847; Radical M.P., 1862–84; treasurer of Jamaica Committee, 1867, and of the Eastern Question Association; proprietor of the *Examiner*, 1873–4; pres., People's International League; pioneer of international arbitration and payment of M.P.s.

TORRENS, Sir Robert Richard (1814–84), son of Robert Torrens, the political economist; emigrated to South Australia, 1840; member of Legislative Council and Collector of Customs, 1851; Registrar-General, 1852; Colonial Treasurer, 1856–7; member of House of Assembly, 1855–8; Premier and Colonial Treasurer, South Australia, 1857; Lib. M.P., 1868–74.

TORRENS, William Torrens McCullagh (1813–94), Ind. Lib. M.P., 1848–52, 1857, 1865–85.

TREGASKIS, Revd Benjamin (1814–85), superintendent W.M.S. in Sierra Leone and the Gambia, 1864–75.

WELD, Sir Frederick Aloysius (1823–91), emigrated to New Zealand, 1844; member of the legislature, 1853; Minister for Native Affairs, 1860–1; Premier, 1864–5; Gov. of Western Australia, 1869–74; Tasmania, 1875–80; Straits Settlements, 1880–7.

WESTGARTH, William (1815–89), emigrated to Victoria, 1840; member of New South Wales legislature, 1850; of Legislative Council, 1851–3; 1st pres., Melbourne Chamber of Commerce, 1851; founded Westgarth & Co., colonial brokers, in London, 1857; helped establish London Chamber of Commerce, 1881.

WILSON, Edward (1814–78), emigrated to Melbourne, 1842; partner in cattle station; purchased Melbourne *Argus*, 1847, and incorporated Melbourne *Daily News*, 1851; founded Acclimatisation Society of Victoria, 1861; settled in England, 1864; promoted Cannon Street Hotel meetings.

WODEHOUSE, Sir Philip (1811–87), District Judge, Kandy, Ceylon, 1840; Superintendent, British Honduras, 1851–4; Gov. of British Guiana, 1854–61; Cape of Good Hope and High Commissioner for South Africa, 1861–70; Bombay, 1872–7.

WOLFF, Sir Edward Henry Drummond Charles (1830–1908), private sec. to Sir E. Bulwer-Lytton at C.O., 1858; sec. to High Commissioner for Ionian Islands, 1859–64; Cons. M.P., 1874–85; founded Fourth Party with Lord Randolph Churchill; special commissioner to reorganise Egyptian administration, 1885–6; British envoy to Persia, 1887–91; Bucharest, 1891; Madrid, 1892–1900.

WOLSELEY, Sir Garnet Joseph (1833–1913), 1st Viscount; saw active service in India, Burma, the Crimea, Indian mutiny and China; helped reorganise British army; led expeditions to Red River, 1869; the Gold Coast, 1873; Zululand, 1879; Egypt, 1882, 1884; Commander-in-Chief Ireland, 1890; C.-in-C. British Army, 1895–9.

YOUL, Sir James Arndell (1811–1904), born in New South Wales, moved to Tasmania, 1819; successful agriculturalist, 1827–54; settled in England, 1854; sec. and treasurer to G.A.A.C., 1855–62; Political Agent in London for Tasmania, 1861–3; introduced salmon and trout into Tasmania, 1864, and New Zealand, 1868.

YOUNG, Sir Frederick (1817–1913), chairman, National Colonial and Emigration League, 1867; on committee of National State-Aided Colonisation Society; hon. sec., R.C.I., 1874–86.

YOUNG, Sir John (1807–76), 2nd Baron Lisgar; Lib. M.P., 1831–55; Lord High Commissioner, Ionian Islands, 1855–9; Gov. and Commander-in-Chief, New South Wales, 1860–7; Gov.-General of Canada, 1868–72.

Bibliography

1. *Manuscripts:*
   (a) *Government records*
   (b) *Private papers*

2. *Government Printed Sources:*
   (a) *Confidential prints*
   (b) *Parliamentary Papers*
   (c) *Other official publications*

3. *Contemporary writings:*
   (a) *Newspapers*
   (b) *Periodicals and journals*
   (c) *Contemporary articles of particular interest*
   (d) *Contemporary books, memoirs and pamphlets*

4. *Secondary books and articles:*
   (a) *Biographies*
   (b) *Works of general interest*
   (c) *The Colonial Office and the empire*
   (d) *Regional studies*

5. *Unpublished theses*

1. MANUSCRIPTS

(a) *Government records in the Public Record Office*

Colonial Office	Foreign Office
C.O. 209 New Zealand	F.O. 58 Pacific Islands
C.O. 42 Canada	F.O. 84 Slave Trade
C.O. 60 British Columbia	F.O. 27 France
C.O. 83 Fiji	F.O. 12 Borneo
C.O. 87 Gambia	
C.O. 96 Gold Coast	
C.O. 234 Queensland	
C.O. 48 Cape Colony	*War Office*
C.O. 201 New South Wales	W.O. 32 Ashanti War
C.O. 309 Victoria	W.O. 33 Reports and
C.O. 28 Barbados	Miscellanea

(b) *Private papers*

Aborigines Protection Society Papers, Rhodes House, Oxford.

Anti-Slavery Society Papers, Rhodes House.
Cardwell Papers, Public Record Office, P.R.O. 30/48.
Carnarvon Papers, P.R.O. 30/6.
Gladstone Papers, British Museum, Add. MSS.
Granville Papers, P.R.O. 30/29.
Methodist Missionary Society Archives, Gambia and Fiji files and Calvert Papers.
Newcastle Papers, Nottingham University Library, Manuscripts Department.
Royal Commonwealth Society Papers, General Association for the Australian Colonies Minute Book and Young Papers.

2. GOVERNMENT PRINTED SOURCES
(a) *Confidential prints*
     C.O. 806 African
     C.O. 808 Australian

(b) *Parliamentary Papers*
1865   v   (412) Report from Select Committee on the West African Settlements.
1870   XLIX   (C. 24, C. 51) Correspondence respecting proposed conference of colonial representatives in London.
        XLIX   (C. 80) Return of annual cost of colonies, 1859–68, 1869.
          L   (C. 264, C. 444) Gambia: correspondence concerning proposed cession to France.
1874   XLVI   (C. 100) Gold Coast: despatches concerning domestic slavery.
        XLVI   (C.962) Gold Coast: report on expedition against Ashanti.
1876   LII   (C. 1409, C. 1498) Gambia: correspondence concerning cession.
        LIII   (C. 1539, C. 1559) Barbados: Papers on Disturbances.
        LIV   (C. 1566) Correspondence respecting New Guinea.
1880   LXXVI   (C. 2520) Statistical Abstracts for Colonies, 1864–78.

(c) *Other official publications*
London Gazette
Hansard's Parliamentary Debates, 3rd ser.
Colonial Office Lists

3. CONTEMPORARY WRITINGS
(a) *Newspapers*

Australian and New Zealand Gazette   *Morning Post*
Daily News   *Pall Mall Gazette*
Daily Telegraph   *Standard*
European Mail   *The Colonies*
Evening Standard   *The Times*

Clippings from the following newspapers have also been used: *The Argus* (Melbourne); *New Zealand Advertiser*; *The Globe* (Toronto, weekly and daily); *Montreal Gazette*; *Sydney Morning Herald*; *Sydney Examiner*.

(b) *Periodicals and Journals*
Blackwood's Magazine
Contemporary Review
Fraser's Magazine
Proceedings of the Royal Colonial Institute
Punch

Quarterly Review
Spectator
The Nineteenth Century
Transactions of the National Association for the Promotion of Social Science
Westminster Review

(*c*)   *Contemporary articles of particular interest*

Adderley, C. B., 'How Not to Retain the Colonies', *The Nineteenth Century*, vi (July 1879) 170–8.

——, 'Imperial Federation: Its Impossibility', *The Nineteenth Century*, xvi (Sept. 1884) 505–16.

Blachford, Lord (Sir Frederic Rogers), 'The Integrity of the British Empire', *The Nineteenth Century*, ii (Oct. 1877) 355–65.

Bury, Viscount, 'The Unity of the Empire', *The Nineteenth Century*, xvii (Mar. 1885) 381–96.

Carnarvon, Earl of, 'Imperial Administration', *Fortnightly Review*, xxiv (Dec. 1878) 751–63.

Cunningham, G. C., 'The Federation of the English Empire', *Westminster Review*, lvi (Oct. 1879) 313–34.

Dicey, E., 'Our Route to India', *The Nineteenth Century*, i (June 1877) 665–85.

——, 'The Future of Egypt', *The Nineteenth Century*, ii (Aug. 1877) 3–14.

——, 'Mr Gladstone and Our Empire', *The Nineteenth Century*, ii (Sept. 1877) 292–308.

Gladstone, W. E., 'Aggression on Egypt and Freedom in the East', *The Nineteenth Century*, ii (Aug. 1877) 149–66.

——, 'England's Mission', *The Nineteenth Century*, iv (Sept. 1878) 560–84.

Hill, A. S. 'An Empire's Parliament', *P.R.C.I.*, xi (1880) 136–77.

Jenkins, E., 'Imperial Federalism', *Contemporary Review*, xvi (Jan. 1871) 176–86.

——, 'An Imperial Confederation', *Contemporary Review*, xvii (Apr. 1871) 60–77.

Labilliere, F. P. de, 'What Ought to be the Legal and Constitutional Relations between England and her Colonies?', *T.N.A.P.S.S.* (1869) 114–19.

——, 'The Permanent Unity of the Empire', *P.R.C.I.*, vi (1875) 36–85.

Lowe, R., 'Imperialism', *Fortnightly Review*, xxiv (Oct. 1878) 457 ff.

Macfie, R. A., 'The United Kingdom and the Colonies: One Autonomic Empire', *T.N.A.P.S.S.* (1869) 119–20.

——, 'Imperial and Colonial Policy', *T.N.A.P.S.S.* (1870) 179–80.

Mills, A., 'Our Colonial Policy', *Contemporary Review*, xi (June 1869) 216–39.

[Smith, W. J.], 'Empire or No Empire', *Fraser's Magazine*, vi (Dec. 1872) 667–85.

Spedding, J., 'The Future of the British Empire', *Westminster Review*, xxxviii (July 1870) 47–74.

Vogel, J., 'Greater or Lesser Britain', *The Nineteenth Century*, i (July 1877) 809–31.

——, 'The British Empire: Mr Lowe and Lord Blachford', *The Nineteenth Century*, iii (Apr. 1878) 617–33.

Westgarth, W., 'On the Colonial Question', *P.R.C.I.*, ii (1870) 59–81.

——, 'The Policy of Extending the Empire', *T.N.A.P.S.S.* (1872) 157–9.

Wilson, E., 'Colonies as Fields of Experiment in Government', *T.N.A.P.S.S.* (1870) 175–9.

(d) Contemporary books, memoirs and pamphlets

Adderley, C. B., *Review of 'The Colonial Policy of Lord John Russell's Administration' by Earl Grey, 1853; and of Subsequent Colonial History* (London, 1869).

——, *Our Relations with the Colonies and Crown Colonies* (London, 1870).

Bousfield, W., *The Government of the Empire* (London, 1877).

Bowen, G. F., *Thirty Years of Colonial Government, 1859–88,* 2 vols. (London, 1889).

Buckle, G. E. (ed.), *The Letters of Queen Victoria,* 2nd ser., 3 vols. (London, 1926).

Bury, Viscount, *The Exodus of the Western Nations,* 2 vols. (London, 1865).

Childers, S., *Life and Correspondence of the Rt Hon. H. C. E. Childers, 1827–96,* 2 vols. (London, 1901).

Cobden, R., *Speeches on Questions of Public Policy,* ed. J. Bright and J. E. Thorold Rogers, 2 vols. (London, 1870).

Denison, W., *Varieties of Vice Regal Life* (London, 1870).

Dilke, C. W., *Greater Britain,* 2 vols. (London, 1868).

——, *Mr Dilke M.P. on 'Colonies'* (London, 1869).

Eddy, C. W., *Assisted Colonisation* (London, 1870).

Escott, T. H. S., *Pillars of the Empire* (London, 1879).

Fitzgerald, C., *The Gambia and its Proposed Cession to France* (London, 1875).

Flynn, J. S., *Sir Robert Fowler* (London, 1893).

Forster, W. E., *Our Colonial Empire: An Address* (Edinburgh, 1875).

Froude, J. A., *Short Studies on Great Subjects,* 4 vols. (London, 1891).

Gladstone, W. E., *The Bulgarian Horrors and the Question of the East* (London, 1876).

——, *Political Speeches in Scotland, November and December 1879* (Edinburgh, 1879).

Grant, D., *Home Policies or the Growth of Trade* (London, 1870).

Hogan, J. F., *Robert Lowe, Viscount Sherbrooke* (London, 1893).

Hursthouse, C. F., *Australian Independence: Remarks in Favour of the Six Australasian Colonies* (London, 1870).

Hutcheon, W. (ed.), *Whigs and Whiggism: The Political Writings of Benjamin Disraeli* (New York, 1914).

Hutton, J. F., *The Proposed Cession of the British Colony of the Gambia to France* (Manchester, 1876).

Jenkins, E., *State Emigration: An Essay* (London, 1869).

——, *The Colonies and Imperial Unity* (London, 1871).

——, *Discussions on Colonial Questions* (London, 1872).

——, *The Russo-Turkish War: Janus or the Double Faced Ministry* (London, 1877).

——, *The Blot on the Queen's Head or How Little Ben, the Head Waiter, Changed the Sign of the 'Queen's Inn' to 'Empress Hotel Ltd' and the Consequences Thereof* (London, 1877).

Kebbel, T. E. (ed.), *Selected Speeches of the Late Earl of Beaconsfield,* 2 vols. (London, 1882).

Kimberley, Earl of, 'Journal of Events during the Gladstone Ministry, 1868–74', ed. E. Drus, *C.M.,* xxi (1958).

Knight, W. A. (ed.), *Rectorial Addresses delivered in the University of St Andrews, 1863–93* (London, 1894).

Labilliere, F. P. de, *Imperial or Colonial Federalism* (London, 1871).

——, *Federal Britain: or, Unity and Federation of the Empire* (London, 1894).

Little, J. S., *A World Empire* (London, 1879).

Lucy, H. W., *A Diary of Two Parliaments*, 2 vols. (London, 1885, 1892).

McCullagh, T., *Sir William M'Arthur, K.C.M.G., a Biography* (London, 1891).

Macfie, R. A., *Letter to a Prominent Member of the Cabinet* (London, 1870).

——, *A Glance at the Position and Prospects of the Empire* (London, 1872).

Malmesbury, Earl of, *Memoirs of an ex-Minister*, 2 vols. (London, 1884).

Marindin, G. E., *Letters of Frederic, Lord Blachford, Under-Secretary of State for the Colonies, 1860–71* (London, 1896).

Martineau, J., *Life and Correspondence of Sir Bartle Frere*, 2 vols. (London, 1895).

Mathews, J., *A Colonist on the Colonial Question* (London, 1872).

Merivale, H., *Lectures on Colonisation and Colonies* (London, 1841).

Mill, J. S., *Principles of Political Economy*, 2 vols. (London, 1848).

Morley, J., *The Life of Richard Cobden* (London, 1903).

——, *The Life of William Ewart Gladstone*, 3 vols. (London, 1906).

Morris, E. E., *A Memoir of George Higinbotham, Australian Politician and Chief Justice of Victoria* (London, 1895).

Newton, Lord, *Lord Lyons: A Record of British Diplomacy* (London, 1913).

Pope, Sir J., *The Correspondence of Sir John Macdonald* (Toronto, 1921).

Ramm, A. (ed.), *The Political Correspondence of Mr Gladstone and Lord Granville, 1868–86*, 4 vols. (London, 1952–62).

Ruskin, J., *Lectures on Art* (London, 1894).

Russell, Earl, *Selection from Speeches of Earl Russell, 1817–41, and from Despatches, 1859–65*, 2 vols. (London, 1870).

Seeley, J. R., *The Expansion of England: Two Courses of Lectures* (London, 1883).

Sewell, H., *The Case of New Zealand and our Colonial Policy* (London, 1869).

Skelton, J., *The Table Talk of Shirley* (London, 1895).

Smith, G., *The Empire: A Series of Letters Published in the Daily News, 1862–3* (London, 1863).

——, *Reminiscences* (New York, 1911).

[Thorburn, W. M.], *The Great Game: A Plea for a British Imperial Policy* (London, 1875).

Thring, H., *Suggestions for Colonial Reform* (London, 1865).

Torrens, T. M., *Twenty Years in Parliament* (London, 1893).

Trollope, A., *The West Indies and the Spanish Main*, 2 vols. (London 1859).

——, *North America*, 2 vols. (London, 1862).

——, *Australia and New Zealand*, 2 vols. (London, 1873).

True, H., *Victoria Britannia* (London, 1879).

Weld, F. A., *Notes on New Zealand Affairs* (London, 1869).

Wemyss Reid, T., *Life of the Right Honourable William Edward Forster* (London, 1888).

Wilson, E., *Rambles in the Antipodes* (London, 1864).

Wolff, E. H. D., *The Mother Country and the Colonies* (London, 1869).

——, *Rambling Recollections* (London, 1908).

Young, F., *Imperial Federation of Great Britain and her Colonies* (London, 1876).

Zetland, Marquis of (ed.), *The Letters of Disraeli to Lady Bradford and Lady Chesterfield*, 2 vols. (London, 1929).

4. SECONDARY BOOKS AND ARTICLES
(a) Biographies
Blake, R., Disraeli (London, 1966).
Cecil, Lady G., Life of Robert, Marquis of Salisbury, 4 vols. (London, 1921-32).
Childe-Pemberton, W. S., The Life of Lord Norton: Rt Hon. Sir Charles Adderley, 1814-1905 (London, 1909).
Fitzmaurice, Lord E., The Life of Granville George Leveson Gower, Second Earl Granville, K.G., 2 vols. (London, 1905).
Gathorne Hardy, A. E., A Memoir of Gathorne Hardy, First Earl of Cranbrook, 2 vols. (London, 1910).
Hardinge, A., Life of Henry Howard Molyneux Herbert, Fourth Earl of Carnarvon, 1831-90, 3 vols. (London, 1925).
Hicks Beach, Lady V., Life of Sir Michael Hicks Beach, 2 vols. (London, 1932).
Magnus, Sir P., Gladstone, A Biography (London, 1954).
Monypenny, W. F., and Buckle, G. E., The Life of Benjamin Disraeli, Earl of Beaconsfield, 6 vols. (London, 1910-20).
Skelton, O. D., The Life and Times of Sir Alexander Tilloch Galt (Toronto, 1920).
Trevelyan, G. M., Life of John Bright (London, 1913).

(b) Works of general interest
Arendt, H., Origins of Totalitarianism (London, 1958).
Biddulph, R., Lord Cardwell at the War Office: A History of his Administration, 1868-74 (London, 1904).
Bolt, C., Victorian Attitudes to Race (London, 1970).
Brunschwig, H., French Colonialism: Myths and Realities, 1871-1914 (London, 1966).
Cairncross, A. K., Home and Foreign Investment, 1870-1913 (Cambridge, 1953).
Cairns, H. A. C., The Prelude to Imperialism: British Reactions to Central African Society, 1840-90 (London, 1965).
Ellegård, A., Readership of the Periodical Press in Mid-Victorian Britain, Göteborgs Universitets Arsskrift, vol. LXIII (Gothenburg, 1957).
——, Darwin and the General Reader: The reception of Darwin's Theory of Evolution in the British Periodical Press, 1859-72, Göteborgs Universitets Arsskrift, vol. LXIV (Gothenburg, 1958).
Ensor, R. C. K., England, 1870-1914 (Oxford, 1936).
Fay, C. R., Imperial Economy and its Place in the Foundation of Economic Doctrine, 1600-1932 (Oxford, 1934).
Fieldhouse, D. K., ' "Imperialism": An Historiographical Revision', Econ.H.R., XIV (1961) 187-209.
Findlay, G. G., and Holdsworth, W. W., The History of the Wesleyan Methodist Missionary Society, 5 vols. (London, 1921-4).
Fox Bourne, H. R., The Aborigines Protection Society: Chapters in its History (London, 1899).
Fuchs, C. J., The Trade Policy of Great Britain and her Colonies since 1860 (London, 1905).
Grampp, W. D., The Manchester School of Economics (Berkeley, 1960).
Hanham, H. J., Elections and Party Management: Politics in the Time of Disraeli and Gladstone (London, 1959).
Henkin, L. J., Darwinism and the English Novel, 1860-1910 (New York, 1940).

Hobsbawm, E. J., *Industry and Empire* (London, 1968).

Imlah, A. H., *Economic Elements in the Pax Britannica* (Cambridge, Mass., 1958).

Jenks, L. H., *The Migration of British Capital to 1875* (New York, 1927).

Lowe, C. J., *The Reluctant Imperialists*, 2 vols. (London, 1967).

Marriott, Sir J. A., *Queen Victoria and her Ministers* (London, 1933).

Maunier, R., *The Sociology of Colonies: An Introduction to the Study of Race Contact* (London, 1949).

Platt, D. C. M., *Finance, Trade and Politics in British Foreign Policy, 1815–1914* (London, 1968).

Redford, A., *Manchester Merchants and Foreign Trade*, 2 vols. (Manchester, 1956).

Rostow, W. W., *The British Economy of the Nineteenth Century* (London, 1948).

Schlote, W., *British Overseas Trade from 1700 to the 1930s* (Oxford, 1952).

Shannon, R. T., *Gladstone and the Bulgarian Agitation, 1876* (London, 1963).

Steiner, Z., 'Finance, Trade and Politics in British Foreign Policy, 1815–1914', *H.J.*, XIII (1970) 545–68.

West, K., 'Theorising about "Imperialism": A Methodological Note', *Journal of Imperial and Commonwealth History*, I (1973) 147–54.

(c) *The Colonial Office and the Empire*

Benians, E. A., *et al.* (eds.), *The Cambridge History of the British Empire*, vol. III: *The Empire–Commonwealth, 1870–1919* (Cambridge, 1959).

Blackton, C. S., 'The Cannon Street Episode: An Aspect of Anglo-Australian Relations', *H.S.*, XIII (1969) 520–32.

Blakely, B., *The Colonial Office, 1868–92* (Durham, N.C., 1972).

Bodelsen, C. A., *Studies in Mid-Victorian Imperialism* (Copenhagen, 1924).

Butler, J. R. M., 'Imperial Questions in British Politics, 1868–80', *C.H.B.E.*, III 17–64.

Cheng, S. C. Y., *Schemes for the Federation of the British Empire* (New York, 1931).

Creighton, D. G., 'The Victorians and the Empire', *C.H.R.*, XIX (1938) 138–53.

Cumpston, I. M., 'The Discussion of Imperial Problems in the British Parliament, 1880–85', *T.R.H.S.*, XIII (1962) 29–47.

Eldridge, C. C., 'The Myth of Mid-Victorian "Separatism": The Cession of the Bay Islands and the Ionian Islands in the Early 1860s', *V.S.*, XII (1969) 331–46.

——, 'Forgotten Centenary: The Defence Review of the 1860s', *Trivium*, V (1970) 85–103.

Folsom, A., *The Royal Empire Society* (London, 1933).

Galbraith, J. S., 'The "Turbulent Frontier" as a Factor in British Expansion', *C.S.S.H.*, II (1960) 150–68.

——, 'Myths of the "Little England" Era', *A.H.R.*, LXVII (1961) 39–42.

Gallagher, J. A., and Robinson, R. E., 'The Imperialism of Free Trade', *Econ.H.R.*, 2nd ser., VI (1953) 1–15.

Ghosh, R. N., *Classical Macroeconomics and the Case for Colonies* (Calcutta, 1967).

Hall, H., *The Colonial Office: A History* (London, 1937).

Kittrell, E. R., 'The Development of the Theory of Colonisation in English Classical Political Economy', *Southern Economic Journal*, XXXI (1965) 189–206.

Knaplund, P., *Gladstone and Britain's Imperial Policy* (London, 1927).

Knorr, K. E., *British Colonial Theories, 1750–1850* (Toronto, 1944).

Knox, B. A., 'Reconsidering Mid-Victorian Imperialism', *Journal of Imperial and Commonwealth History*, I (1973) 155–72.

Koebner, R., and Schmidt, H. D., *Imperialism: The Story and Significance of a Political Word, 1840–1960* (Cambridge, 1964).

Landes, D. S., 'Some Thoughts on the Nature of Economic Imperialism', *J.E.H.*, XXI (1961) 496–512.

Macdonagh, O., 'The Anti-Imperialism of Free Trade', *Econ.H.R.*, XIV (1962) 489–501.

Macmillan, D. S., 'The Australians in London, 1857–88', *J.P.R.A.H.S.*, XLIV (1958) 155–81.

Mehrota, S., 'Imperial Federation and India, 1868–1917', *J.C.P.S.*, I (1961) 29–40.

Morison, J. L., 'The Imperial Ideas of Benjamin Disraeli', *C.H.R.*, I (1920) 267–80.

Morrell, W. P., *British Colonial Policy in the Mid-Victorian Age* (London, 1969).

Platt, D. C. M., 'The Imperialism of Free Trade – Some Reservations', *Econ.H.R.*, XXI (1968) 296–306.

——, 'Economic Factors in British Policy during the "New Imperialism"', *P.&P.*, 39 (1968) 120–38.

——, 'Further Objections to an "Imperialism of Free Trade", 1830–60', *Econ.H.R.*, XXVI (1973) 77–91.

Pugh, R. B., 'The Colonial Office, 1801–1923', *C.H.B.E.*, III 711–68.

Reese, T. R., *The History of the Royal Commonwealth Society, 1868–1968* (London, 1968).

Robbins, L., *Robert Torrens and the Evolution of Classical Economics* (London, 1958).

Robinson, R. E., 'Imperial Problems in British Politics, 1880–95', *C.H.B.E.*, III 127–80.

—— and Gallagher, J. A., with Denny, A., *Africa and the Victorians* (London, 1961).

Rutherford, J., *Sir George Grey, 1812–98: A Study in Colonial Government* (London, 1961).

Schuyler, R. L., 'The Climax of Anti-Imperialism', *P.S.Q.*, XXXV (1921) 537–60.

——, *The Fall of the Old Colonial System: A Study in British Free Trade, 1770–1870* (New York, 1945).

Semmel, B., 'The Philosophic Radicals and Colonialism', *J.E.H.*, XXI (1961) 513–25.

——, *The Rise of Free Trade Imperialism: Classical Political Economy, the Empire of Free Trade and Imperialism, 1750–1850* (London, 1970).

Shaw, A. G. L., 'British Attitudes to the Colonies, ca 1820–50', *J.B.S.*, IX (1969) 71–95.

—— (ed.), *Great Britain and the Colonies, 1815–65* (London, 1970).

Shepperson, G., 'Africa, the Victorians and Imperialism', *Revue Belge de Philologie et d'Histoire*, XL (1962) 1228–38.

Stembridge, S. R., 'Disraeli and the Millstones', *J.B.S.*, V (1965) 122–39.

Stengers, J., 'L'Impérialisme colonial de la fin du XIXᵉ siècle: Mythe ou Réalité', *J.A.H.*, III (1962) 469–91.

Stokes, E., *Imperialism and the Scramble for Africa: A New View* (Historical Association of Rhodesia and Nyasaland, 1963).

Sturgis, J. L., *John Bright and the Empire* (London, 1969).

Swinfen, D. B., *Imperial Control of Colonial Legislation, 1813–65* (London, 1970).

Temperley, H., 'Disraeli and Cyprus', *E.H.R.*, xlvi (1931) 274–9.

Thornton, A. P., *The Imperial Idea and its Enemies: A Study in British Power* (London, 1959).

Tyler, J. E., *The Struggle for Imperial Unity, 1868–95* (London, 1938).

Winch, D., *Classical Political Economy and Colonies* (London, 1965).

(d) *Regional studies*

Balfour, Lady E., *History of Lord Lytton's Indian Administration, 1876–80* (London, 1899).

Catala, R., 'La Question de l'Échange de la Gambie Britannique contre les Comptoirs Français du Golfe de Guinée de 1866 à 1876', *Revue des Colonies Françaises*, xxxv (1948) 114–36.

Coupland, R., *Zulu Battle Piece* (London, 1948).

Cowan, C. D., *Nineteenth Century Malaya: The Origins of British Political Control* (Oxford, 1961).

Cowling, M., 'Lytton, the Cabinet and the Russians, August to November 1878', *E.H.R.*, lxxvi (1961) 60–79.

Drus, E., 'The Colonial Office and the Annexation of Fiji', *T.R.H.S.*, xxxii (1950) 87–110.

Eldridge, C. C., 'Newcastle and the Ashanti War of 1863–4: A Failure of the Policy of "Anti-Imperialism" ', *R.M.S.*, xii (1968) 68–90.

——, 'The Imperialism of the "Little England" Era: The Question of the Annexation of the Fiji Islands, 1858–61', *N.Z.J.H.*, i (1967) 171–84.

Farr, D. M., *The Colonial Office and Canada, 1867–87* (Toronto, 1955).

Fraser-Tytler, W. K., *Afghanistan* (Oxford, 1950).

Galbraith, J. S., *The Hudson's Bay Company as an Imperial Factor* (Berkeley, 1957).

Ghose, D. E., *England and Afghanistan* (Calcutta, 1962).

Goodfellow, C. F., *Great Britain and South African Confederation, 1868–81* (Cape Town, 1966).

Gopal, S., *British Policy in India, 1858–1905* (Cambridge, 1965).

Gordon, D. C., *The Australian Frontier in New Guinea, 1870–85* (New York, 1951).

Gray, J. M., *A History of the Gambia* (Cambridge, 1940).

Hamilton, W. B., *Barbados and the Confederation Question, 1871–85* (London, 1956).

Hargreaves, J. D., *Prelude to the Partition of West Africa* (London, 1963).

Harnetty, P., 'The Imperialism of Free Trade: Lancashire and the Indian Cotton Duties, 1859–62', *Econ.H.R.*, xviii (1965) 333–49.

——, *Imperialism and Free Trade: India and Lancashire in the Mid-Nineteenth Century* (London, 1972).

Harrop, A. J., *England and the Maori Wars* (London, 1937).

Holmberg, A., *African Tribes and European Agencies* (London, 1966).

Hyam, R., 'The Partition of Africa', *H.J.*, vii (1964) 154–69.

Jacobs, M. G., 'The Colonial Office and New Guinea, 1874–84', *H.S.A.N.Z.*, v (1952) 106–18.

Kiewiet, C. W. de, *The Imperial Factor in South Africa* (Cambridge, 1937).

McIntyre, W. D., 'Disraeli's Colonial Policy: The Creation of the Western Pacific High Commission, 1874–7', *H.S.A.N.Z.*, ix (1960) 279–94.

——, 'Anglo-American Rivalry in the Pacific: The British Annexation of the Fiji Islands in 1874', *Pacific Historical Review*, xxix (1960) 361–80.

——, 'Disraeli's Election Blunder: The Straits of Malacca Issue in the 1874 Election', *R.M.S.*, v (1961) 76–105.

——, 'Britain's Intervention in Malaya: The Origin of Lord Kimberley's Instructions to Sir Andrew Clarke in 1873', *Journal of South East Asian History*, II (1961) 47–69.

——, 'British Policy in West Africa: The Ashanti Expedition of 1873–4', *H.J.*, v (1962) 19–46.

——, 'New Light on Commodore Goodenough's Mission to Fiji, 1873–4', *H.S.A.N.Z.*, x (1962) 270–88.

——, 'Commander Glover and the Colony of Lagos, 1861–73', *J.A.H.*, IV (1963) 57–79.

——, *The Imperial Frontier in the Tropics, 1865–75: A Study of British Colonial Policy in West Africa, Malaya and the South Pacific in the Age of Gladstone and Disraeli* (London, 1967).

Moore, R. J., 'Imperialism and "Free Trade" Policy in India, 1853–4', *Econ.H.R.*, XVII (1964) 135–45.

——, *Liberalism and Indian Politics, 1872–1922* (London, 1966).

Morrell, W. P., *Britain in the Pacific Islands* (Oxford, 1960).

Morris, D. R., *The Washing of the Spears* (London, 1966).

Newbury, C. W., 'Victorians, Republicans and the Partition of West Africa', *J.A.H.*, III (1962) 493–501.

Parnaby, O. W., 'Aspects of British Policy in the Pacific: The 1872 Pacific Islanders Protection Act', *H.S.A.N.Z.*, VIII (1957) 54–65.

——, *Britain and the Labour Trade in the Southwest Pacific* (Durham, N.C., 1964).

Philips, C. H. (ed.), *The Evolution of India and Pakistan, 1858–1947: Select Documents* (London, 1962).

Rich, E. E., *The History of the Hudson's Bay Company, 1670–1870*, 2 vols. (London, 1958–9).

Robinson, R. E., and Gallagher, J. A., 'The Partition of Africa', *N.C.M.H.* (Cambridge, 1962) XI 593–640.

Ross, A., *New Zealand Aspirations in the Pacific in the Nineteenth Century* (Oxford, 1964).

Scarr, D., *Fragments of Empire: A History of the Western Pacific High Commission, 1877–1914* (Canberra, 1968).

Singhal, D. P., *India and Afghanistan: A Study in Diplomatic Relations, 1876–1907* (Brisbane, 1963).

Uys, C. J., *In the Era of Shepstone: British Expansion in South Africa, 1842–77* (Lovedale, 1933).

Ward, J. M., *British Policy in the South Pacific, 1786–1893* (Sydney, 1948).

5. UNPUBLISHED THESES

Amey, P. M., 'The Nature of the Concern with the Empire of Parliament and Some Leading Journals during Palmerston's Second Ministry', M.Phil. thesis (London, 1971).

Burton, A., 'The Influence of the Treasury on the Making of British Colonial Policy, 1868–80', D.Phil. thesis (Oxford, 1960).

Durrans, P. J., 'The Discussion of Imperial Affairs in the British Parliament, 1868–80', D.Phil. thesis (Oxford, 1970).

Eldridge, C. C., 'The Colonial Policy of the Fifth Duke of Newcastle, 1859–64', Ph.D. thesis (Nottingham, 1966).

Gavin, R. J., 'Palmerston's Policy towards East and West Africa', D.Phil. thesis (Oxford, 1958).

Kirkpatrick, R. L., 'British Imperial Policy, 1874–80', D.Phil. thesis (Oxford, 1953).

Preston, A. W., 'British Military Policy and the Defence of India: A Study of British Military Policy, Plans and Preparations during the Russian Crisis, 1876–80', Ph.D. thesis (London, 1966).

Swaisland, H. C., 'The Aborigines Protection Society and British Southern and West Africa', D.Phil. thesis (Oxford, 1968).

Index

KINNAIRD, Arthur Fitzgerald (1814–87), 10th Baron Kinnaird; private sec. to Earl of Durham, 1837; Lib. M.P., 1837–9, 1852–78; head of banking firm of Ransome, Bouverie & Co.

KNATCHBULL-HUGESSEN, Edward Hugessen (1829–93), 1st Lord Brabourne; Lib. M.P., 1857–80; Under-Sec. at Home Office, 1860, 1866; Under-Sec. for Cols., 1871–4; became a Cons. in 1880.

LABILLIERE, Francis P. de, Victorian colonist; author; instrumental in founding the Imperial Federation League.

LAWSON, Sir Wilfrid (1829–1906), Lib. M.P., 1859–65, 1868–1900, 1903–6; temperance leader.

LOWE, Robert (1811–92), 1st Viscount Sherbrooke; emigrated to Sydney, 1842; member of Legislative Council of New South Wales, 1843–50; leader writer for *The Times*, 1850; Lib. M.P., 1852–80; Chancellor of the Exchequer, 1868–73; Home Sec., 1873–4.

LYTTON, Edward Robert Bulwer, 1st Earl of (1831–91), poet and diplomat, son of Sir Edward Bulwer-Lytton; occupied several posts in British legations at Washington, Florence, The Hague, Vienna, Belgrade, Copenhagen, Athens, Lisbon and Paris; Gov.-General of India, 1876–80; Ambassador at Paris, 1887–91.

M'ARTHUR, Alexander (1814–1909), brother of William M'Arthur; emigrated to Australia, 1841, and began a firm in Sydney; prominent politician in New South Wales legislature; m. daughter of Revd W. B. Boyce, pres. of Australian Methodist Conference; returned to England, 1862–3; Lib. M.P., 1874–80.

M'ARTHUR, Sir William (1809–87), Irish woollen draper in Enniskillen, Londonderry and London; established houses with his brother at Sydney, Melbourne and Auckland; Lib. M.P., 1868–85; chairman, London Wesleyan Conference, 1870; Lord Mayor of London, 1880–1; one of founders of London Chamber of Commerce, 1881.

MACDONALD, Sir John Alexander (1815–91), Canadian politician; 1st Premier of Dominion of Canada, 1867–73; one of commissioners of Treaty of Washington, 1871; Premier and Minister of the Interior, 1878–91.

MACFIE, Robert Andrew (1811–93), sugar refiner, established Macfie & Sons, Liverpool, 1838; original director of Liverpool Chamber of Commerce; trustee of Liverpool Exchange; Lib. M.P., 1868–74.

MACLEAY, Sir George (1809–91), son of former Colonial Sec. of New South Wales, 1825–37, who founded Linnaean Society and gave Botany Bay its name; played important role in promoting foundation of South Australia when, in company with Charles Sturt, he discovered the Murray river; Speaker of Legislative Council of N.S.W., 1843–6.

MANCHESTER, William Drogo Montagu, 7th Duke of (1823–90), former cavalry officer; Cons. M.P., 1848–55; pres., R.C.I., 1871–8.

MEADE, Sir Robert Henry (1835–98), entered F.O., 1859; private sec. to Granville, 1864–6, 1868–70; Assistant Under-Sec. at C.O., 1871–92; Permanent Under-Sec., 1892–6.

MERIVALE, Herman (1806–74), Prof. of Political Economy at Oxford, 1837; Assistant Under-Sec. at C.O., 1847; Permanent Under-Sec. at C.O., 1848–59, and at India Office, 1859–74.

MONSELL, William (1812–94), 1st Baron Emly; Lib. M.P., 1847–74; Under-Sec. for Cols., 1868–70; Postmaster-General, 1871–3.

MUNDELLA, Anthony John (1825–97), hosier manufacturer and director of Bank of New Zealand; Radical M.P., 1868–97; Pres. of Board of Trade, 1886, 1892–4.

NEWCASTLE, Henry Pelham Fiennes Pelham Clinton, 5th Duke of (1811–64), Peelite M.P., 1832–51; Sec. of State for War and Cols., 1852–4; Sec. of State for War, 1854–5; Sec. of State for Cols., 1859–64.

NICHOLSON, Sir Charles (1808–1903), medical practitioner; spent years 1834–62 in New South Wales and Queensland; member of Legislative Council, N.S.W., 1843–59; Speaker, 1847–56; Pres. of Legislative Council, Queensland, 1860; principal founder, Vice-Chancellor and then Chancellor of University of Sydney, 1854–62.

NORMANBY, George Augustus Constantine Phipps, 2nd Marquis of (1819–90), ex-army officer; Lib. M.P., 1847–58; Lieut.-Gov. of Nova Scotia, 1858–67; Gov. of Queensland, 1871–4; New Zealand, 1874–9; Victoria, 1879-84.

NORTHBROOK, Thomas George Baring, 1st Earl of (1826–1904), Under-Sec. at India Office, 1859–61, 1861–4, at War Office, 1861, 1868, and at Home Office, 1864; Sec. to Admiralty, 1866; Gov.-General of India, 1872–6; 1st Lord of the Admiralty, 1880–5; special commissioner to Egypt, 1884.

NORTHCOTE, Sir Stafford Henry (1818–87), 1st Earl of Iddesleigh; Cons. M.P., 1855–85; Sec. of State for India, 1867; Gov. of Hudson's Bay Co., 1869–74; Chancellor of the Exchequer, 1874–80; Foreign Sec., 1886.

PAKINGTON, Sir John Somerset (1799–1880), 1st Baron Hampton; Cons. M.P., 1837–74; Sec. of State for War and Cols., 1852; 1st Lord of the Admiralty, 1858, 1866; Sec. of State for War, 1867–8.

POPE-HENNESSY, Sir John (1834–91), Cons. M.P., 1859–65, 1890–1; Gov. of Labuan, 1867–71; West African Settlements, 1872–3; Bahamas, 1873–4; Windward Islands, 1875–6; Hong Kong, 1877–82; Mauritius, 1883–9.

RICHARD, Henry (1812–88), Congregational pastor, Old Kent Road, London, 1835–50; sec., Peace Society, 1848; Lib. M.P., 1868–88; advocate of international arbitration.

ROBINSON, Sir Hercules George Robert (1824–97), 1st Baron Rosmead; Lieut.-Gov. of St Kitts, 1854–9; Gov. of Hong Kong, 1859–65; Ceylon, 1865–72; New South Wales, 1872–9; New Zealand, 1879–80; Cape of Good Hope and High Commissioner for South Africa, 1880–9, 1895–7.

ROCHE, Alfred R. (1819–76), father editor of *Morning Post*; civil servant in Canada; campaigned for development of North Western Territories of Hudson's Bay Co. under pseudonym 'Assiniboia' in *Montreal Gazette*; hon. sec., R.C.I., 1868–71.

ROGERS, Sir Frederic (1811–89), 1st Baron Blachford; one of founders of the *Guardian*; leader writer for *The Times*; Registrar to Joint Stock Cos., 1844; Colonial Land and Emigration Commissioner, 1846; Permanent Under-Sec. at C.O., 1860–71.

ROGERS, James Edwin Thorold (1823–90), political economist; 1st Tooke Prof. of Statistics and Economic Science, King's College, London, 1859–90; Drummond Prof. of Political Economy, Oxford, 1862–7, 1888; M.P., 1880–6.

SEWELL, Henry (1807–79), sec. and deputy chairman of Canterbury Assoc. for Colonisation of New Zealand, 1850; member of House of Representatives, N.Z., 1853–6, 1860, 1865–6; of Legislative Council, 1861–5, 1870–3; 1st Premier of N.Z., 1856; Colonial Treasurer and Commissioner of Customs, 1856–9; Attorney-General, 1861–2; Minister of Justice, 1864–5, 1869–72.

SHEPSTONE, Sir Theophilus (1817–93), British resident among Fingo, 1839; Agent for Natives in Natal, 1845; Sec. for Native Affairs, 1856; annexed and administered Transvaal, 1877–9; Administrator in Zululand, 1884.

CARNARVON, Henry Howard Molyneux Herbert, 4th Earl of (1831–90), Under-Sec. for Cols., 1858–9; Sec. of State for Cols., 1866–7, 1874–8; Chairman of Commission on Imperial Defence, 1879–82.

CAVE, Stephen (1820–86), Cons. M.P., 1859–80; Paymaster-General, 1866–8; chairman, West India Committee, and director of Bank of England.

CHESSON, Frederick William (1833–88), journalist prominent in many philanthropic societies; wrote for *Morning Star, Daily News, Adelaide Observer, South Australia Register and Evening Journal*; edited for short while *The Dial*; assistant sec., A.P.S., 1854–66; sec., 1866–88; organised Manchester Peace Conference, 1853; founded London Emancipation Society, 1859; member of N.A.P.S.S.; Law Society; Jamaica, Gambia, Fiji, Afghan and Greek Committees; Anti-Opium Society; helped organise Eastern Question Conference and Association.

CHILDERS, Hugh Culling Eardley (1827–96), emigrated to Melbourne, 1850; prominent politician in Victoria to 1856; 1st Vice-Chancellor of University of Melbourne; Agent for Victoria in London, 1857; Lib. M.P., 1860–92; 1st Lord of the Admiralty, 1868–71; Chancellor of Duchy of Lancaster, 1872–3; Sec. of State for War, 1880–2; Chancellor of the Exchequer, 1882–5; Home Sec., 1886.

CHURCHILL, Lord Alfred (1824–93), Cons. M.P., 1845–7; supporter of Palmerston, 1857–65; chairman, African Aid Society.

CLIFFORD, Sir Charles, member of House of Representatives, N.Z., 1853–60; Speaker, House of Representatives, 1854–60.

CORRY, Montagu William Lowry (1838–1903), 1st Baron Rowton; private sec. to Disraeli, 1866–81; founder of poor man's hotel, 'Rowton Houses'.

DENISON, Sir William (1804–71), colonial governor; Tasmania, 1847–55; New South Wales, 1855–61; Madras, 1861–6.

DICEY, Edward James Stephen (1823–1911), author and journalist; leader writer for *The Times*, 1861; editor *Daily News*, 1870; editor *The Observer*, 1870–89.

DILKE, Sir Charles Wentworth (1843–1911), Lib. M.P., 1868–86, 1892–1911; Under-Sec. at F.O., 1880–2; Pres. of Local Government Board, 1882–5; ruined by divorce case, 1886.

EASTWICK, Edward Backhouse (1814–83), Prof. of Hindustani at Haileybury College, 1845; Assistant Political Sec., India Office, 1859; private sec. to Lord Cranbourne at India Office, 1866–7; Cons. M.P., 1868–74.

EDDY, Dr Charles W. (1821–74), Oxford M.B., 1849; held Ratcliffe Travelling Fellowship for 10 years during which time he lived in Europe, Australia and Canada; sec. to Danube & Black Sea Railway Co., 1862–74; hon. sec., R.C.I., 1871–4.

ERSKINE, Admrl John E. (1806–87), Lib. M.P., 1865–74; author of *Journal of a Cruise among the Islands of the Western Pacific*; associated with W.M.S.

FORSTER, William Edward (1818–86), Yorkshire woollen manufacturer; left Quakers in 1850; Lib. M.P., 1861–86; Under-Sec. for Cols., 1865–6; Vice-Pres. of Privy Council, 1870–4; Chief Sec. for Ireland, 1880–2; 1st chairman, Imperial Federation League, 1884.

FORTESCUE, Chichester Samuel (1823–98), Lord Carlingford; Lib. M.P., 1847–74; Under-Sec. for Cols., 1857–8, 1859–65; Chief. Sec. for Ireland, 1865–6, 1868–71; Pres. of Board of Trade, 1871–4; Lord Privy Seal, 1881–3; Lord Pres. of the Council, 1883–5.

FOWLER, Sir Robert Nicholas (1828–91), from Quaker banking family (became Anglican, 1858); Cons. M.P., 1868–74, 1880–91; chairman, Anti-Opium Society; twice Lord Mayor of London.

FRERE, Sir Henry Bartle Edward (1815–84), served in Indian Civil Service, 1834–61; Gov. of Bombay, 1862–7; member of Council of India, 1867; commissioner to Zanzibar to negotiate slave-trade treaty, 1872; Gov. of Cape Colony and High Commissioner for South Africa, 1877–80.

FROUDE, James Anthony (1818–94), historian; editor *Fraser's Magazine*, 1860–74; travelled in South Africa, 1874–5; Regius Prof. of Modern History at Oxford, 1892–4.

GORST, Sir John Eldon (1835–1916), emigrated to New Zealand, 1859; served as civil commissioner in Waikato, 1862, wrote classic account of the Maori king; Cons. M.P., 1866–8, 1875–1906; reorganised Conservative party machinery, 1868–74; helped found Fourth Party, 1880; Solicitor-General, 1885; Under-Sec. at India Office, 1886.

GOSCHEN, George Joachim (1831–1907), 1st Viscount Goschen; Lib. M.P., 1863–85; Lib. Unionist M.P., 1886–1900; Pres. of Poor Law Board, 1868–71; 1st Lord of the Admiralty, 1871–4, 1895–1900; investigated financial position of Egypt, 1876; Chancellor of the Exchequer, 1886–92.

GRANVILLE, Granville George Leveson-Gower, 2nd Earl (1815–91), Colonial Sec., 1868–70, 1886; Foreign Sec., 1851–2, 1870–4, 1880–5.

GREY, Sir George (1812–98), colonial governor; explored north-western Australia, 1837; Resident Magistrate, Albany, Western Australia; Gov. of South Australia, 1841–5; New Zealand, 1845–53, 1861–8; Cape of Good Hope, 1854–61; Superintendent of Auckland, 1875; Member of House of Representatives, N.Z., 1875–9, 1880–95; Premier, 1877–9.

GREY, Sir Henry George, Viscount Howick, 3rd Earl (1802–94), Under-Sec. for Cols., 1830–3; Under-Sec. at Home Office, 1834–5; Sec.-at-War, 1835–9; Sec. of State for War and Cols. 1846–52.

HARCOURT, Sir William George Granville Venables Vernon (1827–1904), Whewell Prof. of International Law, 1869–87; Lib. M.P., 1868–1904; Solicitor-General, 1873–4; Home Sec., 1880–5; Chancellor of the Exchequer, 1886, 1892–5.

HAY, Rear-Admiral Sir John (1821–1908), Cons. M.P., 1862–5, 1866–85; a Lord of the Admiralty, 1866–8.

HERBERT, Sir Robert George Wyndham (1831–1905), Colonial Office official; private sec. to Gladstone, 1855; Colonial Sec., Queensland, 1859; member of Legislative Council and 1st Premier of Queensland, 1860–5; Assistant Under-Sec. at C.O., 1870; Permanent Under-Sec., 1871–92; Agent-General for Tasmania, 1893–6.

HICKS BEACH, Sir Michael Edward (1837–1916), 1st Earl of St Aldwyn; Cons. M.P., 1864–1906; Chief. Sec. for Ireland, 1874, 1886–7; Col. Sec., 1878–80; Chancellor of the Exchequer, 1885, 1895–1902.

HUTTON, James F., Manchester merchant; pres., Manchester Chamber of Commerce, 1884–5; Cons. M.P., 1885–6; director of United Africa Co. and British East Africa Co.

JENKINS, John Edward (1838–1910), lived in Canada many years, father a prominent Presbyterian minister in Montreal; barrister; General Resident Agent and Superintendent of Colonisation for Dominion of Canada in London, 1874–6; Radical M.P., 1874–80.

KIMBERLEY, John Wodehouse, 1st Earl of (1826–1902), Under-Sec. at Foreign Office, 1852–6, 1859–61; British Minister at St Petersburg, 1856–8; Lord Privy Seal, 1868–70; Sec. of State for Cols., 1870–4, 1880–2; Sec. of State for India, 1882–5, 1886, 1892–4; Foreign Sec., 1894–5.